AZURE ZERO TO HERO

KICKSTART YOUR CLOUD CAREER

FIRST EDITION

Preface

In today's digital age, the cloud has become a transformative force, reshaping how businesses operate, developers build, and users interact with applications and services. As organizations continue to migrate to the cloud, Microsoft Azure stands out as a powerful and versatile platform that offers an extensive suite of services. This book is designed to provide a comprehensive, practical, and up-to-date guide to learning Microsoft Azure from the ground up.

Whether you're an aspiring cloud professional, a seasoned IT administrator, or a developer exploring new horizons, this book serves as your roadmap to mastering Azure. Beginning with the fundamentals of cloud computing, the book steadily progresses into deeper technical subjects including core Azure services, security, infrastructure as code, automation, monitoring, and governance. It doesn't stop there—dedicated chapters for developers, real-world applications, and guidance for certifications and careers ensure this is not just a technical manual, but a companion for your journey into the cloud ecosystem.

Each chapter builds upon the last, ensuring you gain both conceptual understanding and practical skills. From setting up your first Azure subscription to deploying resilient, secure applications, every section is structured to deliver value, complete with code examples, industry insights, and best practices. Furthermore, appendices offer reference material, project templates, and curated resources to expand your learning.

We've also placed a strong emphasis on aligning your learning path with career growth. With cloud-related roles in high demand, knowing how to position yourself with the right certification and experience can make a significant difference.

Our goal with this book is to demystify Azure and empower you with the knowledge to innovate, deploy, and manage cloud solutions with confidence. By the time you reach the final chapter, you won't just understand Azure — you'll be ready to apply it effectively in professional settings.

Let's begin this journey into the cloud, one chapter at a time.

Table of Contents

Chapter 1: Introduction to Cloud Computing and Azure

What is Cloud Computing?

Cloud computing is a paradigm shift in the way technology infrastructure is delivered and consumed. Traditionally, organizations relied on physical servers and data centers to host applications, manage data, and run business processes. This approach was often capital intensive, complex to scale, and required continuous maintenance and upgrades.

With cloud computing, those physical assets are replaced or augmented by on-demand, scalable resources available over the internet. Instead of owning the hardware, users rent computing power, storage, and services from cloud providers like Microsoft Azure, Amazon Web Services (AWS), and Google Cloud Platform (GCP). This shift enables organizations to be more agile, cost-efficient, and innovative.

At its core, cloud computing allows access to shared pools of configurable resources — such as servers, storage, networks, applications, and services — that can be provisioned and released rapidly with minimal management effort. These resources are made available in data centers that are distributed globally, ensuring high availability and redundancy.

The Characteristics of Cloud Computing

There are five essential characteristics that define cloud computing, according to the National Institute of Standards and Technology (NIST):

1. **On-demand self-service**: Users can provision resources like computing power and storage without requiring human interaction with a service provider.

2. **Broad network access**: Resources are accessible over the network using standard mechanisms — such as laptops, smartphones, and tablets.

3. **Resource pooling**: Providers serve multiple consumers with dynamically assigned resources based on demand.

4. **Rapid elasticity**: Capabilities can be elastically scaled outward and inward commensurate with demand.

5. **Measured service**: Cloud systems automatically control and optimize resource use by leveraging metering capabilities.

Cloud Service Models

Cloud computing is generally delivered through three primary service models:

- **Infrastructure as a Service (IaaS)**: This provides virtualized computing resources over the internet. Users can rent virtual machines (VMs), storage, and networking capabilities. It offers flexibility and control, making it suitable for IT administrators and developers.

- **Platform as a Service (PaaS)**: PaaS abstracts much of the infrastructure management. It provides a platform allowing customers to develop, run, and manage applications without dealing with servers, storage, or networking.

- **Software as a Service (SaaS)**: SaaS delivers fully functional software applications over the internet. Examples include Microsoft 365, Google Workspace, and Salesforce. The user simply accesses the application — everything else is handled by the provider.

Each model serves different use cases and levels of control. Understanding the distinctions is essential for selecting the right approach for your projects.

Deployment Models

There are also several cloud deployment models:

- **Public Cloud**: Resources are owned and operated by third-party cloud service providers and delivered over the internet. Azure, AWS, and GCP are examples.

- **Private Cloud**: A cloud infrastructure is operated solely for a single organization, either on-premises or hosted by a third party. It offers more control and security.

- **Hybrid Cloud**: This combines public and private clouds, enabling data and applications to be shared between them. It offers flexibility and optimization for existing infrastructure.

- **Multi-Cloud**: Involves using services from multiple cloud providers. Organizations might choose this model to avoid vendor lock-in or leverage the best features of each provider.

Benefits of Cloud Computing

The rapid adoption of cloud computing is driven by its numerous advantages:

- **Cost Efficiency**: Pay-as-you-go models reduce capital expenditure and eliminate over-provisioning.

- **Scalability**: Instantly scale applications and infrastructure based on demand.

- **Performance**: Access high-performance resources with global distribution and redundancy.

- **Speed and Agility**: Accelerate development, testing, and deployment cycles.

- **Reliability**: Data backup, disaster recovery, and fault tolerance are built into the architecture.

- **Security**: Cloud providers invest heavily in security features and compliance certifications.

Real-World Use Cases

Cloud computing is not just theoretical — it powers everyday applications and critical business operations across industries:

- **Healthcare**: Storing and analyzing patient records, enabling telemedicine, and running health-related AI models.

- **Finance**: Running risk modeling systems, fraud detection, and regulatory reporting.

- **Education**: Delivering virtual classrooms, managing student data, and supporting research collaboration.

- **Retail**: Managing inventory, running e-commerce platforms, and analyzing customer behavior.

Understanding Cloud Economics

Cloud economics involves understanding how to manage and optimize costs in the cloud. Azure provides detailed pricing calculators and cost analysis tools, helping users plan and budget effectively. Key principles include:

- **Right-sizing resources** to avoid over-provisioning

- **Utilizing reserved instances** for predictable workloads

- **Auto-scaling** to handle variable demand

- **Tagging resources** for accountability and tracking

- **Setting budgets and alerts** to avoid surprises

For example, you might use the Azure Pricing Calculator to estimate monthly costs for a web app hosted in Azure App Service with a Standard App Service Plan:

```
az appservice plan create --name MyPlan --resource-group
MyResourceGroup \
  --sku S1 --is-linux
```

The Role of Virtualization

At the heart of cloud computing lies virtualization. By decoupling hardware from the operating system, virtualization allows multiple operating systems to run concurrently on a single physical machine. Hypervisors like Microsoft Hyper-V, VMware vSphere, and KVM are commonly used in cloud environments to enable resource sharing and isolation.

This is a fundamental concept, especially when provisioning Virtual Machines (VMs) in Azure. Users choose the OS, CPU cores, memory, and disk space, all within minutes — compared to days or weeks in traditional setups.

Cloud-Native and Serverless Concepts

The rise of **cloud-native** development brings new architectural patterns such as microservices, containers, and serverless computing. These patterns are designed to take full advantage of cloud platforms:

- **Containers** (e.g., Docker, Kubernetes) provide consistent runtime environments.

- **Microservices** architecture separates applications into small, loosely coupled services.

- **Serverless** computing (e.g., Azure Functions) allows you to write code that runs in response to events without managing infrastructure.

These paradigms enable developers to build scalable, resilient applications faster than ever before.

Summary

Cloud computing is no longer an emerging technology — it's the new normal. Understanding its core principles, models, and benefits lays the groundwork for mastering Azure and leveraging it to create impactful solutions. As we progress through this book, you'll gain hands-on knowledge of Azure's services, tools, and architectures, equipping you for real-world cloud challenges and career opportunities.

The Rise of Microsoft Azure

Microsoft Azure has emerged as one of the leading public cloud platforms in the world, serving millions of customers and providing an extensive range of services across computing, storage, networking, machine learning, and more. What began as a platform-as-a-service (PaaS) initiative called "Windows Azure" in 2010 has evolved into a full-fledged cloud ecosystem, capable of supporting everything from small startups to Fortune 500 enterprises.

The growth and adoption of Azure is rooted in several factors: Microsoft's legacy enterprise customer base, its vast global infrastructure, continuous innovation, and its integration with industry standards and open-source technologies. In this section, we explore how Azure became what it is today, why it continues to grow rapidly, and how its evolution impacts businesses, developers, and IT professionals worldwide.

Early Beginnings and Strategic Vision

When Azure launched in 2010 as Windows Azure, its primary goal was to offer developers a platform for building and deploying applications without managing infrastructure. At the time, cloud computing was still gaining traction, and Microsoft's entry was met with both interest and skepticism. Amazon Web Services (AWS) had already captured early adopters, but Microsoft brought something different to the table — a strong presence in the enterprise space, an extensive partner ecosystem, and a trusted brand.

Microsoft quickly recognized the need to expand Azure beyond PaaS to include Infrastructure as a Service (IaaS), allowing customers to run virtual machines and traditional workloads in the cloud. This transition, along with the rebranding to Microsoft Azure in 2014, signaled a shift toward a broader, more inclusive cloud strategy.

Building a Global Footprint

Azure's growth has been underpinned by an aggressive global expansion strategy. Today, Azure operates in more than 60 regions and over 160 data centers, offering customers data residency and compliance options in virtually every major geography. Microsoft refers to these as *Azure Regions*, each consisting of one or more datacenters equipped with independent power, cooling, and networking.

This global footprint enables Azure to provide:

- **High Availability**: Applications can be deployed across multiple regions for redundancy.

- **Low Latency**: Proximity to users ensures faster access and performance.

- **Compliance**: Organizations can choose to store data in specific jurisdictions to meet legal and regulatory requirements.

For example, a multinational enterprise can host its web front-end in the US, its APIs in the UK, and its customer database in Germany — all using Azure.

You can list available Azure regions using the Azure CLI:

```
az account list-locations -o table
```

Service Offerings and Innovation

Azure is not just a hosting environment. It is a platform that enables innovation across verticals. As of this writing, Azure offers over 200 products and cloud services, organized into several categories:

- **Compute**: Virtual Machines, App Services, Functions, Kubernetes Service (AKS)

- **Storage**: Blob, Queue, Table, Disk, and File Storage

- **Networking**: Virtual Networks, Load Balancer, Application Gateway, ExpressRoute

- **Databases**: Azure SQL Database, Cosmos DB, MySQL, PostgreSQL

- **AI & Machine Learning**: Azure Machine Learning, Cognitive Services, Bot Services

- **DevOps**: Azure DevOps, GitHub Actions for Azure, CI/CD pipelines

- **Security**: Azure Active Directory, Key Vault, Sentinel, Defender for Cloud

- **IoT**: IoT Hub, Azure Sphere, Digital Twins

- **Analytics**: Azure Synapse Analytics, Data Lake, Stream Analytics, Databricks

Azure also supports numerous programming languages, frameworks, and platforms. Whether you're developing in .NET, Java, Python, Node.js, or Go — Azure has first-class tooling and support.

Hybrid and Multi-Cloud Strategy

Microsoft has always embraced the hybrid cloud model — allowing customers to run workloads on-premises, in the cloud, or in a combination of both. Azure Arc and Azure Stack are flagship offerings in this domain.

- **Azure Arc** allows you to manage on-premises, multi-cloud, and edge environments as if they were native Azure resources. This unifies governance and simplifies operations.

- **Azure Stack** brings Azure services and capabilities to your own data center. It's ideal for disconnected environments or compliance-heavy industries.

This hybrid approach has made Azure particularly appealing to industries like government, finance, and healthcare, where data sovereignty, security, and latency are critical.

Additionally, Azure has increased its support for **multi-cloud** strategies. With tools like Azure Arc and the ability to integrate with AWS and GCP resources, Microsoft acknowledges that many enterprises will adopt multiple providers for different workloads.

Enterprise and Developer Focus

Microsoft's success in the enterprise space has been a major growth driver for Azure. Organizations already invested in Microsoft technologies (e.g., Windows Server, SQL Server, Active Directory, SharePoint, Office 365) find it easier to transition to Azure because of compatibility and integration.

Azure provides benefits such as:

- **Seamless identity management** with Azure Active Directory

- **License portability** with Hybrid Use Benefits

- **Direct integration** with Microsoft 365 and Dynamics 365

- **Enterprise Agreements and cost savings** for large-scale deployments

From a developer perspective, Azure's integration with Visual Studio, GitHub, and VS Code offers a frictionless development experience. Azure DevOps provides an end-to-end toolchain for CI/CD, agile planning, and code management.

Here's an example of deploying a .NET application to Azure App Service using GitHub Actions:

```
name: Build and Deploy .NET App to Azure

on:
  push:
    branches:
      - main

jobs:
  build-and-deploy:
    runs-on: ubuntu-latest
    steps:
      - uses: actions/checkout@v2
      - name: Setup .NET
        uses: actions/setup-dotnet@v1
        with:
          dotnet-version: '7.0.x'
      - name: Build
```

```
      run: dotnet build MyApp.sln
    - name: Deploy to Azure Web App
      uses: azure/webapps-deploy@v2
      with:
        app-name: 'my-webapp-name'
        publish-profile: ${{ secrets.AZURE_WEBAPP_PUBLISH_PROFILE
}}
        package: '.'
```

Security, Compliance, and Trust

Microsoft Azure places heavy emphasis on security and compliance, investing over $1 billion annually in cybersecurity. Azure's security features include:

- **Azure Security Center**: Unified security management and threat protection.

- **Azure Key Vault**: Secure storage of keys, secrets, and certificates.

- **Azure Policy**: Enforce organizational standards and assess compliance.

- **Microsoft Defender for Cloud**: Threat detection across hybrid and cloud environments.

Azure is also certified for more than 90 compliance offerings including:

- ISO/IEC 27001, 27017, 27018

- SOC 1/2/3

- FedRAMP

- GDPR

- HIPAA

- PCI DSS

These certifications make Azure a viable platform for organizations with stringent regulatory requirements.

Market Share and Competitive Landscape

While AWS was the pioneer in cloud computing, Azure has significantly closed the gap. As of recent reports, Azure holds the second-largest market share globally, with strong momentum in sectors like government, education, and regulated industries.

Azure's ability to provide comprehensive hybrid solutions, leverage existing Microsoft ecosystems, and invest in cutting-edge technologies (like AI, quantum computing, and edge computing) continues to differentiate it in a competitive space.

Azure's Ecosystem and Community

Azure isn't just a product — it's an ecosystem. From certifications to community forums, Microsoft has invested in creating a rich learning and support environment.

- **Microsoft Learn**: Interactive training modules and certifications

- **Azure Marketplace**: A catalog of third-party solutions and templates

- **Microsoft Q&A and Tech Community**: Peer and expert support

- **GitHub**: Microsoft's acquisition of GitHub has deepened Azure's connection with the open-source community

There's also a strong presence of meetups, conferences, and user groups focused on Azure. These foster learning, networking, and collaboration.

Looking Ahead

Azure continues to evolve rapidly. With its focus on AI (Azure OpenAI, Cognitive Services), edge computing (Azure IoT, Azure Stack Edge), sustainability (carbon-negative goals), and quantum computing (Azure Quantum), Microsoft is investing in the future.

Azure's relevance is only growing as businesses increasingly rely on the cloud for innovation, agility, and scalability. Learning Azure today not only positions you to understand modern technology but equips you to participate in the digital transformation of tomorrow.

Summary

The rise of Microsoft Azure is a story of adaptability, scale, and vision. From its roots as a platform-as-a-service offering to a vast ecosystem supporting every aspect of IT and application development, Azure is central to the cloud computing landscape.

Whether you're an IT professional looking to migrate workloads, a developer deploying applications, or a student building your skills, Azure offers the tools and opportunities to succeed. With deep integrations, robust services, and a global presence, Microsoft Azure is more than just a cloud provider — it's a platform for the future.

Career Opportunities in the Azure Ecosystem

The cloud computing revolution has fundamentally changed the IT job landscape, introducing new roles and expanding traditional ones into the digital-first age. Microsoft Azure, as one of the top cloud platforms globally, is a centerpiece in this transformation. Organizations across the world are embracing Azure to build, deploy, and manage applications — and in doing so, they are fueling the demand for professionals with Azure expertise.

This section explores the breadth of career opportunities available in the Azure ecosystem, spanning technical, managerial, and strategic roles. We'll examine core responsibilities, skills required, career progression, certifications, and the realities of working in an Azure-powered environment. Whether you're new to IT or looking to pivot your current career toward cloud technologies, Azure offers a clear and compelling path forward.

The Demand for Azure Professionals

As companies migrate from on-premises environments to cloud-first or hybrid infrastructures, they need skilled professionals who can navigate the Azure platform confidently. Microsoft reports that over 95% of Fortune 500 companies use Azure in some form, and the platform is expanding its reach in government, education, healthcare, retail, and financial services.

According to leading job portals, roles requiring Azure skills have seen double-digit growth year over year. These include both hands-on engineering roles and higher-level positions in architecture, governance, and strategic cloud transformation.

Several factors drive this demand:

- Rapid digital transformation across industries

- The complexity of hybrid and multi-cloud environments

- A need for automation and DevOps practices

- Growing emphasis on security and compliance

- The rise of AI, data analytics, and IoT use cases

Azure Career Paths and Roles

The Azure ecosystem offers a diverse range of roles suited to different skill sets and interests. Below are some of the most in-demand careers you can pursue:

Cloud Administrator

Responsibilities:

- Managing Azure subscriptions and resources

- Configuring virtual networks, VMs, and storage

- Monitoring system health and performance

- Implementing backup and disaster recovery

Skills Required:

- Familiarity with the Azure portal, CLI, and PowerShell

- Understanding of networking, virtualization, and security

- Experience with tools like Azure Monitor and Azure Backup

Tools Used:

```
az vm create --resource-group MyResourceGroup \
  --name MyVM --image UbuntuLTS \
  --admin-username azureuser --generate-ssh-keys
```

Azure Developer

Responsibilities:

- Building and deploying apps using Azure App Services, Functions, and APIs

- Integrating services like Azure Cosmos DB, Key Vault, and Event Grid

- Writing scalable and secure serverless solutions

Skills Required:

- Proficiency in programming languages like C#, JavaScript, Python

- Familiarity with REST APIs and SDKs

- Knowledge of Azure DevOps and CI/CD pipelines

Example:

```
[FunctionName("HttpTrigger")]
public static async Task<IActionResult> Run(
    [HttpTrigger(AuthorizationLevel.Function, "get", "post", Route =
null)] HttpRequest req,
```

```
    ILogger log)
{
    log.LogInformation("C# HTTP trigger function processed a
request.");
    string name = req.Query["name"];
    return new OkObjectResult($"Hello, {name}");
}
```

Azure Solutions Architect

Responsibilities:

- Designing scalable, secure, and cost-effective Azure solutions

- Translating business requirements into technical specifications

- Overseeing cloud migrations and modernization efforts

Skills Required:

- Deep knowledge of IaaS, PaaS, networking, identity, and storage

- Experience with architecture frameworks and cost optimization

- Familiarity with hybrid and multi-cloud strategies

Certifications Recommended:

- Microsoft Certified: Azure Solutions Architect Expert

- Microsoft Certified: Azure Administrator Associate

DevOps Engineer

Responsibilities:

- Automating builds, tests, and deployments using Azure Pipelines

- Managing infrastructure as code using ARM, Bicep, or Terraform

- Monitoring performance and ensuring CI/CD best practices

Skills Required:

- Proficiency with scripting (PowerShell, Bash) and version control (Git)

- Experience with YAML pipelines, Docker, Kubernetes (AKS)

- Strong understanding of development and operations processes

Example YAML Snippet:

```
trigger:
  branches:
    include:
      - main

jobs:
- job: BuildAndDeploy
  pool:
    vmImage: ubuntu-latest
  steps:
  - task: DotNetCoreCLI@2
    inputs:
      command: 'build'
      projects: '**/*.csproj'
```

Data Engineer / Data Scientist

Responsibilities:

- Designing and maintaining data pipelines with Azure Data Factory

- Performing ETL and data integration from various sources

- Analyzing data using Azure Synapse, Machine Learning, and Databricks

Skills Required:

- Knowledge of SQL, Python, Spark, and big data tools

- Familiarity with data lakes, data warehouses, and governance

- Ability to build and deploy machine learning models

Common Tools:

- Azure Data Factory

- Azure Synapse Analytics

- Azure Machine Learning Studio

- Power BI

Security Engineer

Responsibilities:

- Securing Azure resources and enforcing compliance policies

- Managing identity and access using Azure AD and RBAC

- Monitoring and mitigating threats with Microsoft Defender

Skills Required:

- Understanding of security best practices and threat modeling

- Familiarity with SIEM tools like Azure Sentinel

- Experience with network security, encryption, and identity management

Security Rule Creation Example:

```
az network nsg rule create \
  --resource-group MyResourceGroup \
  --nsg-name MyNSG \
  --name AllowSSH \
  --protocol Tcp \
  --direction Inbound \
  --source-address-prefix '*' \
  --source-port-range '*' \
  --destination-address-prefix '*' \
  --destination-port-range 22 \
  --access Allow \
  --priority 1000
```

Certification as a Career Catalyst

Microsoft has developed a well-structured certification path tailored to each career role. These certifications not only validate your skills but also significantly enhance your employability and earning potential.

Some popular certifications include:

- **AZ-900: Microsoft Azure Fundamentals**

- **AZ-104: Azure Administrator Associate**

- **AZ-204: Azure Developer Associate**

- **AZ-305: Azure Solutions Architect Expert**

- **DP-203: Data Engineering on Microsoft Azure**

- **SC-300: Identity and Access Administrator Associate**

- **AZ-400: Azure DevOps Engineer Expert**

Certifications are not just resume boosters — they demonstrate to employers that you're serious about your career and committed to staying current in a fast-evolving field.

Salaries and Earning Potential

Azure professionals enjoy competitive salaries across roles and regions. Here are approximate figures (subject to location, experience, and organization):

- **Azure Administrator**: $70,000 – $100,000+

- **Azure Developer**: $80,000 – $120,000+

- **Solutions Architect**: $110,000 – $160,000+

- **DevOps Engineer**: $90,000 – $140,000+

- **Data Engineer/Scientist**: $95,000 – $150,000+

- **Security Engineer**: $100,000 – $150,000+

Freelancers and consultants with Azure expertise can also command premium hourly rates, especially those who hold multiple certifications or specialize in niche domains like compliance or hybrid architecture.

Soft Skills and Professional Development

While technical knowledge is vital, successful Azure professionals also cultivate key soft skills:

- **Communication**: Explaining technical concepts to non-technical stakeholders

- **Problem-solving**: Diagnosing complex issues and designing practical solutions

- **Project Management**: Managing timelines, risks, and priorities

- **Teamwork**: Collaborating across departments and teams

Many organizations now look for T-shaped professionals — individuals with deep expertise in one area and broad knowledge across others.

Career Progression

Azure professionals often find themselves on fast-tracked career paths. A typical progression might look like this:

- Junior Azure Admin → Senior Admin → Architect or Cloud Manager

- Azure Developer → Lead Developer → DevOps Engineer → CTO

- Support Engineer → Consultant → Solution Architect → Practice Lead

As your experience grows, you can transition from hands-on roles to strategy, governance, and leadership positions — or even become an independent consultant, trainer, or author.

Breaking into the Azure Ecosystem

If you're just starting out, here are practical steps to begin your Azure career:

1. **Start with AZ-900**: Learn the fundamentals of cloud computing and Azure services.

2. **Create an Azure Free Account**: Practice hands-on using the $200 in free credits.

3. **Follow Microsoft Learn Paths**: Interactive, free modules tailored by role.

4. **Work on Real Projects**: Deploy web apps, automate tasks, or analyze data.

5. **Join the Community**: Attend meetups, follow Azure blogs, and contribute to forums.

6. **Document Your Learning**: Use a blog or GitHub portfolio to showcase your skills.

7. **Prepare for Certification Exams**: Use practice tests, official guides, and study groups.

Summary

The career opportunities in the Azure ecosystem are vast, lucrative, and constantly evolving. As more organizations migrate to the cloud, the demand for skilled Azure professionals will only continue to rise. Whether you're passionate about development, infrastructure, data, security, or automation, Azure provides a platform to build a rewarding career.

With the right mix of skills, certifications, and real-world experience, you can position yourself at the forefront of the cloud computing revolution. The journey starts with curiosity and commitment — and there's no better time to begin than now.

Prerequisites and Mindset for Learning Azure

Embarking on a journey to master Microsoft Azure involves more than simply studying cloud services or passing certification exams. It requires building a solid technical foundation, developing practical problem-solving skills, and most importantly, cultivating the right mindset. Cloud computing — and Azure in particular — is a fast-moving domain that demands continuous learning, adaptability, and a strong understanding of both theoretical and applied concepts.

In this section, we'll examine the knowledge and tools that serve as prerequisites for learning Azure effectively. We'll also explore the learning strategies, mindset shifts, and best practices that help learners at all levels — from beginners to seasoned IT professionals — succeed in their Azure journey.

Foundational Technical Skills

Before diving into Azure's vast array of services, it's essential to build or strengthen your understanding in several core areas. These skills will not only help you grasp Azure concepts more effectively but also empower you to design better solutions and troubleshoot issues with confidence.

1. Operating Systems

Familiarity with both Windows and Linux is vital. Azure supports both platforms across virtual machines, containers, app hosting, and serverless environments.

- Know how to use the command line or terminal

- Understand basic file system navigation, user permissions, and service management

- Learn to write simple scripts (e.g., PowerShell for Windows, Bash for Linux)

Example: Connecting to a Linux VM via SSH

```
ssh azureuser@your-vm-ip
```

2. Networking Fundamentals

Cloud services heavily depend on virtual networks, subnets, IP addressing, DNS, and routing. A foundational understanding of networking is critical for tasks such as securing services, creating hybrid connections, and deploying scalable applications.

Key concepts include:

- TCP/IP, DNS, DHCP

- NAT and firewalls

- Load balancing and traffic routing

- VPN and ExpressRoute

Example: Creating a virtual network in Azure using the CLI

```
az network vnet create \
  --name MyVNet \
  --resource-group MyResourceGroup \
  --subnet-name MySubnet
```

3. Virtualization and Containers

Virtual machines are a core Azure service. Understanding how virtualization works helps with sizing, performance tuning, and cost optimization.

- Learn about hypervisors (Type 1 and 2)

- Understand VM lifecycles and configuration options

- Get comfortable with Docker containers (important for microservices and DevOps)

4. Programming and Scripting

While you don't need to be a software engineer to use Azure, having basic knowledge of programming or scripting significantly enhances your capabilities — especially in automation, DevOps, and serverless computing.

- Recommended languages: PowerShell, Bash, Python, C#, JavaScript

- Learn how to interact with REST APIs

- Write scripts to automate resource provisioning and deployments

5. Security Basics

Security is paramount in the cloud. Concepts like identity, authentication, authorization, and encryption are integral to working with Azure securely.

- Understand how Azure Active Directory works

- Learn about Role-Based Access Control (RBAC)

- Know basic encryption (in transit and at rest)

- Explore secure coding and threat modeling practices

Recommended Tools and Platforms

Getting hands-on is one of the most effective ways to learn Azure. Here are tools and resources to make your journey smoother:

Azure Portal

The graphical web-based UI for managing and configuring Azure resources. It's the most beginner-friendly starting point.

Azure CLI

A cross-platform command-line tool to manage Azure resources. Ideal for automation and scripting.

```
az login
az group create --name MyResourceGroup --location eastus
```

Azure PowerShell

PowerShell modules tailored for Azure management, favored by Windows administrators.

```
Connect-AzAccount
New-AzResourceGroup -Name MyResourceGroup -Location "East US"
```

Visual Studio Code

A lightweight, extensible code editor with Azure extensions for resource management, debugging, and deployment.

GitHub and Azure DevOps

Version control and CI/CD platforms integrated with Azure. Knowing Git and GitHub Actions or Azure Pipelines can greatly enhance your DevOps skills.

Microsoft Learn

A free platform with interactive tutorials, sandboxes, and learning paths mapped to certifications and roles.

Learning Approaches That Work

How you approach learning Azure is just as important as what you learn. Here are effective strategies to maximize your growth.

1. Hands-on First

Azure learning should be practical. Theory without application will lead to superficial understanding. Use the Azure free tier and sandbox environments to deploy and test real services.

- Create virtual machines

- Host a simple website using App Services

- Set up a serverless function triggered by an HTTP call

- Connect a database to a web app

2. Break Things (Safely)

One of the best ways to learn is by breaking and fixing things. Try deploying resources with incorrect parameters, or explore how access permissions affect resource behavior.

Just be sure to clean up unused resources to avoid charges:

```
az group delete --name MyResourceGroup
```

3. Learn in Layers

Don't try to learn everything at once. Focus first on understanding core services: compute, storage, networking, and identity. Then gradually move into advanced areas like automation, monitoring, containers, and AI.

4. Work on Projects

Apply your knowledge by building something tangible. Examples include:

- A blog hosted on Azure App Service

- A task tracker with a serverless backend

- A chatbot using Azure Bot Service and Cognitive Services

- A CI/CD pipeline using GitHub and Azure Pipelines

5. Join the Community

Learning with others accelerates progress. Consider:

- Attending local or virtual meetups

- Participating in online forums like Microsoft Q&A or Stack Overflow

- Following Azure experts on LinkedIn and Twitter

- Contributing to open-source projects on GitHub

The Growth Mindset

Perhaps the most important prerequisite for learning Azure is adopting a growth mindset. The cloud is always changing. Today's best practices may evolve tomorrow. To thrive, you must stay curious, resilient, and humble.

Key principles of the growth mindset in cloud learning:

- **Embrace challenges**: Learning something new will be uncomfortable. Lean into that discomfort.

- **Be patient**: Azure is vast. You won't understand everything immediately — and that's okay.

- **Reflect and iterate**: After each hands-on experience, ask: What did I learn? What could I do better?

- **Celebrate progress**: Even small wins matter. Successfully deploying your first VM is a milestone worth acknowledging.

Common Pitfalls to Avoid

Here are a few common mistakes Azure learners make — and how to avoid them:

- **Focusing only on certifications**: Certifications are valuable, but hands-on experience is what really prepares you for real-world scenarios.

- **Ignoring costs**: Always monitor your usage, even on free accounts. Accidental provisioning of premium resources can incur charges.

- **Overcomplicating early projects**: Start simple. A basic CRUD app on Azure App Service is better than an overly complex microservice architecture when you're just beginning.

- **Learning in isolation**: Collaborate, share, and ask questions. The Azure community is vast and supportive.

Staying Current

Azure evolves rapidly. New features are released monthly. Stay up to date by:

- Subscribing to Azure blog and release notes

- Following Microsoft's "What's New in Azure" updates

- Attending Microsoft Ignite, Build, and other conferences

- Enrolling in refresher courses annually

Microsoft Learn also includes "role-based learning paths" that evolve with service updates and certification changes.

Summary

Learning Azure is not a one-time event — it's a continuous journey. Having the right technical prerequisites certainly helps, but it's your approach, mindset, and dedication to practical experience that will determine your success.

Start with foundational skills in networking, virtualization, scripting, and security. Use the tools Microsoft provides — the Portal, CLI, VS Code, and Learn — to gain hands-on familiarity. Build projects, ask questions, and challenge yourself to solve real-world problems.

Most importantly, adopt a mindset of growth, curiosity, and persistence. The Azure cloud is vast, but every expert was once a beginner who kept showing up, kept learning, and kept experimenting.

Welcome to your Azure journey — it starts here, but it can take you anywhere.

Chapter 2: Getting Started with Microsoft Azure

Creating and Configuring Your Azure Account

Creating and configuring your Azure account is the essential first step to becoming proficient in Microsoft's powerful cloud platform. Whether you're a developer, an IT professional, or a student exploring the cloud for the first time, setting up your Azure environment correctly from the beginning sets a solid foundation for everything that follows. This section walks you through the complete process—from registering for an account, understanding the free tier, exploring the Azure Portal, and configuring essential settings like regions and defaults, all the way to preparing your development and automation environments.

Setting Up a Microsoft Azure Account

To get started with Azure, you'll need a Microsoft account. If you already use services like Outlook, Xbox, or Skype, you already have one. Otherwise, creating one is simple.

1. Visit https://azure.microsoft.com.

2. Click on **Start Free** or **Try Azure for Free**.

3. Sign in with your Microsoft account or create one.

4. Complete the sign-up form. You'll need:

   ○ A phone number (for identity verification)

   ○ A valid credit/debit card (for identity verification only; you won't be charged for free-tier services)

   ○ A valid email address

After registering, Microsoft offers a generous **Azure Free Account**, which includes:

- $200 USD in credits for the first 30 days

- Free limited-tier access to certain services for 12 months (e.g., B1S VM, 250 GB SQL DB storage)

- Always free services (with usage caps)

It's important to be aware of what falls within the free tier to avoid unexpected charges.

Azure Account Hierarchy and Structure

Once your account is active, understanding the structural hierarchy is essential.

- **Account**: Your root identity, which contains all your resources.

- **Subscriptions**: Logical containers for resources. Billing and usage are tied to subscriptions.

- **Resource Groups**: Containers that hold related resources.

- **Resources**: Instances of services like VMs, databases, or storage accounts.

For example, a virtual machine, a storage account, and a virtual network created for a single app might all be housed in a single resource group.

You can have multiple subscriptions under a single account—useful for separating billing by department, environment (e.g., dev, test, prod), or project.

Navigating the Azure Portal

The **Azure Portal** is a web-based, graphical interface for managing your Azure resources. After logging in at https://portal.azure.com, you'll see:

- **Dashboard**: Customizable with tiles for your favorite services and resources.

- **Search Bar**: Quickly find any resource, service, or documentation.

- **Left-hand Menu**: Quick access to commonly used services (like Virtual Machines, Storage, and App Services).

- **Notifications Bell**: Alerts, deployment status, and errors.

- **Cloud Shell**: Embedded command-line interface supporting both Bash and PowerShell.

Creating Your First Resource: A Virtual Machine

To make your setup more concrete, let's walk through creating a simple Windows VM.

1. From the portal home page, click **Create a resource** > **Compute** > **Virtual Machine**.

2. Fill out the **Basics** tab:

   - Subscription: Free Trial

   - Resource Group: Create a new one, e.g., MyFirstRG

   - Virtual machine name: TestVM01

   - Region: Select the closest or most relevant Azure region

   - Image: Windows Server 2022

   - Size: Use a free-tier eligible size like B1S

   - Administrator Account: Enter a username and password

3. In the **Disks** tab, leave the default settings.

4. In **Networking**, allow selected ports (e.g., RDP - 3389).

5. Review + Create > Create

This spins up a VM you can RDP into. Azure also gives you pricing details and an estimated monthly cost—critical for managing costs effectively.

Understanding Azure Regions and Availability Zones

Azure has data centers around the world. When creating resources, you must choose a **region**—which affects latency, availability, and compliance.

Regions are geographic areas like:

- **East US**

- **West Europe**

- **Southeast Asia**

Some services aren't available in all regions, and pricing varies by location. Use the Azure Products by Region page to verify.

Availability Zones are unique physical locations within a region. For highly available apps, deploy across multiple zones.

Azure Resource Naming Conventions

Azure recommends consistent and meaningful naming conventions to ensure clarity and manageability across large environments.

For example:

- VMs: `vm-web-uks-prod-001`

- Resource groups: `rg-ecommerce-dev`

- Storage accounts: `staccmediafiles01`

Following a standard improves collaboration, automation, and cost tracking.

Working with Azure Cloud Shell

Azure Cloud Shell is your browser-based command-line interface. It supports both **Bash** and **PowerShell**, comes preloaded with Azure CLI, and automatically authenticates to your account.

To start Cloud Shell:

1. Click the **Shell icon** at the top of the portal.

2. Choose Bash or PowerShell.

3. Create a storage account if prompted (Cloud Shell uses it to persist files).

Example: List all resource groups in your subscription:

```
az group list --output table
```

Or create a new one:

```
az group create --name MyFirstRG --location eastus
```

This method is ideal for scripting and automation without needing to install anything locally.

Using Azure CLI Locally

While Cloud Shell is powerful, many users prefer using the Azure CLI locally.

Install the CLI:

- **Windows**: Download and run the installer: https://aka.ms/installazurecliwindows

macOS:

```
brew update && brew install azure-cli
```

-

Linux:

```
curl -sL https://aka.ms/InstallAzureCLIDeb | sudo bash
```

-

Authenticate:
```
az login
```

A browser window will open. After login, CLI commands are available.

Configuring Default Settings with Azure CLI

To avoid repeating subscription and location info, set defaults:

```
az configure --defaults group=MyFirstRG location=eastus
```

Now, subsequent commands like creating a storage account will inherit those defaults.

```
az storage account create --name mystorageacct001 --sku Standard_LRS
```

Azure Subscription and Billing Alerts

To prevent budget overruns, configure billing alerts and budgets in the **Cost Management + Billing** section:

1. Go to **Subscriptions** > select your subscription

2. Click **Budgets**

3. Add a budget (e.g., $50/month)

4. Set email alerts for thresholds (50%, 75%, 100%)

This helps manage the free credits and avoid unexpected charges once your trial ends.

Summary

Creating and configuring your Azure account is more than just signing up—it's about understanding Azure's structure, using the right tools, and taking precautions to manage resources and costs effectively. From choosing your region and subscription to navigating the portal and automating tasks via Cloud Shell or the CLI, your initial setup defines your experience in Azure. As you proceed through this book, you'll build on this strong foundation to create robust, scalable, and cost-efficient solutions.

Navigating the Azure Portal

The Azure Portal is the primary graphical interface for interacting with Microsoft Azure's vast array of services. It provides an intuitive, browser-based UI that enables developers, administrators, and analysts to manage cloud resources without needing to rely solely on command-line tools. Whether you're deploying a virtual machine, monitoring application performance, setting up security policies, or managing billing, the portal is your centralized control hub.

This section will explore the layout of the Azure Portal, explain how to access and organize resources, customize dashboards, manage subscriptions, use helpful productivity tools, and utilize diagnostic capabilities—all essential to becoming fluent in Azure.

Accessing the Azure Portal

The Azure Portal is accessible through any modern browser at:

https://portal.azure.com

To log in, use your Microsoft account or the credentials provided by your organization's Azure Active Directory tenant. Once authenticated, you'll be redirected to the default dashboard.

The portal operates entirely in the browser, meaning there is no need to install client software. It is mobile-friendly and can be accessed from smartphones and tablets, although certain UI components are best suited to desktops and laptops.

Azure Portal Layout

After logging in, you'll notice the portal is split into several key components:

- **Global Search Bar** (top): Used to search for services, resources, documentation, and help.

- **Left-Hand Menu (Azure Services Menu)**: Quick access to frequently used Azure services such as Virtual Machines, Storage Accounts, App Services, and more.

- **Dashboard**: The main area in the center that can be customized to show resource tiles, monitoring graphs, shortcuts, and recent activity.

- **Notifications Bell**: Located in the top-right corner, it shows deployment status, alerts, updates, and errors.

- **Settings and Directory Switcher**: Also in the top-right, for changing themes, managing account settings, or switching between Azure directories and tenants.

- **Cloud Shell Access**: A command-line terminal embedded directly into the portal.

The layout is highly customizable to support different workflows.

Searching and Filtering Resources

The global search bar is one of the most powerful tools in the portal. You can type almost anything—service names, resources, marketplace offers, documentation links—and it will provide real-time suggestions.

Example: Typing "vm" shows quick links to Virtual Machines, Marketplace VMs, and related documentation.

Every list of resources includes **filter** and **sort** capabilities. For instance, when viewing all Virtual Machines, you can filter by:

- Subscription

- Resource Group

- Region

- Status (running/stopped)

- OS type

This becomes especially important as your cloud footprint grows.

Creating Resources in the Portal

To create a new resource, you can click:

- **Create a Resource** from the left menu or the top bar

- **+** icon in service-specific pages (e.g., "+ Add" on the Virtual Machines page)

This opens a guided **blade** (a panel that slides out) where you configure all required fields.

Example: Creating a Storage Account

1. Click **Create a Resource > Storage > Storage Account**

2. Fill in the basics:

   o Resource Group: MyResourceGroup

   o Storage Account Name: myuniquestorageacct

   o Region: UK South

   o Performance: Standard

   o Redundancy: LRS (Locally Redundant Storage)

3. Click **Review + Create**

4. Click **Create**

Once deployed, you can navigate to the resource, view its properties, configure settings, or delete it.

Customizing the Dashboard

The Dashboard acts as your personal workspace. It's particularly useful for:

- Monitoring resource health

- Viewing charts and alerts

- Pinning frequently used items for easy access

To customize:

1. Click **Dashboard** in the left menu.

2. Click **Edit** at the top of the dashboard.

3. Add tiles using **+ Tile** or pin them from resource pages.

4. Resize and move tiles by dragging.

5. Click **Done Customizing** to save.

You can create **multiple dashboards** for different environments or roles (e.g., "Production Monitoring", "Dev Tools", "Finance View") and share them with your team.

Managing Resources

You can manage all your Azure resources from the **All Resources** page.

Navigation:

- Click **All Resources** from the left menu.

- Filter by **Resource Type**, **Subscription**, or **Tag**.

Clicking on a resource opens its overview blade. Common actions available from here include:

- Start/Stop/Restart (for VMs)

- Metrics and Logs

- Access Control (IAM)

- Tags

- Diagnostic Settings

For example, a Web App will show options to scale out, change app settings, or view deployment logs.

Resource Groups and Tagging

Resource Groups are organizational units that contain logically related resources. Managing by group allows bulk operations such as:

- Applying policies

- Deleting a project

- Assigning RBAC roles

Tags are name-value pairs you can assign to resources for metadata purposes. Useful tags include:

- `Environment = Production`

- `Owner = JohnDoe`

- `CostCenter = IT`

From the portal, tags can be applied at creation or added afterward via the **Tags** blade in any resource.

Using Azure Marketplace

The Azure Marketplace lets you deploy third-party solutions or preconfigured environments directly from the portal.

Steps:

1. Click **Create a Resource**

2. Search or browse the Marketplace

3. Select a solution (e.g., WordPress, Ubuntu Server, Fortinet Firewall)

4. Fill out the deployment wizard

These offerings often save time by avoiding manual configuration and can be integrated with other Azure services seamlessly.

Monitoring and Troubleshooting in the Portal

Every Azure resource comes with a set of monitoring tools. From the resource's blade, click **Monitoring** to access:

- **Metrics**: Real-time performance data

- **Alerts**: Custom thresholds that trigger emails or actions

- **Logs**: Diagnostic logs, activity logs, and audit trails

You can create custom alerts such as:

- CPU > 85% for 10 minutes

- Storage account nearing quota

- VM shut down unexpectedly

These alerts can trigger email, webhook, or Azure Logic App workflows.

Productivity Tools in the Portal

The Azure Portal is equipped with tools to boost productivity:

- **Cloud Shell**: Use Bash or PowerShell directly in your browser.

- **Azure Resource Graph Explorer**: Query your resources using Kusto Query Language (KQL).

- **Task Center**: Monitor progress of deployments, policy assignments, and updates.

- **Quickstart Center**: Guided onboarding experiences for common tasks like migrating servers or configuring networks.

- **Bastion**: Browser-based secure SSH/RDP access to VMs without needing public IPs.

For example, open Cloud Shell and run:

```
az vm list --output table
```

to see all your VMs.

Or use Resource Graph:

```
Resources
| where type == "microsoft.compute/virtualmachines"
| project name, location, resourceGroup
```

Managing Subscriptions and Directories

If you're managing multiple clients, departments, or environments, you may be part of more than one **subscription** or **Azure AD tenant**.

To switch:

1. Click your profile icon in the top-right corner.

2. Select **Switch Directory**.

3. Use the **Directory + Subscription** blade to filter resources by the current context.

This is essential for MSPs, consultants, or large enterprises using **Enterprise Agreements** or **CSP programs**.

Accessibility and Dark Mode

Azure Portal supports accessibility features:

- Screen reader compatibility

- Keyboard shortcuts

- Dark and high-contrast themes

To change theme:

1. Click your profile icon.

2. Choose **Portal Settings** > **Theme** > Select **Dark**, **Light**, or **High Contrast**.

Custom themes are saved per user and synchronized across devices.

Exporting Templates and Automation

Every resource created in the portal can be exported as an **ARM (Azure Resource Manager) template**, allowing you to automate future deployments.

From any resource:

1. Click **Export Template**

2. View/edit the JSON configuration

3. Download and reuse it with Azure CLI or DevOps pipelines

Example use case:

- Create a sample VM in the portal

- Export the ARM template

- Use it to deploy multiple VMs with minor changes (e.g., different names or sizes)

Summary

Navigating the Azure Portal effectively transforms a novice user into a productive Azure administrator or developer. With a combination of powerful graphical interfaces, embedded automation tools, and integrated monitoring, the portal allows you to build, manage, and troubleshoot complex environments with ease.

Mastering the portal means understanding its layout, customizing dashboards for workflows, managing resource access, monitoring usage, and even exporting configurations for automation. As you continue your Azure journey, this fluency in the portal will be your anchor for working efficiently and confidently in the cloud.

Understanding Azure Subscriptions and Billing

Microsoft Azure operates on a pay-as-you-go pricing model, where you are billed for the resources and services you use. At the heart of this billing model lies the concept of **subscriptions**, which act as logical containers for Azure resources and usage tracking. Understanding how subscriptions work, how they interact with resource groups, billing accounts, and cost management tools is critical for ensuring transparency, controlling expenses, and maintaining accountability in cloud environments.

In this section, we will explore the different types of Azure subscriptions, how to manage them, the role of billing accounts, setting up budgets and alerts, viewing invoices and cost analysis, and using built-in tools to forecast and optimize expenses.

What Is an Azure Subscription?

An Azure subscription is a logical container that holds Azure resources like virtual machines, databases, and networks. It is tied to a billing account and defines boundaries for:

- **Billing**: Each subscription has its own billing relationship.

- **Access Control**: You can assign different permissions to different subscriptions.

- **Quotas and Limits**: Resources are governed by limits at the subscription level (e.g., VM cores, storage accounts).

A single Azure account (identity) can manage multiple subscriptions, making it easy to separate environments like development, staging, and production or to isolate client workloads.

Types of Azure Subscriptions

Azure offers various types of subscriptions to suit individuals, businesses, and enterprises:

1. Free Trial

- $200 in Azure credits for the first 30 days.

- Limited to certain regions and quotas.

- Can be upgraded to a Pay-As-You-Go subscription.

2. Pay-As-You-Go

- Charges based on resource usage per second or per transaction.

- No upfront costs.

- Ideal for individuals and small organizations.

3. Azure for Students

- Includes $100 in credit for 12 months.

- No credit card required.

- Limited to students with a verified academic email.

4. Microsoft Customer Agreement (MCA)

- Billing directly with Microsoft.

- Suitable for SMBs and larger orgs with centralized billing needs.

5. Enterprise Agreement (EA)

- For large organizations committing to high usage.

- Offers volume discounts and enterprise-scale benefits.

- Involves a dedicated Microsoft account manager.

6. Cloud Solution Provider (CSP)

- Managed by a Microsoft partner.

- Resellers provide support and billing.

- Common among SMBs working with MSPs.

Each subscription type has its own billing rules, access control structure, and management interface.

Azure Subscription Hierarchy and Billing Structure

Understanding how subscriptions relate to the broader Azure billing architecture is essential.

- **Billing Account**: The top-level container. May be associated with a company or an individual.

- **Billing Profile**: Contains payment methods and invoices.

- **Invoice Section**: Specific grouping within a billing profile for invoicing purposes.

- **Subscription**: Where usage and costs accumulate.

Example hierarchy:

```
Billing Account: Contoso Ltd.
├── Billing Profile: R&D Department
│   ├── Invoice Section: Dev Projects
│   │   ├── Subscription: Dev-Env-1
│   │   └── Subscription: Dev-Env-2
```

Assigning Users and Roles to Subscriptions

Each subscription can have multiple users with different levels of access using **Role-Based Access Control (RBAC)**.

Common roles:

- **Owner**: Full management rights, including access and billing.

- **Contributor**: Manage resources but not permissions.

- **Reader**: View-only access.

To assign a user to a subscription:

1. Navigate to **Subscriptions** in the Azure Portal.

2. Select your subscription.

3. Click **Access Control (IAM)**.

4. Click **+ Add Role Assignment**.

5. Choose role, user, and scope.

You can also restrict users to only see resources within specific subscriptions, enhancing governance and security.

Managing Multiple Subscriptions

Organizations often use multiple subscriptions for isolation or billing separation.

Examples:

- Separate subscriptions for dev/test/prod

- One subscription per department or business unit

- Dedicated subscriptions per customer in multi-tenant apps

Switching between subscriptions:

1. Click your profile in the portal.

2. Click **Switch Directory** or **Directory + Subscription**.

3. Filter the resources shown by current subscription context.

Using **Management Groups**, you can apply governance policies and access controls across multiple subscriptions.

Cost Analysis in Azure Portal

Azure provides detailed cost tracking capabilities through the **Cost Management + Billing** section of the portal.

Steps to access:

1. Go to the portal.

2. Navigate to **Cost Management + Billing** > **Cost Analysis**.

3. Choose a subscription.

4. View charts and breakdowns by:

   - Resource

- o Region

- o Service

- o Tags

- o Time period

You can also export the data to Excel or Power BI.

Example: View cost per service

```
az consumption usage list --subscription "MySub" --output table
```

This command shows cost data in CLI for scripting or automation.

Setting Budgets and Alerts

Budgets allow you to define a spending threshold and receive notifications when you approach or exceed it.

To create a budget:

1. Navigate to **Cost Management + Billing**.

2. Click **Budgets > + Add**.

3. Choose:

   - o Subscription

   - o Budget name

   - o Reset period (monthly, quarterly)

   - o Amount (e.g., $200)

   - o Filters (e.g., by service, resource group, or tag)

4. Add alert conditions (e.g., 50%, 75%, 100%)

5. Assign email recipients or trigger automation

This helps prevent surprise charges and promotes financial discipline in cloud usage.

Reviewing Invoices and Downloading Billing Statements

Azure automatically generates monthly invoices per billing profile.

To review:

1. Navigate to **Cost Management + Billing**.

2. Select **Invoices** under the billing profile.

3. Download:

    ○ PDF invoice

    ○ CSV usage data

    ○ Tax details

Invoices are archived for up to 36 months and show detailed breakdowns including discounts, taxes, and adjustments.

Forecasting Future Costs

Azure provides predictive forecasting tools based on historical usage.

Steps:

1. Go to **Cost Management + Billing** > **Cost Analysis**.

2. Enable **Forecast** toggle in chart view.

3. Use the drop-down to forecast:

    ○ This month

    ○ Next quarter

    ○ By resource or tag

Forecasting is useful for budgeting and preparing for scale-out scenarios.

Tagging for Cost Attribution

To attribute costs effectively, use **Tags**.

For example:

- Tag all marketing-related resources with `Department = Marketing`.

- Tag dev VMs with `Environment = Dev`.

In **Cost Analysis**, you can group and filter by tag to see how much each department or project is spending.

To assign tags:

1. Open any resource.

2. Go to **Tags > + Add Tag**.

3. Enter key and value.

4. Save.

Use **Policy** to enforce tagging at creation time for governance.

Azure Pricing Calculator and TCO Estimator

Before deploying, use the **Azure Pricing Calculator** to estimate costs:

https://azure.microsoft.com/en-us/pricing/calculator

You can add services, adjust usage, and export a detailed pricing sheet. Useful for:

- Business case approvals

- Client proposals

- Scenario comparisons

For larger migrations, use the **Total Cost of Ownership (TCO) Estimator**:
https://azure.microsoft.com/en-us/pricing/tco/

Automation with Azure CLI and Billing APIs

Azure CLI and REST APIs allow you to automate cost tracking and alerts.

Example: List budgets

```
az consumption budget list --subscription "MySub"
```

Example: Query usage details

```
az consumption usage list --start-date 2024-03-01 --end-date 2024-03-31
```

You can schedule these scripts with Logic Apps or Azure Automation to send daily or weekly cost summaries via email.

Summary

Azure subscriptions are the backbone of account structure, usage tracking, and cost management. By understanding how subscriptions operate, how billing is calculated and attributed, and how to use built-in tools to monitor and forecast expenses, you can maintain control of your cloud spending and optimize costs over time.

From setting up multi-tiered billing hierarchies and tagging strategies to leveraging cost analysis, alerts, and automation, mastering subscription and billing management is crucial for running efficient and accountable cloud operations.

Azure CLI and PowerShell Basics

Azure provides multiple tools to interact with and manage resources programmatically. Two of the most powerful and widely-used command-line tools are **Azure Command-Line Interface (CLI)** and **Azure PowerShell**. While both serve similar purposes, they differ in syntax, platform integration, and scripting paradigms. This section delves deep into understanding and using both tools effectively to manage Azure resources, automate tasks, and streamline cloud workflows.

You will learn how to install and configure Azure CLI and PowerShell, authenticate and set defaults, run essential commands, use automation scripts, and determine which tool is best suited for your use case. Practical examples and best practices are provided throughout.

Installing Azure CLI

Azure CLI is a cross-platform command-line tool designed for managing Azure resources in a simple, consistent way. It works on Windows, macOS, and Linux.

Installation:

- **Windows**
  Download and run the installer:
  https://aka.ms/installazurecliwindows

macOS
Using Homebrew:

```
brew update && brew install azure-cli
```

-

Ubuntu/Debian

```
curl -sL https://aka.ms/InstallAzureCLIDeb | sudo bash
```

-

Check installation

```
az --version
```

-

This should return the installed version and available extensions.

Installing Azure PowerShell

Azure PowerShell is ideal for users familiar with Windows PowerShell or PowerShell Core. It enables scripting and automation with deep Windows integration.

Installation (PowerShell 7+ recommended):

Install module:

```
Install-Module -Name Az -AllowClobber -Scope CurrentUser
```

-

Verify installation:

```
Get-Module -Name Az -ListAvailable
```

-

Update module:

```
Update-Module -Name Az
```

-

Azure PowerShell works on Windows, macOS, and Linux through PowerShell Core.

Logging In and Authenticating

Azure CLI:

```
az login
```

This opens a browser window to authenticate. If running in a headless environment:

```
az login --use-device-code
```

Azure PowerShell:

```
Connect-AzAccount
```

Both tools support service principal authentication for automation:

```
az login --service-principal -u APP_ID -p PASSWORD --tenant
TENANT_ID

$securePassword = ConvertTo-SecureString "PASSWORD" -AsPlainText -
Force
$cred = New-Object System.Management.Automation.PSCredential
("APP_ID", $securePassword)
Connect-AzAccount -ServicePrincipal -Credential $cred -Tenant
"TENANT_ID"
```

Setting Subscription and Defaults

In environments with multiple subscriptions, always set the active one to avoid confusion.

Azure CLI:

```
az account set --subscription "Subscription Name"
```

Set defaults:

```
az configure --defaults group=MyResourceGroup location=westeurope
```

Azure PowerShell:

```
Set-AzContext -SubscriptionName "Subscription Name"
```

To view all subscriptions:

```
az account list --output table
```

```
Get-AzSubscription
```

Core Resource Management Commands

Let's explore how to manage common Azure resources using CLI and PowerShell.

Resource Groups

Create:

```
az group create --name MyResourceGroup --location eastus
```

```
New-AzResourceGroup -Name "MyResourceGroup" -Location "EastUS"
```

List:

```
az group list --output table
```

```
Get-AzResourceGroup
```

Delete:

```
az group delete --name MyResourceGroup --yes --no-wait
```

```
Remove-AzResourceGroup -Name "MyResourceGroup" -Force
```

Virtual Machines

Create a VM (CLI):

```
az vm create \
  --resource-group MyResourceGroup \
  --name MyVM \
  --image UbuntuLTS \
  --admin-username azureuser \
  --generate-ssh-keys
```

Create a VM (PowerShell):

```
New-AzVM `
  -ResourceGroupName "MyResourceGroup" `
  -Name "MyVM" `
  -Location "EastUS" `
  -VirtualNetworkName "MyVNet" `
  -SubnetName "MySubnet" `
  -SecurityGroupName "MyNSG" `
  -PublicIpAddressName "MyPublicIP" `
  -OpenPorts 22
```

Scripting with Azure CLI

Azure CLI scripts can be used in .sh files for automation.

Example: Script to create a storage account and container

```
#!/bin/bash

group="MyResourceGroup"
location="westeurope"
storage="mystorageacct$(date +%s)"

az group create --name $group --location $location
az storage account create --name $storage --resource-group $group --
location $location --sku Standard_LRS
az storage container create --name mycontainer --account-name
$storage --public-access off
```

Run it with:

```
bash setup-storage.sh
```

Scripting with Azure PowerShell

PowerShell scripts are written in `.ps1` files and can include loops, conditionals, and error handling.

Example: Creating a storage account and blob container

```
$resourceGroup = "MyResourceGroup"
$location = "EastUS"
$storageName = "mystorage$(Get-Random)"

New-AzResourceGroup -Name $resourceGroup -Location $location
New-AzStorageAccount -ResourceGroupName $resourceGroup -Name
$storageName -Location $location -SkuName "Standard_LRS" -Kind
"StorageV2"
$ctx = New-AzStorageContext -StorageAccountName $storageName -
UseConnectedAccount
New-AzStorageContainer -Name "mycontainer" -Context $ctx -Permission
Off
```

Run in PowerShell:

```
.\setup-storage.ps1
```

Azure Cloud Shell Integration

Both Azure CLI and PowerShell are available in **Azure Cloud Shell**, accessible via the Azure Portal. Benefits include:

- Pre-installed tools and modules

- Persistent file storage via Azure Files

- Instant access to your authenticated session

Choose between Bash (for CLI) and PowerShell when launching.

To upload and run a script:

1. Open Cloud Shell.

2. Click **Upload/Download** > **Upload**.

Choose your script and run it:

```
bash setup-vm.sh
```

3.

Or in PowerShell:

```
.\setup-network.ps1
```

Managing Identity and Access

You can assign roles and manage identities via the CLI and PowerShell.

CLI Example: Assign RBAC Role

```
az role assignment create --assignee user@example.com --role
Contributor --scope
/subscriptions/{subId}/resourceGroups/MyResourceGroup
```

PowerShell Example:

```
New-AzRoleAssignment -ObjectId "user-object-id" -RoleDefinitionName
"Reader" -Scope
"/subscriptions/{subId}/resourceGroups/MyResourceGroup"
```

Comparing CLI vs PowerShell

Feature	Azure CLI	Azure PowerShell
Syntax Style	Linux/Unix command-line	PowerShell-based
Platform	Cross-platform	Windows and PowerShell Core

Scripting Language	Shell/Bash	PowerShell
Learning Curve	Easier for new users	Preferred by .NET/Windows professionals
Cloud Shell Availability	Yes (Bash)	Yes (PowerShell)

Both tools can coexist. Some teams prefer CLI for scripting in CI/CD pipelines and PowerShell for automation in hybrid environments.

Debugging and Output Formats

Azure CLI supports multiple output formats:

```
az vm list --output table
az vm list --output json
az vm list --output yaml
```

Azure PowerShell uses standard PowerShell objects, which can be piped and formatted:

```
Get-AzVM | Format-Table Name, Location
```

For verbose output:

```
az vm start --name MyVM --resource-group MyGroup --debug

Start-AzVM -Name "MyVM" -ResourceGroupName "MyGroup" -Debug
```

Summary

Azure CLI and Azure PowerShell are essential tools for any cloud practitioner. Mastering both gives you the flexibility to automate deployments, manage resources efficiently, and integrate with CI/CD pipelines or other external systems.

Use Azure CLI when working in cross-platform environments or scripting with Bash. Choose PowerShell when deep integration with Windows, scripting with .NET objects, or working in hybrid data centers is needed.

Both tools empower you to go beyond the portal and take full control of your Azure infrastructure. By building proficiency in CLI and PowerShell, you're laying the groundwork for scalable, repeatable, and automated cloud operations.

Chapter 3: Core Azure Services Explained

Compute Services: VMs, App Services, and Functions

In the vast ecosystem of Microsoft Azure, compute services are the backbone of deploying and running applications. These services provide the processing power and infrastructure required to support anything from simple web apps to complex enterprise-grade systems. Azure offers multiple compute options, and understanding each is crucial for selecting the right one for your workloads. The most widely used compute services in Azure are Virtual Machines (VMs), Azure App Services, and Azure Functions. Each of these services caters to different use cases, levels of abstraction, and management responsibilities.

Virtual Machines (VMs)

Azure Virtual Machines are Infrastructure-as-a-Service (IaaS) offerings that allow you to create and manage your own virtualized computing environments in the cloud. With VMs, you have full control over the operating system, software, and configurations.

Key Features:

- Choice of Windows or Linux OS

- Persistent disks (managed or unmanaged)

- Custom VM sizes for CPU, memory, and disk

- Availability Zones and Sets for high availability

- Integration with virtual networks and firewalls

Use Cases:

- Hosting legacy applications

- Development and test environments

- Domain controllers and file servers

- Application backends with complex dependencies

Creating a VM using Azure CLI:

```
az vm create \
```

```
--name MyVM \
--resource-group MyResourceGroup \
--image UbuntuLTS \
--admin-username azureuser \
--generate-ssh-keys
```

This command deploys a basic Ubuntu VM with SSH key authentication. Azure provides images from its own gallery or allows you to use custom ones.

Cost Considerations:

VMs are charged based on the time they are running. You can save costs by using spot instances for non-critical workloads, resizing VMs appropriately, and shutting them down when not in use.

Best Practices:

- Use managed disks for better performance and reliability.

- Implement backup and disaster recovery strategies using Azure Backup.

- Leverage Azure Monitor to track performance and usage metrics.

Azure App Services

App Services are Platform-as-a-Service (PaaS) solutions designed for hosting web apps, RESTful APIs, and mobile backends. Azure abstracts away the infrastructure management, allowing you to focus solely on the application code.

Advantages of App Services:

- Automatic scaling and load balancing

- Integrated development tools (Visual Studio, GitHub)

- SSL, custom domains, and authentication support

- Easy deployment via GitHub Actions, Azure DevOps, or CLI

- Staging environments for zero-downtime deployments

Common Plans:

- **Free and Shared**: Limited testing environments

- **Basic**: Entry-level production workloads

- **Standard and Premium**: High-performance and scalable apps

Deploying an App using Azure CLI:

```
az webapp up --name my-webapp --resource-group MyResourceGroup --
runtime "NODE|18-lts"
```

This simple command deploys a Node.js application to Azure with a single CLI line. App Services automatically detect the runtime and configure the environment accordingly.

App Settings and Configuration:

App Services support environment variables and connection strings which can be managed directly from the Azure Portal or via CLI. This makes it easier to deploy applications consistently across environments.

```
az webapp config appsettings set \
  --name my-webapp \
  --resource-group MyResourceGroup \
  --settings "APP_ENV=production" "DB_CONN=xxxxx"
```

Custom Domains and SSL:

App Services allow easy configuration of custom domains and provide free SSL certificates via Azure-managed certificates.

Best Practices:

- Enable autoscale based on metrics such as CPU or request count.

- Use deployment slots for testing in production environments without impacting users.

- Monitor performance with Azure Application Insights.

Azure Functions

Azure Functions represent a Serverless compute model, where developers write code that executes in response to events. Azure manages the infrastructure, automatically scaling up or down based on demand.

Benefits:

- Pay only for the time your code runs

- Event-driven (e.g., HTTP requests, timers, message queues)

- Supports multiple languages (C#, JavaScript, Python, etc.)

- Integrated with Azure services like Blob Storage, Event Grid, and Service Bus

When to Use Functions:

- Lightweight APIs or webhooks

- Background tasks like data processing or notifications

- Integrating disparate systems via triggers

- Automation and reactive business logic

Creating a Basic Function with Azure CLI:

```
az functionapp create \
  --resource-group MyResourceGroup \
  --consumption-plan-location westeurope \
  --runtime node \
  --functions-version 4 \
  --name my-function-app \
  --storage-account mystorageaccount
```

Once created, you can write your code in the Functions portal or use local tools like VS Code.

Example of a Timer-Triggered Function (JavaScript):

```
module.exports = async function (context, myTimer) {
  const timeStamp = new Date().toISOString();
  context.log('Timer trigger function ran!', timeStamp);
};
```

Trigger Types:

- HTTP Trigger

- Timer Trigger

- Blob Trigger

- Queue Trigger

- Cosmos DB Trigger

Durable Functions:

These are an extension of Azure Functions that allow you to write stateful workflows in a serverless environment. They're useful for orchestrating complex tasks, like order processing or data migration.

Best Practices:

- Use retry policies to handle transient failures.

- Group related functions into the same Function App for efficiency.

- Monitor executions with Application Insights.

- Secure functions with API keys or OAuth tokens.

Choosing the Right Compute Option

Criteria	Virtual Machines	App Services	Azure Functions
Control	Full control over OS	Managed PaaS	Minimal, code-only focus
Scalability	Manual or auto-scale	Auto-scale built-in	Event-driven, auto-scale
Pricing Model	Per second when running	Tier-based, per instance	Pay-per-execution
Use Case	Legacy apps, full control	Web apps, APIs	Background jobs, triggers
Setup Time	Minutes to hours	Minutes	Seconds
Management Overhead	High	Medium	Low

Conclusion

Understanding compute services in Azure is foundational for architects, developers, and administrators. Virtual Machines offer full control but require more management. App Services simplify the deployment of web applications with integrated scalability and development tools. Azure Functions take abstraction to the next level, enabling you to build applications that react to events and scale automatically with minimal infrastructure concerns.

Choosing the right compute model depends on the specific requirements of your application—its architecture, scalability needs, performance expectations, and cost sensitivity. Often, real-world solutions will combine multiple compute models to achieve the desired outcome. For example, a web app hosted on App Services might invoke Functions for background processing and communicate with a VM-hosted legacy database.

In the next section, we'll explore Azure's storage services, which are equally essential to delivering scalable and reliable applications.

Storage Solutions: Blob, Table, Queue, and File Storage

Microsoft Azure provides a comprehensive set of storage services that are highly available, durable, secure, and massively scalable. These services are foundational for virtually all cloud-based applications, offering the flexibility to store and retrieve different types of data — structured, unstructured, semi-structured — in efficient and cost-effective ways. In this section, we'll delve deep into the core Azure Storage services: Blob Storage, Table Storage, Queue Storage, and File Storage.

Each of these services targets specific use cases and patterns, and selecting the right one is critical to achieving optimal performance, scalability, and cost-efficiency.

Azure Storage Overview

Azure Storage is a cloud storage solution for modern data storage scenarios. It includes:

- **Blob Storage** – For storing large volumes of unstructured data like images, videos, backups, logs, etc.

- **Table Storage** – A NoSQL key-value datastore for semi-structured data.

- **Queue Storage** – For building scalable, decoupled messaging between components.

- **File Storage** – Fully managed shared file system accessible via SMB protocol.

All storage services are part of the Azure Storage Account. You can create a general-purpose v2 storage account which gives access to all these services.

```
az storage account create \
  --name mystorageacct \
  --resource-group MyResourceGroup \
  --location eastus \
  --sku Standard_LRS \
  --kind StorageV2
```

Blob Storage

Azure Blob Storage is optimized for storing massive amounts of unstructured data, such as media files, backups, and big data objects. It supports three types of blobs:

- **Block blobs**: Best for text and binary files, often used for documents, images, etc.

- **Append blobs**: Optimized for append operations — perfect for logging scenarios.

- **Page blobs**: Designed for frequent read/write operations, used for VHD files.

Common Use Cases:

- Media streaming and file delivery

- Backup and disaster recovery

- Static content for web apps

- Big data analytics storage

Creating a Blob Container:

```
az storage container create \
  --name mycontainer \
  --account-name mystorageacct \
  --public-access off
```

Uploading a File to Blob Storage:

```
az storage blob upload \
  --account-name mystorageacct \
  --container-name mycontainer \
  --name myfile.txt \
  --file ./localpath/myfile.txt
```

Blob Tiers:

Azure Blob Storage supports different access tiers:

- **Hot** – For frequently accessed data

- **Cool** – For infrequently accessed data

- **Archive** – For rarely accessed, long-term data

Each tier has different pricing and availability trade-offs. You can set the tier when uploading or change it later.

Best Practices:

- Use lifecycle management rules to automatically transition blobs between tiers.

- Enable soft delete to recover accidentally deleted blobs.

- Use SAS (Shared Access Signatures) to securely grant time-limited access.

Table Storage

Azure Table Storage is a NoSQL datastore that stores semi-structured data using key-value pairs. It is schema-less, fast, and highly scalable, suitable for storing structured datasets without complex relationships.

Key Characteristics:

- Rows are called "entities"

- Each entity has a partition key and row key

- Supports OData for querying

Typical Use Cases:

- Audit logs

- User metadata

- Product catalogs

- Configuration data

Creating a Table and Adding Data (via Azure SDK):

```
CloudStorageAccount storageAccount =
CloudStorageAccount.Parse(connectionString);
CloudTableClient tableClient =
storageAccount.CreateCloudTableClient();
CloudTable table = tableClient.GetTableReference("myTable");

await table.CreateIfNotExistsAsync();

CustomerEntity customer = new CustomerEntity("Smith", "001")
{
    Email = "smith@example.com",
    PhoneNumber = "123-456-7890"
};

TableOperation insertOperation = TableOperation.Insert(customer);
await table.ExecuteAsync(insertOperation);
```

Advantages:

- Cost-effective for large-scale storage

- Partitioning allows fast access and horizontal scaling

- Easy integration with .NET and Azure SDKs

Limitations:

- Limited querying capabilities compared to relational databases

- No joins or complex querying

Best Practices:

- Design partition keys carefully to avoid hot partitions

- Use batch operations for inserting multiple entities

- Apply retry logic for transient faults

Queue Storage

Azure Queue Storage provides a simple but powerful message queueing service for storing large numbers of messages that can be accessed from anywhere via authenticated calls. It is often used to build decoupled and scalable distributed systems.

Features:

- Messages can be up to 64 KB

- Queues can hold millions of messages

- Supports message TTL and visibility timeout

Common Use Cases:

- Decoupling front-end from back-end

- Asynchronous background processing

- Reliable command dispatching

Creating a Queue and Sending Messages:

```
az storage queue create \
  --name myqueue \
  --account-name mystorageacct

az storage message put \
  --account-name mystorageacct \
  --queue-name myqueue \
  --content "Hello, Azure Queue!"
```

Processing Messages in C#:

```csharp
CloudQueue queue = queueClient.GetQueueReference("myqueue");
CloudQueueMessage retrievedMessage = await queue.GetMessageAsync();

Console.WriteLine("Message content: " + retrievedMessage.AsString);

// Delete after processing
await queue.DeleteMessageAsync(retrievedMessage);
```

Security Considerations:

- Always access queues via secure endpoints (HTTPS)

- Use Shared Access Signatures to delegate fine-grained permissions

Best Practices:

- Use poison queues for messages that fail multiple times

- Monitor queue length to auto-scale consumers

- Encrypt messages in transit and at rest

File Storage

Azure File Storage provides shared file storage in the cloud using the standard Server Message Block (SMB) protocol. It allows you to mount cloud-based file shares on-premises or in the cloud.

Use Cases:

- Lift-and-shift legacy applications

- Centralized file share across VMs

- Replace on-premises file servers

- CI/CD artifacts and logs

Creating a File Share:

```
az storage share create \
  --name myfileshare \
  --account-name mystorageacct
```

Mounting in Windows:

```
net use Z: \\mystorageacct.file.core.windows.net\myfileshare
/u:mystorageacct <storage-key>
```

Mounting in Linux:

```
sudo mount -t cifs //mystorageacct.file.core.windows.net/myfileshare
/mnt/azure \
  -o vers=3.0,username=mystorageacct,password=<storage-
key>,dir_mode=0777,file_mode=0777,serverino
```

Integration with Azure File Sync:

Azure File Sync allows you to cache Azure File shares on Windows Servers for fast local access, then sync changes back to the cloud.

Best Practices:

- Use Premium File Shares for IO-intensive workloads

- Enable snapshots for file versioning and backup

- Set NTFS ACLs to control access permissions

Securing and Monitoring Azure Storage

Security is a fundamental concern when dealing with data in the cloud. Azure Storage offers several capabilities to help secure and monitor access:

- **Encryption**: All data is encrypted at rest using Microsoft-managed or customer-managed keys.

- **Access Control**: Support for Azure AD, Shared Keys, and SAS tokens.

- **Firewalls and Virtual Networks**: Restrict access to trusted sources.

- **Monitoring**: Azure Monitor and Storage Analytics provide detailed logs and metrics.

Enabling Soft Delete for Blobs:

```
az storage blob service-properties delete-policy update \
  --account-name mystorageacct \
  --enable true \
  --days-retained 7
```

Setting Storage Metrics:

Storage metrics provide insights into request rates, latency, success/failure rates, and capacity usage. These are essential for troubleshooting and optimization.

Conclusion

Azure's storage solutions are designed to support virtually every storage need that a cloud-based application could have. Whether it's unstructured object data, structured NoSQL data, temporary messages, or traditional file shares, Azure provides a robust, scalable, and secure platform to manage them.

- Use **Blob Storage** for massive object data.

- Use **Table Storage** for quick key-value access at scale.

- Use **Queue Storage** to build loosely coupled systems.

- Use **File Storage** when you need a shared filesystem experience.

By leveraging the right service for the right scenario, you ensure better performance, lower costs, and cleaner architecture. Storage is more than just persistence — it's an enabler of scalability, reliability, and innovation in the cloud.

Networking Essentials: Virtual Networks, Load Balancers, and NSGs

In Azure, networking is the glue that ties all services together. It enables secure, performant, and scalable communication between applications, services, users, and the internet. Whether you're deploying a multi-tier application, setting up a hybrid cloud, or securing your infrastructure, Azure's networking components provide the tools you need. In this section, we'll cover three foundational networking services: **Virtual Networks (VNets)**, **Load Balancers**, and **Network Security Groups (NSGs)**.

Understanding these services is crucial for both developers and infrastructure professionals. They determine how your applications connect with each other and the outside world, how traffic is routed and secured, and how scalable your solutions are under real-world conditions.

Virtual Networks (VNets)

Virtual Networks are the fundamental building blocks of Azure networking. A VNet is an isolated, private network in the Azure cloud where you can host your Azure resources.

Think of it as a cloud-based equivalent of your on-premises network, complete with subnets, IP address ranges, routing, and security controls.

Key Characteristics

- **Isolation**: VNets are isolated from one another by default.

- **Subnets**: Resources are grouped into subnets with defined IP ranges.

- **IP Addressing**: Supports public and private IPs.

- **Name Resolution**: Internal DNS resolution within the VNet.

- **Hybrid Connectivity**: Connect VNets to on-premises via VPN or ExpressRoute.

Creating a VNet Using Azure CLI

```
az network vnet create \
  --name MyVNet \
  --resource-group MyResourceGroup \
  --address-prefix 10.0.0.0/16 \
  --subnet-name MySubnet \
  --subnet-prefix 10.0.1.0/24
```

Use Cases

- Hosting virtual machines, databases, and apps in a secured and segmented network.

- Enabling hybrid cloud connectivity with on-premises data centers.

- Application tiering with different subnet-level access.

Subnet Design Best Practices

- Separate subnets for front-end, middle-tier, and back-end services.

- Use Network Security Groups (NSGs) for fine-grained traffic control.

- Allocate IP ranges that allow room for growth and subnet expansion.

Load Balancers

In any cloud-native solution, scaling horizontally is key to performance and reliability. Azure Load Balancer provides high availability and network performance by distributing incoming traffic across healthy instances.

Azure provides two types of Load Balancers:

- **Public Load Balancer**: Routes traffic from the internet to your virtual machines.

- **Internal Load Balancer**: Balances traffic within a VNet, often between tiers of an application.

Key Features

- **Layer 4 (TCP/UDP)** load balancing

- **Health Probes** to check instance availability

- **Automatic failover**

- **Outbound rules** for controlling SNAT traffic

Creating a Basic Public Load Balancer

```
az network lb create \
  --resource-group MyResourceGroup \
  --name MyLoadBalancer \
  --sku Basic \
  --frontend-ip-name MyFrontEnd \
  --backend-pool-name MyBackEndPool
```

Adding a Health Probe

```
az network lb probe create \
  --resource-group MyResourceGroup \
  --lb-name MyLoadBalancer \
  --name MyHealthProbe \
  --protocol tcp \
  --port 80
```

Configuring a Load Balancing Rule

```
az network lb rule create \
  --resource-group MyResourceGroup \
  --lb-name MyLoadBalancer \
  --name MyHTTPRule \
```

```
--protocol tcp \
--frontend-port 80 \
--backend-port 80 \
--frontend-ip-name MyFrontEnd \
--backend-pool-name MyBackEndPool \
--probe-name MyHealthProbe
```

Use Cases

- Web applications requiring high availability.

- Backend APIs balanced across multiple compute instances.

- Internal microservices routing between tiers.

Load Balancer vs Application Gateway

Feature	Load Balancer	Application Gateway
OSI Layer	Layer 4 (TCP/UDP)	Layer 7 (HTTP/HTTPS)
Protocol Awareness	No	Yes
SSL Termination	No	Yes
Path-based Routing	No	Yes
Use Case	VM balancing, general-purpose	Web applications

Network Security Groups (NSGs)

NSGs are essential to controlling traffic flow in and out of Azure resources. They act as virtual firewalls at both the subnet and NIC (Network Interface Card) level.

Key Features

- Allow or deny inbound/outbound traffic.

- Rules evaluated in priority order.

- Granular control via protocol, port, IP range, and direction.

Example: Creating an NSG and Adding Rules

```
az network nsg create \
  --resource-group MyResourceGroup \
  --name MyNSG

az network nsg rule create \
  --resource-group MyResourceGroup \
  --nsg-name MyNSG \
  --name AllowHTTP \
  --priority 100 \
  --direction Inbound \
  --access Allow \
  --protocol Tcp \
  --source-address-prefixes '*' \
  --source-port-ranges '*' \
  --destination-address-prefixes '*' \
  --destination-port-ranges 80
```

Associating NSG with a Subnet

```
az network vnet subnet update \
  --vnet-name MyVNet \
  --name MySubnet \
  --resource-group MyResourceGroup \
  --network-security-group MyNSG
```

Use Cases

- Restrict access to only required ports (e.g., 80, 443).

- Block all outbound traffic and whitelist specific destinations.

- Apply different policies for front-end and back-end subnets.

NSG Rule Best Practices

- Avoid overly permissive rules (* for source/destination).

- Prioritize deny rules where applicable.

- Document each rule with purpose and expiration dates if temporary.

- Regularly audit NSG rules using Azure Policy or Azure Security Center.

Common Networking Patterns in Azure

Multi-tier Application Architecture

- **Front-end subnet** with an NSG allowing HTTP/HTTPS.

- **App subnet** restricted to internal traffic, protected by NSG.

- **Database subnet** locked down with no internet access, only app subnet allowed.

Hybrid Networking

- Site-to-Site VPN or ExpressRoute connects on-prem to Azure.

- VNets peered across regions for global deployments.

- Network Virtual Appliances (NVAs) used for traffic inspection or advanced routing.

VNet Peering

Allows traffic between VNets without going over public internet. Fast, secure, and private.

```
az network vnet peering create \
  --name Peer1To2 \
  --resource-group MyResourceGroup \
  --vnet-name VNet1 \
  --remote-vnet VNet2 \
  --allow-vnet-access
```

Monitoring and Security in Azure Networking

Azure Network Watcher

- Packet capture and flow logs

- Topology visualization

- Connection troubleshooting

- IP flow verify

```
az network watcher flow-log configure \
  --resource-group MyResourceGroup \
  --nsg MyNSG \
  --enabled true \
  --storage-account mystorageacct \
  --retention 7
```

Azure Firewall vs NSGs

Feature	NSG	Azure Firewall
Stateful inspection	No	Yes
Threat intelligence	No	Yes
Application filtering	No	Yes
Centralized control	No (decentralized)	Yes (centralized)
Logging	Limited	Full logging and analytics

Conclusion

Azure networking is not just a foundational layer—it is an essential part of building reliable, secure, and performant applications in the cloud. Mastering **Virtual Networks**, **Load Balancers**, and **Network Security Groups** equips you with the tools to design resilient architectures, enforce security boundaries, and manage traffic flow efficiently.

- **Virtual Networks** provide the logical isolation and connectivity backbone.

- **Load Balancers** enable horizontal scaling and high availability.

- **NSGs** offer strong control over traffic at the subnet and VM level.

When combined, these services offer immense flexibility and control. Whether you're deploying a simple app or a global, enterprise-grade solution, your networking choices will have a direct impact on your architecture's success. Understanding and leveraging these tools wisely is a critical skill in your Azure journey.

Databases: Azure SQL, Cosmos DB, and More

Data is the lifeblood of any application. Whether it's structured, semi-structured, or unstructured, applications need reliable, secure, and scalable databases to store, retrieve, and analyze data. Microsoft Azure offers a wide array of database services that cater to diverse workloads—from traditional relational systems to globally distributed NoSQL solutions. In this section, we explore the most widely used database services in Azure: **Azure SQL Database**, **Azure Cosmos DB**, and a selection of other offerings such as **Azure Database for PostgreSQL**, **MySQL**, and **Table Storage**.

Choosing the right database depends on the nature of your application, its scale, availability requirements, and the structure of your data. Azure's database services provide integrated security, automated scaling, high availability, backup, and monitoring, reducing much of the administrative overhead.

Azure SQL Database

Azure SQL Database is a fully managed Platform-as-a-Service (PaaS) offering built on the latest version of Microsoft SQL Server. It is ideal for cloud-native applications requiring relational data storage with full T-SQL support.

Key Features

- Fully managed with built-in high availability

- Intelligent performance tuning

- Automatic backups and point-in-time restore

- Geo-replication for disaster recovery

- Built-in security features: data encryption, firewalls, auditing

Deployment Models

1. **Single Database** – Isolated, single instance with dedicated resources.

2. **Elastic Pool** – Share resources across multiple databases.

3. **Managed Instance** – Close to on-prem SQL Server with greater control.

Creating a SQL Database

```
az sql server create \
  --name my-sql-server \
  --resource-group MyResourceGroup \
  --location eastus \
  --admin-user azureuser \
  --admin-password MyP@ssw0rd123

az sql db create \
  --resource-group MyResourceGroup \
  --server my-sql-server \
  --name mydatabase \
  --service-objective S0
```

Connecting to Azure SQL

```
var connectionString = "Server=tcp:my-sql-
server.database.windows.net;Database=mydatabase;User
ID=azureuser;Password=MyP@ssw0rd123;";
SqlConnection conn = new SqlConnection(connectionString);
conn.Open();
```

Security Best Practices

- Use **Azure AD Authentication** for centralized identity management.

- Enable **Advanced Threat Protection** to detect vulnerabilities and anomalies.

- Configure **firewall rules** to restrict IP access.

Performance Tuning Tools

- **Query Performance Insight** for bottleneck detection

- **Automatic Index Management**

- **Extended Events** and **Query Store**

Azure Cosmos DB

Azure Cosmos DB is Microsoft's globally distributed, multi-model NoSQL database service. It offers turnkey global distribution, elastic scaling, and guaranteed low latency and high availability.

Key Models Supported

- **Core (SQL) API** – Document database model with SQL-like query language

- **MongoDB API** – Wire protocol compatibility with MongoDB clients

- **Cassandra API** – Column-family store for Cassandra workloads

- **Gremlin API** – Graph-based data models

- **Table API** – Key-value store like Azure Table Storage

Core Concepts

- **Containers**: Logical units for storing items (documents, etc.)

- **Databases**: Logical grouping of containers

- **Partition Keys**: Define the data distribution

- **Request Units (RUs)**: Measure throughput and cost

Creating a Cosmos DB Account (SQL API)

```
az cosmosdb create \
  --name mycosmosdb \
  --resource-group MyResourceGroup \
  --kind GlobalDocumentDB \
  --locations regionName=eastus failoverPriority=0
isZoneRedundant=False
```

Creating a Container

```
az cosmosdb sql database create \
  --account-name mycosmosdb \
  --name mydatabase \
  --resource-group MyResourceGroup

az cosmosdb sql container create \
  --account-name mycosmosdb \
  --database-name mydatabase \
```

```
--name mycontainer \
--partition-key-path "/userId"
```

Sample Document (JSON)

```json
{
  "id": "1",
  "userId": "u123",
  "name": "Alice",
  "email": "alice@example.com",
  "createdAt": "2025-04-01T10:00:00Z"
}
```

Benefits

- Multi-region replication with consistency models

- Millisecond latency for reads/writes

- No schema constraints

- Horizontal scaling via partitions

- Time-to-live (TTL) and automatic indexing

Use Cases

- Real-time analytics

- IoT telemetry

- Product catalogs and recommendation engines

- User profile and session management

Azure Database for PostgreSQL and MySQL

Azure also supports managed open-source relational databases, providing familiar environments with cloud benefits.

PostgreSQL

- Fully managed, community edition support

- Hyperscale (Citus) for horizontal partitioning

- JSONB support for semi-structured data

- Advanced indexing: GIN, GiST, etc.

MySQL

- Managed MySQL servers with high availability

- Performance tiers: Basic, General Purpose, Memory Optimized

- Replication and backups included

Creating PostgreSQL Server

```
az postgres server create \
  --resource-group MyResourceGroup \
  --name mypgserver \
  --location westus \
  --admin-user pgadmin \
  --admin-password MyStrongP@ssword \
  --sku-name B_Gen5_2
```

Connecting with a Client

```
psql -h mypgserver.postgres.database.azure.com -U pgadmin@mypgserver
-d mydatabase
```

Common Use Cases

- Legacy app migration

- Analytics dashboards

- ERP and CRM systems

- Open-source app hosting (WordPress, Drupal)

Other Azure Database Services

Azure Synapse Analytics

- Integrated analytics platform for big data and SQL

- Data warehousing with massive parallel processing

- Supports Spark, T-SQL, Data Lake

Azure Table Storage

- Key-value store

- Massively scalable and fast

- Ideal for logs, telemetry, and metadata

Azure Data Explorer

- Optimized for log and telemetry analysis

- Kusto Query Language (KQL) for fast analytics

Azure Cache for Redis

- In-memory data structure store

- Low latency caching, pub/sub messaging

- Ideal for session storage, real-time apps

Data Security and Compliance

Azure offers enterprise-grade security across all its database services. Key features include:

- **Transparent Data Encryption (TDE)**: Encrypts data at rest.

- **Always Encrypted**: Ensures sensitive data is encrypted during processing.

- **Private Endpoints**: Restrict traffic to your databases over a private network.

- **Network Rules**: IP firewall, VNet rules, service endpoints.

- **Role-Based Access Control (RBAC)**: Fine-grained identity and access management.

```
az sql server firewall-rule create \
  --resource-group MyResourceGroup \
  --server my-sql-server \
  --name AllowMyIP \
  --start-ip-address 203.0.113.5 \
  --end-ip-address 203.0.113.5
```

Monitoring and Performance Insights

Azure databases come with built-in observability:

- **Azure Monitor** and **Log Analytics** for metric and log collection

- **Query Performance Insight** (SQL) to detect expensive queries

- **Alerts** and **Auto-scaling** for Cosmos DB RUs

- **Advisor Recommendations** for index and performance tuning

Backup and Restore

All Azure databases support automatic backups with configurable retention. Point-in-time restore (PITR) allows you to restore a database to any second within the retention window.

- SQL Database: up to 35 days PITR

- Cosmos DB: continuous backups or periodic backups

- PostgreSQL/MySQL: geo-redundant backups

Conclusion

Microsoft Azure provides a rich and diverse database ecosystem that supports nearly every application scenario, from transactional systems to real-time analytics and high-throughput NoSQL workloads.

- **Azure SQL** is perfect for traditional relational workloads with minimal overhead.

- **Cosmos DB** shines in global, scalable, NoSQL environments.

- **PostgreSQL/MySQL** cater to open-source flexibility with managed capabilities.

- **Synapse and Redis** cover big data and in-memory caching respectively.

By understanding the strengths and trade-offs of each service, you can design highly performant, scalable, and cost-effective architectures. Each database offering integrates with other Azure services—like networking, identity, monitoring, and DevOps—making it easier to build and manage complete cloud-native solutions.

Chapter 4: Identity, Access, and Security

Introduction to Azure Active Directory

In today's digital-first world, managing identity and access is one of the most crucial components of any secure infrastructure. As organizations increasingly move to the cloud, traditional methods of managing user identities and securing access to resources become insufficient. This is where **Azure Active Directory (Azure AD)** comes into play—a comprehensive cloud-based identity and access management service from Microsoft.

Azure AD is not just a directory like the traditional on-premises Active Directory; it's an identity platform that enables single sign-on (SSO), multi-factor authentication (MFA), conditional access, identity protection, and seamless integration with thousands of SaaS applications, on-premises apps, and cloud resources. Whether you're an enterprise, small business, or independent developer, understanding and using Azure AD is fundamental for securing cloud environments.

What Is Azure Active Directory?

At its core, Azure AD is Microsoft's cloud-based identity and access management service. It helps your employees sign in and access resources:

- External resources, such as Microsoft 365, the Azure portal, and thousands of other SaaS applications.

- Internal resources, such as apps on your corporate network and intranet, along with any cloud apps developed by your organization.

Unlike the classic on-prem Active Directory (AD DS), which is focused on domain-joined infrastructure, Azure AD is designed for cloud-native environments.

Key features include:

- **Authentication and authorization**

- **Single Sign-On (SSO)**

- **Device registration and management**

- **User and group management**

- **Integration with on-prem Active Directory**

- Support for modern authentication protocols (OAuth2, OpenID Connect, SAML, WS-Fed)

Key Concepts of Azure AD

Understanding Azure AD begins with a few fundamental concepts:

- **Tenant**: A dedicated and trusted instance of Azure AD for an organization. Think of it as your organization's "cloud directory."

- **Directory**: The actual structure that holds users, groups, and other identity objects.

- **User**: Represents an individual identity. This can be a person in your organization or an external partner.

- **Groups**: Used to manage access and permissions collectively.

- **Applications**: Azure AD allows you to register and manage apps, giving them the ability to authenticate and access APIs securely.

- **Roles**: Define the permissions granted to users and groups within the directory.

- **Service Principals**: Identity for use with apps, services, and automation tools.

Setting Up Azure AD

You can begin working with Azure AD via the Azure Portal, CLI, PowerShell, or SDKs. Let's walk through the basics.

Creating an Azure AD Tenant

1. Navigate to the Azure portal.

2. Search for "Azure Active Directory."

3. Click "Create a tenant."

4. Choose "Azure Active Directory" as the tenant type.

5. Provide organization name, initial domain name, and country/region.

6. Click "Create."

Each tenant can have multiple domains and users.

Adding and Managing Users

You can manually add users, sync from on-prem AD, or federate identities.

Adding a User via Azure Portal

1. Go to Azure AD → Users → + New User.

2. Choose "Create user."

3. Fill in user details (name, username, password).

4. Assign groups or roles as needed.

5. Click "Create."

Using Azure CLI

```
az ad user create --display-name "John Doe" \
--password "P@ssw0rd123!" \
--user-principal-name johndoe@yourdomain.onmicrosoft.com \
--force-change-password-next-login true
```

Groups and Access Control

Groups simplify permission management. Assign users to groups, then assign permissions to the group.

Create a Group (Portal)

1. Azure AD → Groups → + New Group.

2. Choose group type (Security or Microsoft 365).

3. Enter name and description.

4. Add members.

5. Click "Create."

Assigning Group Access

Groups can be assigned access to:

- Azure resources (via RBAC)

- Applications

- Microsoft 365 services

Application Management

Azure AD lets you manage app identities, permissions, and access policies.

Registering an App

1. Azure AD → App registrations → + New registration.

2. Provide name and redirect URI.

3. Choose supported account types (single or multi-tenant).

4. Click "Register."

This gives you an **Application (client) ID**, **Directory (tenant) ID**, and **Object ID**. You can use these in your apps to authenticate users or call APIs.

Single Sign-On (SSO)

SSO enables users to log in once and gain access to multiple applications. Azure AD supports SSO for:

- Microsoft apps (Outlook, Teams)

- SaaS apps (Salesforce, ServiceNow)

- Custom apps (via SAML or OpenID Connect)

Enabling SSO for an App

1. Azure AD → Enterprise Applications → Select App.

2. Go to "Single sign-on."

3. Choose method (SAML, OpenID Connect).

4. Configure metadata and claims.

5. Test and enable.

Multi-Factor Authentication (MFA)

MFA requires users to provide two or more verification methods:

- Password

- Phone call/text

- Authenticator app

- Biometrics

Enabling MFA

1. Azure AD → Security → MFA.

2. Click "Additional cloud-based MFA settings."

3. Enable desired options.

You can enforce MFA using **Conditional Access** policies.

Conditional Access

Conditional Access helps you enforce access policies based on conditions like:

- User/group

- Device state

- Location

- Application

- Risk level

Creating a Policy

1. Azure AD → Security → Conditional Access → + New Policy.

2. Name the policy.

3. Assign users/groups.

4. Select apps.

5. Configure conditions (e.g., sign-in risk, location).

6. Grant controls (require MFA, block access, etc.).

7. Enable the policy.

Example: Require MFA for users accessing Azure Portal from outside your corporate network.

Integrating with On-Premises Active Directory

Many organizations use **Azure AD Connect** to sync their on-prem identities with Azure AD.

Key Sync Features

- Password hash sync

- Pass-through authentication

- Federation with AD FS

- Write-back capabilities (group, password, device)

Azure AD Connect can be configured to sync specific OU (Organizational Units), use filtering, and schedule sync frequency.

Roles and Administrative Units

Azure AD has built-in roles like:

- Global Administrator

- User Administrator

- Application Administrator

- Security Reader

Roles can be assigned at the directory or administrative unit level. For least privilege, only grant the minimum necessary access.

Use **Privileged Identity Management (PIM)** for just-in-time role assignments and access reviews.

Securing Azure AD

Azure AD is a key target for attackers. Implement the following best practices:

- Enable MFA for all users, especially admins.

- Monitor sign-ins and set up alerts.

- Use Conditional Access policies.

- Regularly audit permissions and role assignments.

- Enable Identity Protection to detect risky sign-ins.

- Restrict legacy authentication protocols.

Monitoring and Auditing

Azure AD integrates with Azure Monitor and Log Analytics. Important logs include:

- Sign-in logs

- Audit logs

- Risky users and sign-ins

Set up alerts for:

- Unusual sign-in locations

- High sign-in failures

- Sign-ins from anonymized IPs

You can use **Workbooks** for dashboards and visualizations.

Summary

Azure Active Directory is foundational to Microsoft's identity and access strategy. It provides robust capabilities for managing users, groups, roles, and application access, all while enabling strong security through multi-factor authentication, conditional access, and monitoring. Whether you're an IT admin, security architect, or developer, mastering Azure AD unlocks critical capabilities to build secure and scalable cloud solutions.

In the next section, we'll explore **Role-Based Access Control (RBAC)**—a core model for managing granular permissions to Azure resources.

Role-Based Access Control (RBAC)

Role-Based Access Control (RBAC) in Azure is a vital mechanism used to regulate access to resources. Rather than relying on traditional identity and access management techniques that might offer full access or none at all, RBAC introduces a granular and flexible model where users, groups, and services are granted only the permissions they need to perform specific actions.

RBAC helps enforce the principle of least privilege, which significantly reduces the risk of accidental or malicious misuse of resources. In Azure, RBAC is tightly integrated into the platform, making it an essential component for any secure cloud deployment.

What is RBAC?

RBAC allows you to manage **who** has access to **what** resources and **what they can do** with those resources. It enables the following core principles:

- **Segregation of duties** — limit what individuals can access or modify

- **Least privilege access** — users get the minimum access required

- **Operational efficiency** — delegate tasks securely across teams

At its heart, RBAC consists of three core components:

- **Security Principal**: The object requesting access (user, group, service principal, managed identity).

- **Role Definition**: A collection of permissions.

- **Scope**: The boundary within which the role applies (subscription, resource group, or resource).

Security Principals

Security principals are identities that can request access to Azure resources. Azure supports several types:

- **User**: An individual with a Microsoft Entra (Azure AD) identity.

- **Group**: A collection of users. Roles assigned to a group apply to all its members.

- **Service Principal**: A security identity for apps or services to access resources.

- **Managed Identity**: An identity automatically managed by Azure for use with Azure services.

Role Definitions

A role definition is a set of permissions. Roles define what actions can be performed, such as reading, writing, or deleting resources.

Azure provides **built-in roles**, and you can also create **custom roles**.

Common Built-in Roles:

- **Owner**: Full management rights, including the right to delegate access.

- **Contributor**: Can create and manage all types of resources but can't assign roles.

- **Reader**: Can view existing resources.

- **User Access Administrator**: Can manage user access to Azure resources.

Each role is defined in JSON and contains permissions across four categories:

- **Actions**: Allowed operations.

- **NotActions**: Excluded operations.

- **DataActions**: Allowed data operations.

- **NotDataActions**: Excluded data operations.

Example JSON snippet of a built-in Reader role:

```
{
  "Name": "Reader",
  "IsCustom": false,
  "Description": "View all resources, but does not allow making
changes.",
  "Actions": [
    "*"
  ],
  "NotActions": [
    "*"
  ],
  "DataActions": [],
  "NotDataActions": []
}
```

Scope

The **scope** defines where access applies. Azure uses a hierarchical model:

- **Management group** (top level)

- **Subscription**

- **Resource group**

- **Resource** (lowest level)

You can assign a role at any of these levels. A role assignment at a higher level applies to all resources within that level.

For example:

- Assigning at the subscription level affects all resource groups and resources in the subscription.

- Assigning at the resource level affects only that specific resource.

Role Assignment

To grant access, you **assign a role** to a security principal at a specific scope.

Role Assignment = Security Principal + Role Definition + Scope

Assigning a Role in Azure Portal

1. Navigate to the resource (e.g., subscription or resource group).

2. Click **Access control (IAM)**.

3. Click **+ Add → Add role assignment**.

4. Select the role (e.g., Contributor).

5. Assign to a user, group, or service principal.

6. Click **Review + assign**.

Using Azure CLI
```
az role assignment create \
  --assignee johndoe@yourdomain.com \
  --role "Contributor" \
  --scope /subscriptions/xxxx-xxxx-
xxxx/resourceGroups/MyResourceGroup
```

Using Azure PowerShell
```
New-AzRoleAssignment `
```

```
  -ObjectId "user-object-id" `
  -RoleDefinitionName "Reader" `
  -Scope "/subscriptions/xxxx-xxxx-
xxxx/resourceGroups/MyResourceGroup"
```

Custom Roles

If built-in roles don't meet your specific requirements, Azure allows you to create **custom roles**.

Creating a Custom Role

1. Define a role in JSON.

2. Use Azure CLI, PowerShell, or the portal to create the role.

Example: A custom role to allow only VM start/stop actions

```json
{
  "Name": "VM Operator",
  "IsCustom": true,
  "Description": "Can start and stop VMs.",
  "Actions": [
    "Microsoft.Compute/virtualMachines/start/action",
    "Microsoft.Compute/virtualMachines/deallocate/action"
  ],
  "NotActions": [],
  "DataActions": [],
  "NotDataActions": [],
  "AssignableScopes": ["/subscriptions/xxxx-xxxx-xxxx"]
}
```

Create with Azure CLI
```
az role definition create --role-definition ./vm-operator-role.json
```

Data Plane vs. Control Plane Permissions

Azure RBAC applies to the **control plane**, which governs management operations (e.g., create VM, delete database). It does not control access to data inside the resource (data plane), such as reading files in Blob Storage.

For data plane access (e.g., Storage, Key Vault), Azure often uses **Access Control Lists (ACLs)** or separate IAM mechanisms.

Example: RBAC role that allows managing Blob Storage but not reading data within it.

To read blob data, you may need to grant **Storage Blob Data Reader** role.

Auditing Role Assignments

Monitoring role assignments is vital for compliance and security.

Audit via Azure Portal

1. Go to **Azure AD → Audit Logs**.

2. Filter for activity types related to role assignments.

3. Review time, user, and changes made.

Audit with Azure CLI

```
az role assignment list \
  --all \
  --query "[].{Role:roleDefinitionName, Assignee:principalName,
Scope:scope}"
```

Best Practices for Using RBAC

1. **Follow the Principle of Least Privilege**
   Only assign the permissions necessary for the user or application to function.

2. **Use Groups for Access Management**
   Assign roles to groups instead of individuals for easier management.

3. **Avoid Overusing Owner Role**
   This role has unrestricted access; limit it to a few administrators.

4. **Audit Regularly**
   Review role assignments and activity logs frequently to detect misconfigurations.

5. **Segment Access by Scope**
   Define scopes based on organizational boundaries or project needs to minimize

exposure.

6. **Implement Just-in-Time Access with PIM**
   Use Azure AD Privileged Identity Management to grant temporary permissions.

7. **Use Custom Roles Where Needed**
   Don't force-fit a built-in role when a tailored one is more secure.

RBAC vs Azure AD Roles

It's important not to confuse **Azure RBAC roles** with **Azure AD roles**.

- **Azure RBAC**: Applies to Azure resource management.

- **Azure AD roles**: Apply to Azure AD services and management (e.g., User Administrator, Global Administrator).

For example, to manage Azure VMs, use an RBAC role like **Contributor**. To create users in Azure AD, use an **Azure AD User Administrator** role.

Troubleshooting Access Issues

If a user cannot access a resource:

1. **Check Role Assignments**
   Ensure the user has a role assignment at the correct scope.

2. **Verify Scope Inheritance**
   Access granted at a parent scope (e.g., subscription) should propagate.

3. **Inspect Role Permissions**
   Confirm the assigned role includes necessary actions.

4. **Use the "Check Access" Tool**
   In the Azure Portal under **Access Control (IAM)**, select **Check access** to validate permissions.

Summary

Role-Based Access Control is a cornerstone of Azure's security and governance strategy. It offers a powerful way to grant fine-grained access to resources based on clearly defined roles and scopes. With RBAC, organizations can reduce risk, improve operational efficiency, and enforce policy consistently across environments. By understanding how to apply, manage, and audit role assignments, you ensure that your cloud infrastructure remains secure, scalable, and compliant.

In the next section, we will dive into **Azure Policies and Blueprints**, which offer even more sophisticated governance capabilities by allowing you to define and enforce organizational standards across Azure resources.

Azure Policies and Blueprints

Azure Policies and Blueprints are critical tools in the governance and compliance toolkit of any organization leveraging Microsoft Azure. While Role-Based Access Control (RBAC) governs **who** can do **what**, Azure Policies and Blueprints govern **what** can and **should** be done. These services ensure that cloud environments stay compliant with internal standards, regulatory requirements, and best practices, all while enabling scalable, automated, and repeatable deployments.

This section dives deep into both services, exploring how they are used independently and together to ensure secure, consistent, and compliant Azure environments.

Azure Policy Overview

Azure Policy is a governance tool that allows you to create, assign, and manage policies that enforce specific rules or effects on your Azure resources. Policies help you ensure resources are compliant with corporate standards and service-level agreements (SLAs).

You can use Azure Policy to:

- Enforce specific configurations (e.g., require tags or specific SKUs).

- Deny deployments that do not meet rules.

- Audit existing resources for compliance.

- Automatically remediate non-compliant resources.

- Enforce security controls (e.g., encryption or location constraints).

Key Concepts of Azure Policy

Policy Definition

A **policy definition** is a rule that describes the desired behavior. It contains:

- **Display Name**

- **Description**

- **Mode** (All, Indexed, Microsoft.Kubernetes.Data)

- **Policy Rule**

- **Parameters** (optional)

Example: A policy to allow only specific locations

```json
{
  "properties": {
    "displayName": "Allowed locations",
    "description": "This policy enables you to restrict the
locations your organization can specify when deploying resources.",
    "mode": "All",
    "parameters": {
      "listOfAllowedLocations": {
        "type": "Array",
        "metadata": {
          "description": "The list of allowed locations",
          "displayName": "Allowed locations"
        }
      }
    },
    "policyRule": {
      "if": {
        "not": {
          "field": "location",
          "in": "[parameters('listOfAllowedLocations')]"
        }
      },
      "then": {
        "effect": "deny"
      }
    }
  }
}
```

}

Policy Assignment

Once a policy is defined, it must be **assigned** to take effect. Assignments can be made at various scopes: management group, subscription, resource group, or individual resources.

You can also **parameterize** assignments to make reusable policies for different scopes.

Initiatives (Policy Sets)

An **initiative** is a collection of policy definitions grouped together. Useful for enforcing multiple policies as a single unit.

Example: You may have an initiative called **"Security Baseline"** containing:

- Require resource tags

- Restrict locations

- Enforce HTTPS on App Services

Policy Effects

Azure Policy supports several effects:

- **Deny**: Prevent the resource from being created or updated.

- **Audit**: Log non-compliant resources without blocking.

- **Append**: Add properties during resource creation.

- **DeployIfNotExists**: Automatically deploy a resource if it doesn't exist.

- **AuditIfNotExists**: Log if a resource doesn't meet requirements.

Assigning Azure Policies

Using the Azure Portal

1. Go to **Azure Policy** in the portal.

2. Click **Definitions** to find or create a policy.

3. Go to **Assignments** and click **+ Assign Policy**.

4. Select the scope and policy definition.

5. Set parameters (if any).

6. Review and create.

Using Azure CLI

```
az policy assignment create \
  --name "allow-locations" \
  --policy "policyDefinitionID" \
  --params '{ "listOfAllowedLocations": { "value": [ "eastus",
"westeurope" ] } }' \
  --scope "/subscriptions/xxxx-xxxx-xxxx"
```

Auditing and Compliance with Azure Policy

Once policies are assigned, Azure continuously evaluates resources for compliance.

- **Compliance dashboard**: View which resources are compliant or not.

- **Drill-down**: See specific policy violations.

- **Remediation tasks**: Automatically bring non-compliant resources into compliance.

Common Use Cases

- **Tag enforcement**: Ensure all resources have owner or environment tags.

- **Region restrictions**: Limit deployments to approved geographic locations.

- **SKU enforcement**: Prevent usage of expensive or unauthorized VM SKUs.

- **Encryption enforcement**: Require data encryption at rest for storage accounts.

- **Monitoring enforcement**: Ensure all resources have diagnostics enabled.

Azure Policy Best Practices

1. **Start with audit mode**: Use `Audit` effect to monitor without blocking.

2. **Scope appropriately**: Apply to specific resource groups or subscriptions to limit impact.

3. **Use initiatives**: Group related policies for easier management.

4. **Monitor compliance regularly**: Use dashboards to identify issues early.

5. **Automate remediation**: Where possible, use `DeployIfNotExists` to enforce compliance.

Azure Blueprints Overview

While Azure Policy governs behavior, **Azure Blueprints** go a step further by allowing you to **orchestrate the deployment of entire environments** — including policies, role assignments, ARM templates, and resource groups — in a repeatable and controlled manner.

Azure Blueprints is ideal for:

- Enterprise-scale deployments

- Regulated environments

- Standardized environment creation

Blueprints are like **infrastructure templates** that enforce governance from day one.

Blueprint Components

1. **Artifacts**: These are building blocks in a blueprint and can include:

   - Role assignments

   - Policy assignments

- ARM templates

- Resource groups

2. **Blueprint Definition**: A package that includes all artifacts.

3. **Blueprint Assignment**: Applying a blueprint definition to a subscription.

Creating and Assigning a Blueprint

Via Azure Portal

1. Go to **Azure Blueprints**.

2. Click **Blueprint Definitions → Create blueprint**.

3. Select a **definition location** (e.g., management group or subscription).

4. Add artifacts:

   - Add policy assignments (e.g., tag enforcement).

   - Add role assignments (e.g., Reader for auditors).

   - Add resource group declarations.

   - Add ARM templates (e.g., deploy a baseline network).

5. Save and publish the blueprint.

6. Assign it to a subscription and provide required parameters.

Using Blueprints for Compliance

Blueprints are especially useful for enforcing compliance in regulated industries like finance or healthcare. A typical compliance blueprint might include:

- Only deploy resources in compliant regions.

- Require all storage to be encrypted.

- Restrict access using RBAC.

- Deploy a pre-approved network architecture.

- Set audit policies for security and tagging.

Managing Blueprint Lifecycle

Blueprints have versions and can be updated over time.

- **Draft**: Editable state of the blueprint.

- **Published**: Ready for assignment.

- **Locked**: Enforced state that prevents modification outside the blueprint.

This lifecycle helps manage controlled changes across multiple environments.

Blueprint vs. ARM Templates vs. Policy

Feature	Blueprint	ARM Template	Policy
Scope	Environment	Resource	Behavior
Reusable	Yes	Yes	Yes
Governance	High	Low	Very High
Includes RBAC	Yes	No	No
Includes Policy	Yes	No	Yes
Includes Resource Deployment	Yes	Yes	No

Use Blueprints to **enforce structure**, ARM templates to **deploy infrastructure**, and Policies to **control behavior**.

Best Practices for Blueprints

1. **Define baseline blueprints** for different workloads (e.g., dev, prod).

2. **Version control** your blueprints for traceability.

3. **Integrate policies and role assignments** directly into blueprints.

4. **Use parameters** for flexible, reusable blueprints.

5. **Test in lower environments** before assigning to production.

Real-World Scenario: Enforcing Organizational Standards

Imagine an organization wants all environments to include:

- A pre-configured virtual network

- Logging and monitoring

- Resource tagging

- Specific allowed locations

- Cost control policies

This is achieved by:

1. Creating policies for tags and location.

2. Defining an ARM template for the network.

3. Assigning reader roles to the compliance team.

4. Packaging all into a blueprint and assigning it to new subscriptions.

Result: Every new environment is **secure**, **compliant**, and **consistent**.

Summary

Azure Policies and Blueprints provide foundational capabilities for governance, compliance, and standardization in the cloud. Policies enforce rules and remediate drift, while Blueprints bring those policies together with other artifacts to create repeatable, secure environments. Leveraging both in combination helps organizations scale securely while ensuring they meet business, technical, and regulatory standards.

Next, we'll focus on **Implementing Secure Practices in Azure**, where we bring together identity, access, monitoring, and policy controls to harden your cloud infrastructure.

Implementing Secure Practices in Azure

Ensuring the security of your Azure environment is an ongoing process that requires vigilance, best practices, layered defenses, and continuous monitoring. In this section, we explore a comprehensive set of secure practices that should be implemented at all layers of your Azure environment—from identity and network, to compute, storage, and governance.

These practices combine strategic decisions, technical configurations, and operational processes designed to minimize attack surface, enforce compliance, and proactively detect threats.

Identity and Access Security

Identity is the new perimeter. With a shift to cloud-based, identity-driven architectures, controlling who has access and what they can do is the foundation of cloud security.

Enforce Multi-Factor Authentication (MFA)

Multi-Factor Authentication is essential for all accounts—especially those with privileged access.

Best practices:

- Enable MFA for all users via Conditional Access.

- Use Microsoft Authenticator or hardware-based MFA (e.g., FIDO2).

- Disable legacy authentication protocols (POP, IMAP, SMTP).

Implement Conditional Access Policies

Conditional Access (CA) enforces access control based on contextual factors.

Examples:

- Block access from high-risk countries.

- Require MFA from non-compliant devices.

- Enforce access only from hybrid-joined or compliant devices.

```
az ad conditionalaccess policy create \
  --display-name "Require MFA for External Access" \
  --conditions
'{"users":{"include":["All"],"exclude":["Admins"]},"locations":{"inc
lude":["AllTrustedLocations"],"exclude":[]},"clientAppTypes":["Brows
er"]}' \
  --grant-controls '{"operator":"OR","builtInControls":["mfa"]}' \
  --state "enabled"
```

Least Privilege via RBAC

- Assign permissions at the **lowest possible scope**.

- Prefer **role assignments to groups**, not individuals.

- Use **custom roles** where necessary.

- Periodically **review and audit** role assignments.

- Enable **Azure AD Privileged Identity Management (PIM)** to manage and audit elevated access.

Secure Networking Practices

Azure networking must be configured to restrict unnecessary exposure and ensure controlled connectivity.

Use Network Security Groups (NSGs)

NSGs act as firewalls at subnet or NIC level.

Best practices:

- Deny all inbound traffic by default; allow only what's necessary.

- Restrict access to management ports (SSH, RDP) using jumpboxes or Azure Bastion.

- Log and monitor NSG flows using **Network Watcher**.

Segment Networks with Subnets and NSGs

Use subnets to isolate workloads by function (web, app, DB) and apply NSGs at subnet level for enforceable control.

```
az network nsg rule create \
  --resource-group MyResourceGroup \
  --nsg-name MyNSG \
  --name AllowHTTPSInbound \
  --protocol Tcp \
  --direction Inbound \
  --source-address-prefixes Internet \
  --destination-port-ranges 443 \
  --access Allow \
  --priority 100
```

Use Azure Firewall or Third-Party Appliances

- Deploy Azure Firewall for centralized traffic control.

- Configure Application Rules for FQDN-based traffic control.

- Enable threat intelligence to deny traffic from known malicious IPs.

Securing Compute Resources

Virtual machines, containers, and app services are core to workloads and must be hardened appropriately.

Enable Just-In-Time (JIT) VM Access

JIT reduces the risk of brute-force attacks by allowing access only when needed.

- Configure via Azure Security Center.

- Set allowed IPs, ports, and time windows.

Patch Management

- Use **Azure Automation Update Management** to ensure OS patches are applied.

- Enable **Automatic OS updates** on VMs where possible.

- Leverage **Azure Guest Configuration** for compliance.

Secure VM Extensions and Scripts

- Review and restrict use of custom scripts or extensions.

- Ensure only signed or vetted scripts are used.

- Monitor changes via **Azure Defender for Servers**.

Storage and Data Security

Storage accounts, databases, and secrets must be protected to prevent data loss or exfiltration.

Enable Encryption

- Ensure encryption at rest is enabled for all storage accounts and databases.

- Use **customer-managed keys (CMK)** for greater control over encryption keys.

- Enable **encryption in transit** using HTTPS/TLS.

Use Private Endpoints

Expose storage and database services only through private IPs using Private Endpoints.

```
az network private-endpoint create \
  --name myPrivateEndpoint \
  --resource-group MyResourceGroup \
  --vnet-name MyVNet \
  --subnet MySubnet \
  --private-connection-resource-id
"/subscriptions/.../storageAccounts/mystorageaccount" \
  --group-ids blob \
  --connection-name myConnection
```

Access Controls

- Use **Shared Access Signatures (SAS)** with minimum required permissions and expiry.

- Use **role-based access (RBAC)** over access keys where possible.

- Regularly rotate storage account keys and database passwords.

Application Security

Applications deployed to Azure (App Services, Functions, APIs) must follow secure coding and deployment practices.

Secure App Service

- Enforce HTTPS only.

- Use **Managed Identity** for authentication to other Azure services.

- Use **deployment slots** for zero-downtime deployments.

- Enable **static IP restrictions** for sensitive APIs.

Use Azure Key Vault

Azure Key Vault protects secrets, certificates, and encryption keys.

- Store application secrets in Key Vault.

- Integrate with managed identity for secure access.

- Enable logging for audit trails.

```
az keyvault secret set \
  --vault-name "myKeyVault" \
  --name "DbPassword" \
  --value "SuperSecret123"
```

Monitoring and Threat Detection

Visibility into your environment is crucial for detection, response, and auditing.

Azure Monitor & Log Analytics

- Collect metrics and logs from all resources.

- Use **Log Analytics Workspaces** to centralize data.

- Set up **custom dashboards** and **alerts**.

Enable Microsoft Defender for Cloud

Provides continuous assessment and recommendations across compute, data, and networking.

- Enables **threat detection** for VMs, containers, databases, and more.

- Provides **Secure Score** to measure and improve posture.

Azure Sentinel (SIEM)

Use Sentinel to aggregate and analyze logs across Azure and on-prem.

- Use **built-in connectors** for Azure, Microsoft 365, and other sources.

- Create **workbooks** and **analytics rules** for threat detection.

Governance and Compliance

Security must align with organizational standards and regulatory requirements.

Use Azure Policy and Blueprints

- Enforce encryption, allowed SKUs, tag compliance, and more.

- Use Blueprints to define and deploy compliant environments.

Cost Controls and Quotas

- Set budgets and alerts using **Cost Management**.

- Limit resource usage with **quotas and policies**.

Regular Access Reviews

- Schedule reviews for group memberships, app access, and admin roles.

- Use **Access Reviews** in Azure AD and **PIM** for privileged accounts.

Incident Response

Despite best efforts, breaches can occur. A well-prepared response plan is essential.

Key components:

- Clearly defined **roles and responsibilities**.

- **Automated alerts** tied to incident response playbooks.

- Integration with ticketing and response platforms (e.g., ServiceNow).

- Simulations and **tabletop exercises** for readiness.

Use **Azure Logic Apps** to build automated remediation flows when a threat is detected.

Example Logic App steps:

1. Receive alert from Microsoft Defender.

2. Trigger approval request to security officer.

3. If approved, isolate VM or rotate secret.

Secure DevOps and CI/CD

Security must shift left into the development and deployment lifecycle.

Secure Pipelines

- Scan for secrets in code using tools like Microsoft Defender for DevOps.

- Use **service connections** with least privilege.

- Use **signed artifacts** and trusted feeds.

Infrastructure as Code (IaC) Security

- Validate ARM templates or Bicep with **Azure Resource Manager** tooling.

- Use **Terraform Sentinel** or **OPA** for policy as code.

- Perform **pre-deployment scans** for misconfigurations.

Summary

Implementing secure practices in Azure is not a one-time task but a continuous, layered approach that involves planning, configuration, monitoring, and review. From identity and network to storage, compute, and operations, each layer has specific controls and recommendations that, when followed together, form a robust and resilient cloud security posture.

These practices, when implemented thoroughly, drastically reduce the attack surface and ensure that your Azure environment remains secure, compliant, and efficient. In the next chapter, we'll shift focus to **Infrastructure as Code and Automation**, where we'll see how these secure practices can be baked directly into templates and automated workflows.

Chapter 5: Infrastructure as Code and Automation

ARM Templates and Bicep

Infrastructure as Code (IaC) is the practice of managing and provisioning infrastructure through machine-readable definition files, rather than through physical hardware configuration or interactive configuration tools. In Azure, the primary native IaC solutions are **ARM Templates** and **Bicep**. Both allow you to describe resources in a declarative format and provision them consistently across environments.

This section will guide you through the fundamentals and advanced usage of both ARM Templates and Bicep, how they work, their syntax, deployment techniques, benefits, and best practices.

Introduction to ARM Templates

Azure Resource Manager (ARM) Templates are JSON-based files that define the infrastructure and configuration of your Azure solutions. ARM templates allow you to deploy, update, and manage Azure resources in a repeatable manner.

ARM templates use declarative syntax: you describe what resources you need and the Azure platform figures out how to create them.

Key elements of an ARM template:

- `$schema`

- `contentVersion`

- `parameters`

- `variables`

- `resources`

- `outputs`

Sample ARM Template (Creating a Storage Account)

```
{
```

```json
  "$schema": "https://schema.management.azure.com/schemas/2019-04-
01/deploymentTemplate.json#",
  "contentVersion": "1.0.0.0",
  "parameters": {
    "storageAccountName": {
      "type": "string"
    },
    "location": {
      "type": "string",
      "defaultValue": "eastus"
    }
  },
  "resources": [
    {
      "type": "Microsoft.Storage/storageAccounts",
      "apiVersion": "2022-09-01",
      "name": "[parameters('storageAccountName')]",
      "location": "[parameters('location')]",
      "sku": {
        "name": "Standard_LRS"
      },
      "kind": "StorageV2",
      "properties": {}
    }
  ],
  "outputs": {
    "storageAccountName": {
      "type": "string",
      "value": "[parameters('storageAccountName')]"
    }
  }
}
```

ARM Template Deployment Methods

You can deploy ARM templates using:

- Azure Portal

- Azure CLI

- PowerShell

- Azure DevOps

- REST API

Using Azure CLI
```
az deployment group create \
  --resource-group MyResourceGroup \
  --template-file template.json \
  --parameters storageAccountName=mystorageacct
```

Using PowerShell
```
New-AzResourceGroupDeployment `
  -ResourceGroupName "MyResourceGroup" `
  -TemplateFile "template.json" `
  -storageAccountName "mystorageacct"
```

Benefits of Using ARM Templates

- **Consistency**: Avoid manual steps and human error.

- **Idempotency**: Repeated deployments yield the same result.

- **Reusability**: Use parameters to adapt templates to different environments.

- **Versioning**: Store templates in version control systems.

- **Validation**: Templates can be validated before deployment.

Introduction to Bicep

Bicep is a domain-specific language (DSL) for deploying Azure resources declaratively. It's a cleaner, more readable abstraction over ARM templates. Bicep files compile down to ARM JSON templates, but offer a simplified syntax and improved authoring experience.

Why Bicep?

- Easier to read and write than JSON

- Better tooling (IntelliSense, linting, formatting)

- Native support for modularity and code reuse

- Transparent transpilation to ARM

Installing Bicep

You can install Bicep using the Azure CLI:

```
az bicep install
```

Verify installation:

```
az bicep version
```

Sample Bicep File (Storage Account)

```
param storageAccountName string
param location string = 'eastus'

resource storageAccount 'Microsoft.Storage/storageAccounts@2022-09-
01' = {
  name: storageAccountName
  location: location
  sku: {
    name: 'Standard_LRS'
  }
  kind: 'StorageV2'
  properties: {}
}

output name string = storageAccount.name
```

To deploy:

```
az deployment group create \
  --resource-group MyResourceGroup \
  --template-file ./main.bicep \
```

```
--parameters storageAccountName=mystorageacct
```

Key Bicep Features

Parameters and Variables

- Parameters support default values, allowed values, secure values.

- Variables support computed values and reuse.

```
param location string = resourceGroup().location
var storagePrefix = 'myapp'
var accountName =
'${storagePrefix}${uniqueString(resourceGroup().id)}'
```

Modules

Bicep supports reusability via **modules**, making it easy to compose infrastructure.

main.bicep:

```
module storageModule './storage.bicep' = {
  name: 'storageDeploy'
  params: {
    storageAccountName: 'modulestorage'
    location: 'eastus'
  }
}
```

storage.bicep:

```
param storageAccountName string
param location string

resource storage 'Microsoft.Storage/storageAccounts@2022-09-01' = {
  name: storageAccountName
  location: location
  sku: {
    name: 'Standard_LRS'
  }
  kind: 'StorageV2'
```

```
  properties: {}
}
```

Conditions and Loops

Bicep allows conditions and loops for dynamic deployments.

```
param createStorage bool = true

resource storage 'Microsoft.Storage/storageAccounts@2022-09-01' = if
(createStorage) {
  name: 'conditionalacct'
  location: 'eastus'
  sku: { name: 'Standard_LRS' }
  kind: 'StorageV2'
  properties: {}
}
```

Comparing ARM Templates and Bicep

Feature	ARM Templates	Bicep
Format	JSON	DSL
Readability	Moderate	High
Tooling	Basic	Rich (VS Code, IntelliSense)
Modularity	Complex	Native support
Compilation	Native	Requires transpilation
Learning Curve	Steep	Gentle

Use Bicep for new projects and maintain ARM Templates for legacy systems or third-party integrations requiring JSON.

Testing and Validation

ARM Template Validation

```
az deployment group validate \
  --resource-group MyResourceGroup \
  --template-file template.json
```

Bicep Validation

Bicep files can be linted and checked for syntax errors before deployment.

```
bicep build main.bicep
az bicep build --file main.bicep
```

Security in IaC

- Use secure parameters for sensitive values.

- Avoid committing secrets to version control.

- Integrate Key Vault references where possible.

```
param adminPassword string {
  secure: true
}
```

- Use **role-based access** to control who can deploy infrastructure.

- Use **Azure Blueprints** or **Policies** to enforce standards.

CI/CD with Bicep and ARM Templates

Integrate deployments into your DevOps pipeline using:

- Azure DevOps Pipelines

- GitHub Actions

- GitLab CI/CD

Example GitHub Action Step:

```
- name: Deploy Bicep
  run: az deployment group create \
      --resource-group ${{ env.RG }} \
      --template-file ./infra/main.bicep \
      --parameters storageAccountName=mystorageacct
```

Best Practices

- **Use Bicep for readability and maintainability.**

- **Structure files modularly** for reuse and testing.

- **Parameterize** for flexibility across environments.

- **Store templates in Git** and integrate into CI/CD workflows.

- **Validate before deploying** to catch errors early.

- **Combine with Policy** to enforce security and compliance.

Summary

ARM Templates and Bicep are powerful tools in Azure's Infrastructure as Code ecosystem. While ARM provides a mature, widely supported JSON format, Bicep introduces a modern, streamlined approach to writing infrastructure. Both support declarative provisioning, automation, and scalability, enabling consistent deployments across your organization.

By adopting Bicep or ARM templates and integrating them into your CI/CD workflows, you can enforce standards, eliminate drift, and deploy reliable cloud infrastructure quickly and securely. In the next section, we'll explore **Azure Automation and Runbooks**, taking automation to the next level with scheduled and event-driven operational tasks.

Azure Automation and Runbooks

Azure Automation is a powerful cloud-based automation service that provides a platform for orchestrating tasks and automating processes across Azure and non-Azure environments. With Automation, you can automate frequent, time-consuming, and error-prone cloud management tasks. One of its most prominent features is **Runbooks**, which are workflows that perform specific operations like restarting virtual machines, cleaning up unused resources, or performing compliance checks.

Runbooks, combined with other features such as Update Management, Desired State Configuration (DSC), and Change Tracking, create a robust toolset for automating IT operations and achieving operational consistency and efficiency.

Key Concepts of Azure Automation

Azure Automation provides several components that work together:

- **Runbooks**: Scripted processes for task automation.

- **Hybrid Worker Groups**: Extend automation to on-prem or other clouds.

- **Update Management**: Automates patching of Windows and Linux systems.

- **Change Tracking**: Monitors configuration drift.

- **Desired State Configuration (DSC)**: Ensures infrastructure stays in a defined state.

- **Schedules**: Trigger runbooks on defined intervals.

- **Webhooks**: Trigger runbooks via HTTP requests.

- **Shared Resources**: Credentials, certificates, variables, and connections.

Creating an Azure Automation Account

Before creating runbooks, you need an Automation Account:

Using the Azure Portal

1. Search for **"Automation Accounts"**.

2. Click **+ Create**.

3. Provide name, region, and resource group.

4. Optionally enable **Azure Defender for Servers** integration.

5. Click **Review + create**.

Using Azure CLI

```
az automation account create \
```

```
--name MyAutomationAccount \
--resource-group MyResourceGroup \
--location eastus
```

Introduction to Runbooks

A **Runbook** is a set of tasks executed sequentially or conditionally. Azure Automation supports multiple types of runbooks:

- **PowerShell**: The most common type, written in PowerShell.

- **Python 2**: Legacy support for Python-based automation.

- **PowerShell Workflow**: Supports checkpoints and parallel execution.

- **Graphical**: Drag-and-drop visual workflows.

- **Graphical PowerShell Workflow**: Visual with PowerShell Workflow behind the scenes.

Authoring Runbooks

You can create runbooks using:

- **Azure Portal Editor**

- **Visual Studio Code with Azure Automation extension**

- **Importing** `.ps1` **files**

- **GitHub or external repositories**

Example: PowerShell Runbook to Start a VM

```
param (
    [string]$ResourceGroupName,
    [string]$VMName
)


Start-AzVM -ResourceGroupName $ResourceGroupName -Name $VMName
```

Runbook Execution Methods

Runbooks can be triggered in multiple ways:

- **Manual execution** from the Azure Portal

- **Scheduled execution**

- **Webhook triggers** (via HTTP)

- **Azure Event Grid/Event Hub triggers**

- **Called from other runbooks** (nested runbooks)

Example: Creating a Webhook Trigger

1. Go to your runbook → **Add webhook**.

2. Generate and save the webhook URL.

3. Set expiration and enable.

You can now trigger this runbook by sending a POST request to the URL.

```
curl -X POST https://s2events.azure-
automation.net/webhooks?token=abc123
```

Scheduling Runbooks

Schedules allow you to run tasks on a recurring basis—daily, weekly, or monthly.

1. Go to your Automation Account → Runbooks → Select a runbook.

2. Click **Link to schedule**.

3. Create or link an existing schedule.

This is ideal for operations like nightly backups, periodic cleanup, or health checks.

Shared Resources

Azure Automation includes a repository of shared resources:

- **Variables**: Reusable parameters (string, int, bool).

- **Credentials**: Secure storage for usernames/passwords.

- **Certificates**: Used for secure API calls.

- **Connections**: Predefined modules to connect to Azure, GitHub, etc.

Example: Using Credentials in a Runbook

```
$creds = Get-AutomationCredential -Name "AzureAdmin"
Connect-AzAccount -Credential $creds
```

Hybrid Runbook Workers

Hybrid Workers allow you to run automation scripts in your own datacenter or on specific VMs in Azure.

Use cases:

- Execute scripts on machines behind firewalls.

- Automate tasks on physical servers.

- Integrate with third-party systems.

Installing Hybrid Worker

1. Download the agent from the Azure Portal.

2. Install on the desired machine.

3. Register it to the Automation Account.

Runbook Best Practices

1. **Use parameters** to make runbooks reusable and dynamic.

2. **Add logging** and error handling to help with troubleshooting.

3. **Test in sandbox** before production use.

4. **Use Checkpoints** in PowerShell Workflows to save state.

5. **Secure your runbooks** with RBAC and shared resource permissions.

6. **Document runbook logic** using comments and naming conventions.

Real-World Scenarios

Automated VM Shutdown for Cost Savings

- Schedule a runbook to shut down non-critical VMs after business hours.

```
$vmList = Get-AzVM
foreach ($vm in $vmList) {
    if ($vm.Tags["AutoShutdown"] -eq "true") {
        Stop-AzVM -ResourceGroupName $vm.ResourceGroupName -Name
$vm.Name -Force
    }
}
```

Periodic Resource Tag Enforcement

- Ensure all resources have required tags like Environment and Owner.

```
$resources = Get-AzResource
foreach ($res in $resources) {
    if (-not $res.Tags.ContainsKey("Owner")) {
        Set-AzResource -ResourceId $res.ResourceId -Tag
@{Owner="AutoAssigned"} -Force
    }
}
```

Alert-Based Remediation

- Integrate with Azure Monitor alerts to automatically scale out or restart services when metrics cross thresholds.

Monitoring and Troubleshooting

Azure Automation provides tools to track and debug runbooks.

- **Job History**: View success/failure, logs, output.

- **Output Streams**: Write-Output, Write-Error, Write-Verbose.

- **Alerts**: Triggered based on job failures.

```
Write-Verbose "Starting VM provisioning"
Write-Output "VM started successfully"
Write-Error "Failed to authenticate"
```

Logs can be forwarded to **Log Analytics Workspaces** for centralized monitoring and analysis.

Integration with Azure DevOps and GitHub

Use source control to version and manage your runbooks.

- **GitHub Integration**: Pull runbooks from repositories.

- **Azure DevOps Pipelines**: Deploy runbooks as part of CI/CD.

- Use the **AzureAutomation@1** task in DevOps to manage accounts and jobs.

```
- task: AzurePowerShell@5
  inputs:
    azureSubscription: 'My Service Connection'
    ScriptType: 'FilePath'
    ScriptPath: 'runbooks/ShutdownVMs.ps1'
    azurePowerShellVersion: 'LatestVersion'
```

Automation and Security

Security is critical in Automation:

- Use managed identities instead of storing credentials in code.

- Assign least-privilege roles to Automation accounts.

- Regularly rotate credentials stored in shared resources.

- Use auditing to detect unauthorized changes or execution.

Summary

Azure Automation and Runbooks empower teams to build reliable, repeatable, and secure cloud operations. By automating routine tasks, enforcing configuration consistency, and integrating with monitoring and alerting systems, you can reduce human error, increase efficiency, and maintain a healthy, compliant environment.

With its rich ecosystem—including schedules, hybrid workers, secure resources, and webhook triggers—Azure Automation can scale from simple scripts to complex operational frameworks. In the next section, we'll dive into **Using Terraform on Azure**, where infrastructure is declared and managed with an open-source, cloud-agnostic language.

Using Terraform on Azure

Terraform is an open-source Infrastructure as Code (IaC) tool developed by HashiCorp that allows users to define and provision infrastructure across multiple cloud providers, including Microsoft Azure, using a declarative configuration language known as HCL (HashiCorp Configuration Language). With Terraform, you can build, change, and manage infrastructure safely and efficiently using configuration files and a state management system.

Azure offers a native Terraform provider that supports a wide range of services, making it an excellent choice for enterprise-scale deployments, multi-cloud infrastructure management, and DevOps automation. This section provides an in-depth look at how to use Terraform to manage Azure resources, from setup and configuration to deployment and best practices.

Key Benefits of Using Terraform with Azure

- **Declarative Syntax**: Describe the desired state, and Terraform handles the provisioning.

- **Provider Agnostic**: Manage resources across multiple cloud providers using the same tool and language.

- **Modular**: Reuse code through modules for efficiency and maintainability.

- **Immutable Infrastructure**: Infrastructure changes result in consistent, repeatable provisioning.

- **State Management**: Tracks deployed resources to detect and apply only necessary changes.

- **Version Control Friendly**: Works well with Git and CI/CD pipelines.

Installing and Setting Up Terraform

Install Terraform

Visit terraform.io to download and install the appropriate version for your operating system.

Verify installation:

```
terraform -version
```

Authenticate Terraform to Azure

You can authenticate Terraform using:

- Azure CLI

- Service Principal

- Managed Identity (for Azure-hosted agents)

Using Azure CLI:

```
az login
```

Terraform will use your current CLI credentials.

Create a Service Principal (for automation)

```
az ad sp create-for-rbac --role="Contributor" --
scopes="/subscriptions/<subscription_id>"
```

Store the output securely; you'll need the client ID, secret, tenant ID, and subscription ID.

Set environment variables:

```
export ARM_CLIENT_ID="..."
export ARM_CLIENT_SECRET="..."
export ARM_SUBSCRIPTION_ID="..."
export ARM_TENANT_ID="..."
```

Basic Terraform Structure

A typical Terraform project includes:

- `main.tf`: Core resource definitions

- `variables.tf`: Input variables

- `outputs.tf`: Outputs

- `terraform.tfvars`: Variable values

- `provider.tf`: Provider configuration

- `.terraform.lock.hcl`: Provider version locking

Sample Terraform Configuration (Storage Account)

main.tf

```
provider "azurerm" {
  features {}
}

resource "azurerm_resource_group" "example" {
  name     = "example-resources"
  location = "eastus"
}

resource "azurerm_storage_account" "example" {
  name                     = "examplestorage123"
  resource_group_name      = azurerm_resource_group.example.name
  location                 = azurerm_resource_group.example.location
  account_tier             = "Standard"
  account_replication_type = "LRS"
```

```
}
```

Running Terraform

Initialize the Working Directory

```
terraform init
```

This installs the required provider plugins.

Validate the Configuration

```
terraform validate
```

Ensures the configuration syntax is correct.

Preview the Changes

```
terraform plan
```

Shows the resources that will be created or modified.

Apply the Configuration

```
terraform apply
```

Provisions the resources. Terraform will ask for confirmation unless -auto-approve is passed.

Managing Terraform State

Terraform uses a **state file** (terraform.tfstate) to track your deployed infrastructure. This file is critical for detecting changes and performing updates efficiently.

Local state is suitable for small, personal projects. For teams, use **remote state** with locking, like Azure Storage.

Remote State with Azure Storage

```
terraform {
  backend "azurerm" {
    resource_group_name  = "tfstate-rg"
    storage_account_name = "tfstatestorageacct"
    container_name       = "tfstate"
```

```
    key                      = "terraform.tfstate"
  }
}
```

Initialize again after setting the backend:

```
terraform init
```

This migrates the state file to Azure Storage.

Variables and Outputs

variables.tf

```
variable "location" {
  type    = string
  default = "eastus"
}
```

terraform.tfvars

```
location = "westeurope"
```

outputs.tf

```
output "resource_group_name" {
  value = azurerm_resource_group.example.name
}
```

Access outputs after apply:

```
terraform output resource_group_name
```

Modules and Reusability

Terraform **modules** let you encapsulate common infrastructure patterns for reuse.

Directory Structure

```
/main
  main.tf
  variables.tf
  outputs.tf
  /modules
    /storage
      main.tf
      variables.tf
      outputs.tf
```

Calling a Module

```
module "storage" {
  source               = "./modules/storage"
  resource_group_name  = "modulerg"
  location             = "eastus"
  storage_account_name = "modulestorage123"
}
```

Modules enhance scalability and reduce duplication across environments.

Provisioning Complex Environments

You can use Terraform to deploy multi-tier applications with networking, security groups, virtual machines, databases, and more.

Example: VM with Network Interface

```
resource "azurerm_network_interface" "example" {
  name                = "nic1"
  location            = azurerm_resource_group.example.location
  resource_group_name = azurerm_resource_group.example.name

  ip_configuration {
    name                          = "internal"
    subnet_id                     = azurerm_subnet.example.id
    private_ip_address_allocation = "Dynamic"
  }
}


resource "azurerm_linux_virtual_machine" "example" {
```

```
name                  = "example-vm"
resource_group_name   = azurerm_resource_group.example.name
location              = azurerm_resource_group.example.location
size                  = "Standard_B1s"
admin_username        = "azureuser"
network_interface_ids = [azurerm_network_interface.example.id]

os_disk {
  caching              = "ReadWrite"
  storage_account_type = "Standard_LRS"
}

source_image_reference {
  publisher = "Canonical"
  offer     = "UbuntuServer"
  sku       = "18.04-LTS"
  version   = "latest"
}

admin_ssh_key {
  username   = "azureuser"
  public_key = file("~/.ssh/id_rsa.pub")
}
}
```

Terraform in CI/CD

Terraform fits well into DevOps pipelines for repeatable deployments.

Common CI/CD Tools:

- GitHub Actions

- Azure DevOps Pipelines

- GitLab CI/CD

- Jenkins

Example GitHub Action

```
jobs:
```

```
terraform:
  runs-on: ubuntu-latest
  steps:
  - uses: actions/checkout@v3
  - uses: hashicorp/setup-terraform@v2
  - run: terraform init
  - run: terraform plan
  - run: terraform apply -auto-approve
```

Azure DevOps Example:

Use the **Terraform Task** from the marketplace to automate workflows.

Best Practices

1. **Use remote state with locking** to prevent corruption.

2. **Use modules** for reusable infrastructure patterns.

3. **Use version constraints** for providers.

4. **Keep secrets out of configs** — use Key Vault or environment variables.

5. **Lint your configs** using tools like `tflint` and `checkov`.

6. **Lock down state files** with proper RBAC and encryption.

7. **Use CI/CD for automation** to reduce human error.

Security Considerations

- Use **Terraform Cloud** or **Azure Storage** for secure state management.

- Rotate **Service Principal secrets** periodically.

- Use **Azure Key Vault** integration for secrets retrieval.

- Enforce **least privilege** on the identities Terraform uses.

- Scan for hardcoded secrets using tools like `git-secrets` or `truffleHog`.

Summary

Terraform is a mature, extensible, and powerful Infrastructure as Code solution that integrates seamlessly with Azure. By codifying infrastructure in version-controlled, declarative files, you gain consistency, repeatability, and the ability to scale your operations efficiently. Through features like remote state, modules, CI/CD integration, and a vast provider ecosystem, Terraform helps modern cloud teams manage even the most complex infrastructure environments with ease and confidence.

In the next section, we'll explore **CI/CD with Azure DevOps**, where you'll learn how to automate the building, testing, and deployment of your Azure applications and infrastructure with industry-standard DevOps practices.

CI/CD with Azure DevOps

Continuous Integration and Continuous Deployment (CI/CD) are the cornerstones of modern software development practices. With CI/CD pipelines, teams can automate the process of building, testing, and deploying code into production environments, resulting in faster releases, fewer bugs, and more reliable deployments. Azure DevOps, Microsoft's comprehensive DevOps platform, provides robust tools for implementing CI/CD pipelines for both applications and infrastructure on Azure.

In this section, we'll explore how to use Azure DevOps to implement CI/CD pipelines for a variety of Azure resources and workloads. You'll learn how to configure build and release pipelines, integrate with repositories, implement quality gates, deploy ARM/Bicep/Terraform templates, and apply best practices for scalable DevOps workflows.

Key Components of Azure DevOps

Azure DevOps consists of several interconnected services:

- **Azure Repos**: Git repositories for source control.

- **Azure Pipelines**: CI/CD automation for applications and infrastructure.

- **Azure Boards**: Agile project management tools.

- **Azure Test Plans**: Manual and exploratory testing tools.

- **Azure Artifacts**: Package management for NuGet, npm, Maven, etc.

For CI/CD, our focus will be on **Azure Repos** and **Azure Pipelines**.

Understanding CI/CD Workflow

Continuous Integration (CI)

- Developers push code to the repository.

- A CI pipeline automatically builds the code.

- Unit and integration tests are run.

- Artifacts (build outputs) are generated.

Continuous Deployment (CD)

- CD pipeline picks up the artifact.

- Deploys to test or staging environments.

- Runs post-deployment validations.

- Optionally promotes to production.

Creating Your First Azure Pipeline

To create a CI/CD pipeline, you can use:

- **Classic Editor** (GUI-based)

- **YAML Pipelines** (code-based)

YAML is recommended for versioning and portability.

Sample YAML Pipeline for .NET Application

```
trigger:
  branches:
    include:
      - main

pool:
  vmImage: 'windows-latest'
```

```yaml
variables:
  buildConfiguration: 'Release'

steps:
- task: UseDotNet@2
  inputs:
    packageType: 'sdk'
    version: '6.x'

- task: DotNetCoreCLI@2
  inputs:
    command: 'restore'
    projects: '**/*.csproj'

- task: DotNetCoreCLI@2
  inputs:
    command: 'build'
    arguments: '--configuration $(buildConfiguration)'
    projects: '**/*.csproj'

- task: DotNetCoreCLI@2
  inputs:
    command: 'test'
    projects: '**/*Tests/*.csproj'
```

This pipeline restores dependencies, builds the project, and runs tests whenever code is pushed to the main branch.

Implementing CD for Azure App Service

Add a **release pipeline** or extend the YAML to include deployment:

```yaml
- task: AzureWebApp@1
  inputs:
    azureSubscription: 'MyServiceConnection'
    appType: 'webApp'
    appName: 'my-app-service'
    package: '$(System.DefaultWorkingDirectory)/**/*.zip'
```

AzureWebApp@1 deploys your build output to the specified App Service.

Deploying Infrastructure with Pipelines

You can deploy ARM, Bicep, or Terraform using Azure Pipelines.

ARM Template Deployment

```
- task: AzureResourceManagerTemplateDeployment@3
  inputs:
    deploymentScope: 'Resource Group'
    azureResourceManagerConnection: 'MyServiceConnection'
    subscriptionId: '$(subscriptionId)'
    action: 'Create Or Update Resource Group'
    resourceGroupName: 'dev-rg'
    location: 'East US'
    templateLocation: 'Linked artifact'
    csmFile: 'infrastructure/azuredeploy.json'
    overrideParameters: '-storageAccountName mystorageacct'
```

Bicep Deployment

```
- task: AzureCLI@2
  inputs:
    azureSubscription: 'MyServiceConnection'
    scriptType: 'bash'
    scriptLocation: 'inlineScript'
    inlineScript: |
      az deployment group create \
        --resource-group dev-rg \
        --template-file main.bicep \
        --parameters storageAccountName=mystorageacct
```

Terraform Deployment

```
- task: TerraformInstaller@0
  inputs:
    terraformVersion: 'latest'

- task: TerraformTaskV4@4
  inputs:
    provider: 'azurerm'
    command: 'init'
    backendServiceArm: 'MyServiceConnection'
```

```
      backendAzureRmResourceGroupName: 'tfstate-rg'
      backendAzureRmStorageAccountName: 'tfstatestorage'
      backendAzureRmContainerName: 'tfstate'
      backendAzureRmKey: 'terraform.tfstate'

- task: TerraformTaskV4@4
  inputs:
    provider: 'azurerm'
    command: 'apply'
    environmentServiceNameAzureRM: 'MyServiceConnection'
    allowTelemetryCollection: true
    vars: |
      location = "eastus"
```

Using Environments and Approvals

Azure DevOps supports environments like **Dev**, **Test**, and **Prod**. You can define approval gates before deploying to production.

1. Navigate to **Pipelines → Environments**.

2. Create environments with deployment targets (VMs, Kubernetes, etc.).

3. Add **manual approval checks** or **pre/post-deployment gates** (e.g., work item check, branch policy).

Quality Gates and Testing

You can integrate testing and quality checks into pipelines:

- **Unit Tests**: DotNetCoreCLI, NUnit, or other test runners.

- **Code Coverage**: Collect and publish test coverage reports.

- **Static Code Analysis**: Integrate tools like SonarQube or ESLint.

- **Security Scans**: Use tools like WhiteSource Bolt, CredScan, or Microsoft Security DevOps.

```
- task: SonarCloudPrepare@1
```

```
  inputs:
    SonarCloud: 'MySonarConnection'
    organization: 'my-org'
    scannerMode: 'MSBuild'
    projectKey: 'my-project'
    projectName: 'MyProject'

- task: SonarCloudAnalyze@1
- task: SonarCloudPublish@1
  inputs:
    pollingTimeoutSec: '300'
```

Storing Secrets Securely

Use **Azure Key Vault** or **pipeline secrets**:

1. Go to **Project Settings → Service Connections** and create a secure connection.

2. Reference secrets in pipelines securely using variables.

```
variables:
  azureSubscription: $(azureSubscription)
  storageAccountKey: $(StorageAccountKey)

steps:
- task: AzureCLI@2
  inputs:
    scriptType: bash
    scriptLocation: inlineScript
    inlineScript: |
      echo "Using storage key: ${{ secrets.StorageAccountKey }}"
```

Avoid storing secrets directly in YAML or repositories.

Git Branching and Triggers

Configure triggers for:

- Pull Requests (PRs)

- Specific branches

- Tags

```
trigger:
  branches:
    include:
      - main
      - release/*
pr:
  branches:
    include:
      - main
```

Use **branch protection rules** to require a successful pipeline before merge.

Deployment Strategies

You can implement advanced deployment strategies:

- **Blue-Green Deployments**: Deploy new version alongside old, switch traffic upon validation.

- **Canary Releases**: Gradually shift traffic to the new version.

- **Rolling Deployments**: Update parts of the infrastructure sequentially.

Use **Azure App Service deployment slots** to support zero-downtime deployments.

Monitoring and Troubleshooting

Azure DevOps provides extensive monitoring features:

- **Build logs**

- **Deployment logs**

- **Test results**

- **Pipeline analytics**

Set up **alerts and notifications** for pipeline failures, approvals, or successes.

Integrate with external tools:

- Microsoft Teams

- Slack

- Email

- Azure Monitor and Log Analytics

Best Practices

1. **Use YAML for pipelines** to version and manage as code.

2. **Keep pipelines in the repo** alongside application code.

3. **Break up large pipelines** into stages and jobs for clarity and reuse.

4. **Use environments and approvals** for production safety.

5. **Parameterize** pipelines for multi-environment deployments.

6. **Scan for vulnerabilities** early in the pipeline.

7. **Use Key Vault for secrets**, never hard-code credentials.

8. **Automate rollbacks** on deployment failure.

Summary

Azure DevOps provides a comprehensive, scalable platform for implementing CI/CD pipelines that can automate the deployment of applications and infrastructure on Azure. Whether you're deploying a simple web app, a microservice-based architecture, or a complex environment using Infrastructure as Code tools like ARM, Bicep, or Terraform, Azure DevOps offers the integrations and extensibility needed to support enterprise-grade DevOps practices.

With YAML pipelines, secure service connections, automated quality gates, and environment approvals, you can build secure, resilient, and highly automated release workflows that accelerate your development lifecycle and reduce time-to-market.

In the next chapter, we'll explore **Monitoring, Management, and Governance**, diving into tools like Azure Monitor, Log Analytics, tagging strategies, and cost control techniques that help maintain operational health and accountability across your cloud estate.

Chapter 6: Monitoring, Management, and Governance

Azure Monitor and Log Analytics

Effective monitoring, management, and governance are critical to maintaining performance, ensuring compliance, and optimizing resources in any cloud environment. Microsoft Azure offers a robust set of tools and services to help organizations stay informed and in control of their infrastructure and applications. At the heart of this is **Azure Monitor**, a comprehensive platform for collecting, analyzing, and acting on telemetry data. Closely integrated with it is **Log Analytics**, a powerful tool for querying and analyzing data across your Azure resources.

In this section, we'll explore what Azure Monitor and Log Analytics are, how they work, and how you can leverage them to maintain visibility and control over your cloud resources.

What is Azure Monitor?

Azure Monitor is Microsoft's unified monitoring solution that delivers full-stack observability across Azure services, applications, and infrastructure. It provides:

- Metrics collection and visualization

- Logs collection and querying

- Alerts and automated actions

- Application performance monitoring

- Network monitoring

- Diagnostic settings for granular control

Azure Monitor supports both platform-level telemetry (e.g., metrics and logs from Azure resources) and application-level telemetry (via Application Insights).

Understanding Metrics vs Logs

Before diving into configuration and usage, it's important to understand the distinction between **metrics** and **logs** in Azure Monitor:

- **Metrics** are numerical values representing aspects of a system at a specific point in time. Examples include CPU usage, disk IOPS, and request count. These are lightweight and optimized for quick visual insights and alerts.

- **Logs** are records of events. They include diagnostic logs, activity logs, and application logs. Logs are more detailed and can be queried using the powerful Kusto Query Language (KQL).

Enabling Azure Monitor

Most Azure resources come with built-in support for monitoring. To start using Azure Monitor:

1. Go to the **Azure Portal**.

2. Navigate to your resource (e.g., a virtual machine).

3. Select **Monitoring > Insights** or **Monitoring > Logs**.

4. Use **Diagnostic Settings** to configure what data gets collected and where it is sent (e.g., Log Analytics workspace, Event Hubs, Storage Accounts).

You can also enable monitoring programmatically via ARM templates or Azure CLI.

Example: Enable Diagnostic Logs with Azure CLI

```
az monitor diagnostic-settings create \
  --name "SendToLogAnalytics" \
  --resource "/subscriptions/<subscription-
id>/resourceGroups/<resource-
group>/providers/Microsoft.Compute/virtualMachines/<vm-name>" \
  --workspace "<log-analytics-workspace-id>" \
  --logs '[{"category": "AllLogs", "enabled": true}]' \
  --metrics '[{"category": "AllMetrics", "enabled": true}]'
```

Log Analytics Workspace

A **Log Analytics Workspace** is an Azure resource where logs from different services are aggregated and analyzed. It is the backend storage and query engine used by Azure Monitor Logs.

Creating a Workspace

You can create a workspace from the Azure Portal:

1. Search for **Log Analytics Workspaces**.

2. Click **+ Create**.

3. Select the subscription, resource group, name, and region.

4. Review and create.

Or use CLI:

```
az monitor log-analytics workspace create \
  --resource-group MyResourceGroup \
  --workspace-name MyWorkspace
```

Querying Logs with KQL

The **Kusto Query Language (KQL)** is used to query data in Log Analytics. It allows you to filter, sort, aggregate, and visualize data.

Example: Get CPU usage over the last hour

```
Perf
| where ObjectName == "Processor"
| where CounterName == "% Processor Time"
| where TimeGenerated > ago(1h)
| summarize avg(CounterValue) by bin(TimeGenerated, 5m), Computer
| render timechart
```

Example: List failed logins

```
SigninLogs
| where ResultType != 0
| project TimeGenerated, UserPrincipalName, ResultDescription
```

These queries can be saved, shared, and used to power alerts and dashboards.

Setting Up Alerts

Alerts help you stay ahead of issues by notifying you when a condition is met. Azure Monitor supports:

- Metric Alerts

- Log Alerts

- Activity Log Alerts

Creating a Metric Alert

1. Go to **Azure Monitor > Alerts > New alert rule**.

2. Select a resource (e.g., VM).

3. Choose a metric (e.g., CPU Percentage).

4. Set condition (e.g., greater than 80% for 5 minutes).

5. Choose an **Action Group** (e.g., send email, call webhook).

6. Name the rule and create it.

Example: Create a Log Alert with CLI

```
az monitor scheduled-query create \
  --name "HighCPUAlert" \
  --resource-group "MyResourceGroup" \
  --workspace "MyWorkspace" \
  --description "Alert on high CPU" \
  --enabled true \
  --query "Perf | where CounterName == '% Processor Time' and
CounterValue > 80" \
  --severity 2 \
  --action /subscriptions/<sub-
id>/resourceGroups/<rg>/providers/microsoft.insights/actionGroups/<a
ction-group>
```

Dashboards and Workbooks

Azure Monitor supports custom **Dashboards** and **Workbooks** for visual representation of metrics and logs.

- **Dashboards**: Tile-based layouts that show charts, logs, and KPIs.

- **Workbooks**: Interactive reports with parameters, KQL queries, and visualizations.

You can access these from **Azure Monitor > Workbooks**, or pin them to your Azure Dashboard.

Example Use Cases

- Show VM performance metrics over time.

- Visualize request trends and error rates in a web app.

- Analyze security events from Azure AD logs.

Integrating with Application Insights

Application Insights extends Azure Monitor by focusing on application-level monitoring. It's ideal for:

- Performance tracking (response times, load times)

- Exception tracking

- User interaction analysis

- Dependency tracking (e.g., databases, APIs)

To enable it:

1. Install the SDK in your app (e.g., for .NET, JavaScript, Java).

2. Configure the Instrumentation Key.

3. View data in **Application Insights > Performance / Failures / Users**.

Example: Track Requests in ASP.NET Core

```
services.AddApplicationInsightsTelemetry(Configuration["APPINSIGHTS
_INSTRUMENTATIONKEY"]);
```

Monitoring Best Practices

- **Set baseline alerts**: Monitor key metrics like CPU, memory, and disk space.

- **Use workbooks for reports**: Create standardized reports for audits or reviews.

- **Automate diagnostics**: Use runbooks or Logic Apps to respond to alerts.

- **Secure access**: Use RBAC to control who can access monitoring data.

- **Consolidate logs**: Send logs from different resources to the same workspace for unified querying.

- **Monitor at multiple layers**: Infrastructure (VMs, networks), platform (App Services), and application (via Application Insights).

Cost Considerations

Monitoring services can incur costs, especially log retention and ingestion.

- Metrics: Free for standard platform metrics.

- Logs: Charged based on ingestion volume and retention period.

- Application Insights: Includes free tier, then charged per GB ingested.

Use **Cost Management + Billing** to track and optimize spending.

Summary

Azure Monitor and Log Analytics are foundational tools for any serious Azure implementation. They offer deep visibility, powerful analysis capabilities, and the automation necessary for modern cloud operations. By leveraging metrics, logs, alerts, and visualizations, you can ensure that your systems are performant, reliable, and secure—while maintaining control over costs and operations.

In the next section, we'll explore how to set up **alerts and dashboards**, and integrate them with your broader governance and operational strategies.

Setting Up Alerts and Dashboards

Monitoring your cloud environment is only effective when it is actionable. While collecting logs and metrics is important, the real power lies in leveraging this data to generate timely alerts and create insightful dashboards that empower operations teams to respond quickly and proactively. In Azure, alerts and dashboards are core components of operational visibility and situational awareness.

In this section, we will explore how to configure alerts based on metrics and log queries, define action groups for notification and automation, and build custom dashboards that consolidate your monitoring data into intuitive, real-time views.

The Role of Alerts in Azure Monitoring

Alerts in Azure provide a mechanism to detect issues, performance degradation, or other anomalies across your cloud infrastructure and applications. They can be triggered by:

- Metric thresholds (e.g., CPU usage > 80%)

- Log query results (e.g., failed login attempts)

- Activity log events (e.g., resource deletion)

Once triggered, alerts can perform actions such as sending emails, calling webhooks, triggering Logic Apps, or invoking automation runbooks.

Key Components of an Alert Rule

1. **Target Resource** – The Azure resource to monitor.

2. **Signal** – The metric, log query, or event to evaluate.

3. **Condition** – The criteria that determine whether the alert fires.

4. **Action Group** – Defines who gets notified or what automated action is taken.

5. **Alert Rule Details** – Name, severity, description, and evaluation frequency.

Creating Metric Alerts

Metric alerts are the most common and are used to monitor the performance and health of resources.

Steps to Create a Metric Alert via Azure Portal

1. Go to **Azure Monitor > Alerts**.

2. Click **+ Create > Alert rule**.

3. Select the **target resource** (e.g., a virtual machine).

4. Choose a **signal type**, such as "Percentage CPU".

5. Define the **alert logic**, e.g., "Greater than 80% for 5 minutes".

6. Attach an **action group** or create a new one.

7. Provide alert rule details and save.

Example: Create a Metric Alert with Azure CLI

```
az monitor metrics alert create \
  --name "HighCPUAlert" \
  --resource-group "MyResourceGroup" \
  --scopes "/subscriptions/<subscription-
id>/resourceGroups/MyResourceGroup/providers/Microsoft.Compute/virtu
alMachines/MyVM" \
  --condition "avg Percentage CPU > 80" \
  --description "Alert when CPU usage exceeds 80%" \
  --action "/subscriptions/<sub-
id>/resourceGroups/<rg>/providers/microsoft.insights/actionGroups/My
ActionGroup"
```

Log Alerts with Custom Queries

Log alerts provide advanced capabilities by allowing you to write custom queries in Kusto Query Language (KQL) and trigger alerts based on query results.

Example: Detecting Unauthorized Access Attempts

```
SigninLogs
| where ResultType != 0
| where TimeGenerated > ago(5m)
| summarize FailedAttempts = count() by UserPrincipalName
| where FailedAttempts > 3
```

Creating a Log Alert

1. Go to **Azure Monitor > Alerts > + New alert rule**.

2. Choose your **Log Analytics workspace** as the target.

3. Select **Custom log search** as the signal.

4. Paste your KQL query.

5. Define the evaluation period and frequency.

6. Attach an action group and finalize.

Action Groups

An **Action Group** is a reusable set of notification preferences and actions. It can include:

- Email/SMS/Push Notifications

- Webhook calls

- Azure Function invocation

- Logic App execution

- ITSM integration

- Automation Runbook execution

Example: Create Action Group via Azure CLI

```
az monitor action-group create \
  --name "OpsTeam" \
  --resource-group "MyResourceGroup" \
  --short-name "ops" \
  --email-receiver name="OpsEmail" email="ops@company.com"
```

You can reuse this group across multiple alert rules to maintain consistent response behavior.

Managing Alerts at Scale

With hundreds or thousands of alert rules across a large organization, it's crucial to manage them efficiently. Use the following practices:

- **Tag your alert rules** for grouping and filtering.

- Use **naming conventions** (e.g., `VM-HighCPU`, `DB-ConnectionErrors`).

- Review and **audit alert history** via the Azure Activity Log.

- Export alert rules as **ARM templates** to standardize and automate deployments.

Exporting Alerts as ARM Templates

In the Azure Portal, each alert rule can be exported as an ARM template. This allows you to store alert configurations in source control and deploy them as part of your infrastructure code.

Introduction to Azure Dashboards

Azure Dashboards provide customizable, interactive views of your resources, metrics, and logs. Dashboards are ideal for NOC (Network Operations Center) environments, executive summaries, and team-specific overviews.

- Fully customizable layout

- Shareable with RBAC control

- Supports charts, grids, metrics, and markdown

- Data from multiple resources in one view

You can create dashboards directly in the Azure Portal or programmatically using ARM templates.

Building a Custom Dashboard

Steps in Azure Portal

1. Go to **Dashboard > + New dashboard**.

2. Add **tiles** such as:

   - Metric charts

   - Log query visualizations

- ○ Resource summaries

- ○ Markdown notes

3. Arrange tiles using drag-and-drop.

4. Save and share the dashboard with appropriate users/groups.

Example: Pinning a Metric to Dashboard

1. Navigate to a resource (e.g., App Service).

2. Go to **Monitoring > Metrics**.

3. Select a metric like "Requests".

4. Configure chart options.

5. Click **Pin to dashboard.**

Workbooks for Interactive Reporting

While dashboards are great for quick visibility, **Azure Workbooks** offer a more dynamic and interactive reporting solution. They allow you to:

- Combine multiple data sources

- Use parameters and dropdowns

- Include narrative with markdown

- Embed charts, logs, metrics, and KPIs

Create a Workbook

1. Go to **Azure Monitor > Workbooks > + New**.

2. Add steps such as:

- ○ Text/Markdown

- ○ Metric visualization

- KQL-based query

- Parameters (e.g., resource group filter)

3. Save and share or pin to dashboard.

Visualizing Logs with Queries

Any KQL query in Log Analytics can be visualized and pinned to a dashboard or included in a workbook.

Example: Visualize Web App Errors

```
AppTraces
| where SeverityLevel >= 3
| summarize count() by bin(TimeGenerated, 10m), OperationName
| render timechart
```

You can convert this chart into a tile and pin it to your dashboard for real-time tracking.

Role-Based Access for Dashboards

You can control access to dashboards using **Azure Role-Based Access Control (RBAC)**. This allows you to:

- Share dashboards with entire teams

- Grant **read-only** or **edit** permissions

- Restrict visibility of sensitive data

Use roles like Reader, Contributor, or custom roles to fine-tune access.

Automation with Dashboards and Alerts

You can integrate alerts and dashboards with automation tools:

- **Logic Apps**: Send Slack/Teams notifications, trigger support tickets.

- **Azure Functions**: Restart services, scale resources, clean up logs.

- **Runbooks**: Perform remediation scripts on VMs or services.

Example: Auto-scale App Service on High CPU

1. Create alert on high CPU usage.

2. Link to Logic App that triggers scale-out operation.

3. Use dashboard to track scale events and performance trends.

Best Practices for Alerts and Dashboards

- **Keep alerts actionable**: Avoid alert fatigue with noisy or vague rules.

- **Prioritize severity**: Use severity levels (0 to 4) wisely for triage.

- **Consolidate views**: Create role-specific dashboards (e.g., Dev, Ops, Security).

- **Automate where possible**: Tie alerts to automation for faster MTTR.

- **Review regularly**: Periodically audit alert effectiveness and dashboard accuracy.

Summary

Alerts and dashboards in Azure turn raw telemetry data into actionable insights and visual intelligence. With properly configured alerts, you can detect and respond to issues in real-time. Dashboards and workbooks provide contextual visibility, helping teams understand system behavior and trends.

When used together, these tools create a resilient monitoring framework, enabling organizations to maintain operational excellence, respond quickly to incidents, and continuously improve system performance and reliability.

Resource Tagging and Management Groups

Efficient resource management is crucial when working in a cloud environment like Microsoft Azure. As organizations scale their infrastructure, it becomes increasingly important to maintain structure, accountability, and governance across all deployed services. Two of the most powerful tools in Azure for achieving this are **resource tagging** and **management groups**.

Resource tagging allows you to assign metadata to resources for categorization and automation, while management groups provide hierarchical organization above subscriptions, enabling large-scale policy enforcement and access control. In this section, we will explore both in depth, covering strategies, best practices, and implementation examples.

What are Azure Tags?

Azure Tags are key-value pairs that you can assign to resources, resource groups, and subscriptions. Tags are used to:

- Organize resources by department, environment, project, owner, or cost center

- Enable detailed cost reporting

- Automate governance tasks (e.g., shutting down dev VMs after hours)

- Filter resources in the Azure Portal or via CLI and API

Example Tag Structure

Key	Value
Environment	Production
Department	Finance
Owner	jdoe@contoso.com
CostCenter	CC-1001
Project	AzureMigration

Applying Tags in the Azure Portal

1. Navigate to any resource (e.g., Virtual Machine).

2. Select the **Tags** blade from the left menu.

3. Add key-value pairs (e.g., `Environment: Test`, `Owner: JaneDoe`).

4. Save changes.

These tags are now associated with the resource and can be used for filtering, reporting, or automation.

Tagging via Azure CLI

Azure CLI provides a straightforward way to manage tags in bulk.

Add Tags to a Resource

```
az resource tag \
  --tags Environment=Dev Owner=admin@contoso.com \
  --resource-group myResourceGroup \
  --name myVM \
  --resource-type "Microsoft.Compute/virtualMachines"
```

List Tags for a Resource

```
az resource show \
  --name myVM \
  --resource-group myResourceGroup \
  --resource-type "Microsoft.Compute/virtualMachines" \
  --query "tags"
```

Remove a Specific Tag

```
az resource update \
  --name myVM \
  --resource-group myResourceGroup \
  --resource-type "Microsoft.Compute/virtualMachines" \
  --remove tags.CostCenter
```

Tag Inheritance and Automation

Tags are not automatically inherited by child resources. For example, tagging a resource group does **not** automatically apply those tags to the resources within it.

To enforce tag inheritance:

- Use **Azure Policy** to apply and inherit tags.

- Use **Azure Automation** or **Azure Functions** to propagate tags programmatically.

Example: Tag Inheritance Policy (ARM Template Snippet)

```
{
  "if": {
    "field": "[concat('tags[', parameters('tagName'), ']')]",
    "exists": "false"
  },
  "then": {
    "effect": "modify",
    "details": {
      "operations": [
        {
          "operation": "add",
          "field": "[concat('tags[', parameters('tagName'), ']')]",
          "value": "[parameters('tagValue')]"
        }
      ]
    }
  }
}
```

This policy adds a tag to resources if it's missing, enabling standardization across teams.

Tag Governance and Best Practices

Tagging is most effective when governed consistently across the organization. Best practices include:

- **Standardize tag keys and values** (e.g., use Environment not Env)

- **Use naming conventions** to avoid duplication or ambiguity

- **Create a tagging policy document** shared across teams

- **Enforce tagging via Azure Policy**

- **Audit tag usage** regularly using reports or scripts

Example: Tag Naming Convention

Key	Description
Environment	dev, test, staging, prod
Owner	email address of responsible party
Application	Short name of the app/service
BusinessUnit	HR, Finance, Marketing, etc.

Using Tags in Cost Management

Azure Cost Management and Billing supports filtering and grouping costs by tags. This enables organizations to:

- Track project or department-level spending

- Allocate shared resource costs

- Identify underutilized or orphaned resources

Example: Cost Report by Tag

1. Go to **Cost Management + Billing > Cost Analysis**

2. Select your scope (e.g., subscription or resource group)

3. Group by **Tags** (e.g., Environment, CostCenter)

4. Filter date range and export the report

This granular visibility enables better budgeting and accountability.

Introduction to Azure Management Groups

Management Groups provide a way to organize and manage access, policies, and compliance across multiple Azure subscriptions. They are especially useful for large enterprises with complex organizational structures.

Hierarchy Example:

```
Root
├── ManagementGroup: Corp
│   ├── Subscription: HR-Prod
│   ├── Subscription: HR-Test
├── ManagementGroup: DevTeams
│   ├── Subscription: Dev1
│   ├── Subscription: Dev2
```

Creating and Managing Management Groups

Assign a Subscription to a Management Group

```
az account management-group subscription add \
  --name "DevTeams" \
  --subscription "00000000-0000-0000-0000-000000000000"
```

Create a Management Group

```
az account management-group create \
  --name "FinanceGroup" \
  --display-name "Finance Department"
```

List All Management Groups

```
az account management-group list
```

You can also manage these through the Azure Portal under **Management Groups** in the search bar.

Applying Policies at Scale with Management Groups

One of the biggest benefits of management groups is the ability to apply **Azure Policies** and **Role-Based Access Control (RBAC)** at a higher level.

Example: Apply a Tag Policy at Management Group Level

1. Go to **Azure Policy**

2. Assign a policy like **"Require tag and its value"**

3. Scope it to the Management Group (e.g., "DevTeams")

4. Configure remediation actions if necessary

This ensures all subscriptions under the group enforce the same governance rules.

Combining Tags and Management Groups

By combining tagging and management groups, you can implement robust governance models:

- Use management groups to define high-level structure and policy enforcement.

- Use tags for resource-level categorization, reporting, and automation.

Example Scenario

You assign the **FinanceGroup** management group a policy that requires all resources to have CostCenter and Owner tags. Subscriptions under that group inherit this policy, ensuring all resources are correctly tagged regardless of the team deploying them.

Real-World Use Cases

Use Case 1: Cost Tracking per Department

- Apply Department and CostCenter tags.

- Use Cost Analysis to report monthly spend per department.

- Automate tagging via policy or deployment scripts.

Use Case 2: Enforce Tag Compliance for Security

- Create a policy that audits for missing tags.

- Assign policy at management group level.

- Use remediation tasks to automatically add missing tags.

Use Case 3: Delegate Access Based on Organizational Structure

- Use management groups to represent departments (e.g., IT, HR, DevOps).

- Assign Reader or Contributor roles to department leads.

- Control access at scale with minimal overhead.

Automation of Tag Management

For dynamic environments, tags can be managed programmatically:

- **Azure Automation Runbooks**: Execute PowerShell scripts to apply tags regularly.

- **Azure Functions**: Trigger on resource creation events to auto-tag.

- **Logic Apps**: Create workflows that apply tags based on conditions.

Example: Auto-Tagging New Resources with Creator's Email

1. Enable **Activity Log** export to Event Grid.

2. Use Event Grid to trigger an Azure Function.

3. The function reads the event, extracts the identity, and applies a tag.

Summary

Resource tagging and management groups are essential components of Azure governance and operational efficiency. Tags enable fine-grained categorization and reporting, while management groups allow centralized control across multiple subscriptions.

By enforcing consistent tag usage and structuring your environment with management groups, you enhance visibility, accountability, and control—laying a solid foundation for cost management, compliance, and scalability. These tools are not optional in large-scale or regulated environments—they are critical to maintaining order and discipline in the cloud.

Cost Management and Optimization

Managing and optimizing cloud costs is one of the most critical responsibilities for IT administrators, architects, and financial stakeholders within an organization. While the cloud provides scalability, flexibility, and innovation at speed, these benefits can quickly lead to inflated bills and inefficiencies without proper cost control mechanisms in place. Azure offers a comprehensive suite of tools under the **Cost Management + Billing** umbrella to monitor, analyze, allocate, and optimize your spending.

In this section, we'll explore the core features of Azure Cost Management, best practices for cost control, automated optimization techniques, and practical examples to help you get the most value from your Azure investment.

Understanding Azure's Pricing Model

Azure pricing is based on a **pay-as-you-go** model with the following key cost areas:

- **Compute**: Virtual Machines (VMs), App Services, Functions

- **Storage**: Blob, File, Table, Premium Storage

- **Networking**: Data transfer, Load Balancers, VPN Gateways

- **Databases**: SQL Database, Cosmos DB, MySQL, PostgreSQL

- **Support Plans**: Basic, Developer, Standard, Professional Direct

Costs vary by **region, SKU, provisioned capacity**, and **usage patterns**. Many services offer both **consumption-based** and **reserved capacity** pricing.

Example: Pricing for Standard B2s VM

- **Per hour**: $0.0464

- **Monthly (24x7)**: ~$33.41

- **With 1-year Reserved Instance**: Up to 55% savings

Azure Cost Management + Billing Overview

Azure Cost Management (ACM) enables you to:

- Monitor cloud spend in real-time

- Forecast future costs

- Set budgets and thresholds

- Allocate costs to teams/projects via tags

- Analyze usage trends

- Identify idle or underutilized resources

Accessible via the **Azure Portal**, **Azure CLI**, and **REST APIs**, ACM provides powerful insights and tools to take control of your cloud finances.

Setting Budgets

Budgets help set spending thresholds on a monthly, quarterly, or annual basis. When budgets are exceeded (or approach their limit), notifications are sent via email or action groups.

Create a Budget in Azure Portal

1. Go to **Cost Management + Billing > Budgets**

2. Click **+ Add**

3. Define:

    - Scope (e.g., subscription, resource group)

    - Time period (monthly, quarterly, custom)

    - Budget amount

    - Alert thresholds (e.g., 80%, 100%)

4. Save the budget

Example: Budget Alert via CLI

```
az consumption budget create \
  --amount 1000 \
  --time-grain monthly \
  --category cost \
```

```
--name DevTeamBudget \
--resource-group myResourceGroup \
--start-date 2025-04-01 \
--end-date 2026-04-01 \
--notifications \
  actual_greater_than_80_percent=true \
  operator=GreaterThan \
  threshold=80 \
  contact_emails="devteam@contoso.com"
```

Cost Analysis

The **Cost Analysis** tool is one of the most used features in Azure. It lets you explore your spending using:

- Grouping by resource, resource group, subscription, tag, location

- Filtering by service name, location, and tags

- Time-based charts for trends and forecasting

- Downloadable CSV or Excel exports

Example Scenario

You're a cloud architect and want to identify the most expensive resource types:

1. Go to **Cost Management > Cost Analysis**

2. Group by **Resource type**

3. Filter to **last 30 days**

4. Export report to share with stakeholders

This quickly highlights services such as Premium Storage, SQL Database, or VMs that may need optimization.

Cost Allocation with Tags

By applying tags (e.g., Environment, CostCenter, Project), you can generate **tag-based reports** in Cost Analysis. This helps allocate spending back to teams, departments, or projects.

Example Use Case

- Finance wants to charge each department for their Azure usage.

- Apply Department and CostCenter tags to all resources.

- Use **Cost Analysis > Group by tag: Department**

- Export and integrate with internal chargeback systems.

This drives accountability and promotes cost-conscious behavior across the org.

Reserved Instances and Savings Plans

Azure offers significant cost reduction via **Reserved Instances (RIs)** and **Savings Plans**:

- **RIs**: Commit to using a VM size for 1 or 3 years.

- **Savings Plans**: Flexible commitment to compute spend across multiple services.

Savings up to 72% compared to pay-as-you-go.

Purchase Reserved Instance

1. Go to **Virtual Machines > Reservations**

2. Select region, VM size, and term (1 or 3 years)

3. Compare pricing and expected savings

4. Purchase and apply to existing workloads

Optimization Recommendations

Azure Advisor provides **personalized recommendations** to optimize cost and performance. These include:

- Right-size or shutdown underutilized VMs

- Purchase reserved capacity

- Remove unused public IPs or disks

- Use autoscaling for App Services

Example: Viewing Recommendations

1. Go to **Azure Advisor**

2. Select **Cost** category

3. Review:

    o Idle resources

    o Over-provisioned VMs

    o Unused disks and NICs

4. Apply changes or automate with scripts

Automating Cost Optimization

You can automate cost control using:

- **Azure Automation**: Runbooks to stop VMs after hours

- **Logic Apps**: Trigger alerts based on cost thresholds

- **Azure Functions**: Clean up unattached disks, expired snapshots

- **Schedules**: Auto-scale App Services or turn off Dev/Test environments

Example: Auto-shutdown VMs

1. Go to **VM > Operations > Auto-shutdown**

2. Set daily shutdown time

3. Configure notification (optional)

Or via CLI:

```
az vm auto-shutdown \
  --resource-group myResourceGroup \
  --name myVM \
  --time 1900 \
  --timezone "Pacific Standard Time"
```

Forecasting and Anomaly Detection

Azure offers cost forecasting based on historical usage trends. This helps in planning and budgeting for future periods.

- View forecast in **Cost Analysis**

- Compare forecast to budget

- Spot anomalies using alerts or third-party tools

Anomaly Detection Example

1. Set up a budget with 50%, 80%, 100% thresholds

2. Receive alert when actual spend exceeds expected trend

3. Investigate resource changes or configuration drift

Enterprise Agreements and CSP

For organizations using **Enterprise Agreements (EA)** or working via a **Cloud Solution Provider (CSP)**, Azure Cost Management integrates additional capabilities:

- Detailed EA usage reporting

- Department/account-level budgeting

- Partner-level visibility and billing for CSPs

- API access to billing data

Use the **EA Portal** or **Partner Center** for more advanced reporting.

Monitoring Costs Across Tenants

Organizations with multiple Azure tenants (e.g., mergers, subsidiaries) can use **Azure Lighthouse** or **Cross-Tenant Cost Management** to manage and monitor costs centrally.

- Set up delegated resource access

- Monitor spend across tenants

- Centralize reporting and budgeting

Third-Party Cost Management Tools

While Azure's built-in tools are powerful, large enterprises often use third-party solutions for advanced analytics:

- **CloudHealth**

- **CloudCheckr**

- **Spot by NetApp**

- **Apptio Cloudability**

These tools integrate with Azure and provide deeper insights, forecasting models, and cost allocation features.

Best Practices for Azure Cost Optimization

1. **Tag Early and Tag Consistently**
   Ensure all resources are tagged at creation.

2. **Set Budgets for All Teams**
   Track spend against limits to prevent overruns.

3. **Review Costs Weekly**
   Use dashboards or reports for visibility.

4. **Automate Shutdowns and Scaling**
   Especially for Dev/Test and seasonal workloads.

5. **Regularly Review Azure Advisor**
   Apply recommendations to improve efficiency.

6. **Use Reservations and Savings Plans**
   Commit where usage is predictable.

7. **Educate Your Teams**
   Awareness drives accountability and better practices.

Summary

Azure Cost Management and Optimization is not just a set of tools—it's a culture of cloud financial discipline. By leveraging budgets, tags, analysis, and automation, organizations can take control of their cloud spending, align it with business goals, and continuously improve cost efficiency. Whether you're a small startup or a global enterprise, adopting a proactive approach to cost governance ensures that your cloud journey remains sustainable and profitable.

Chapter 7: Building and Deploying Web Apps

App Service Plans and Hosting Options

Azure App Service is one of the most popular and versatile offerings for hosting web applications in the cloud. It abstracts away much of the underlying infrastructure management, allowing developers to focus purely on building and deploying applications. Whether you're running a small personal blog or a globally scaled enterprise web app, Azure App Service can meet your needs with flexible hosting plans, scaling options, and integration with other Azure services.

In this section, we'll cover **App Service Plans**, the different **hosting options**, how to select the right tier for your application, and how to optimize your hosting environment for cost, performance, and scalability.

What Is an App Service Plan?

An **App Service Plan** defines the region (Datacenter), the features, the amount of storage, and the compute resources (CPU, memory, etc.) available to your web app. When you create a web app in Azure App Service, you must associate it with an App Service Plan.

All apps within the same App Service Plan share the same compute resources, which makes it easy to host multiple applications under a single plan.

Key Characteristics:

- Determines **pricing tier** (Free, Shared, Basic, Standard, Premium, Isolated)

- Hosts one or more **Web Apps, API Apps, Mobile Apps, and Functions**

- Controls **scaling**, **resource allocation**, and **region**

Hosting Tiers Overview

Azure App Service offers multiple tiers to meet different needs, from hobby projects to enterprise-grade applications:

Free and Shared (Dev/Test)

- Ideal for experiments and proof-of-concept applications.

- Limited CPU and memory.

- No custom domain or SSL support.

Basic

- Dedicated compute resources.

- Good for small production workloads.

- Manual scaling only.

Standard

- Auto-scaling support.

- Daily backups.

- Custom domains and SSL.

- VNET integration.

Premium v2 / v3

- Enhanced performance.

- Premium hardware.

- Autoscaling and advanced networking.

- Zone redundancy and higher storage.

Isolated

- Dedicated environment in your virtual network.

- Suitable for high-security workloads.

- Higher SLA and capacity.

Comparison Example

Tier	Scaling	SSL	Custom Domain	Backups	VNET Support
Free	No	No	No	No	No
Basic	Manual	Yes	Yes	No	No
Standard	Auto	Yes	Yes	Yes	Yes
Premium	Auto + High Perf	Yes	Yes	Yes	Yes
Isolated	Auto + Dedicated	Yes	Yes	Yes	Full

Creating an App Service Plan

You can create an App Service Plan from the portal, CLI, or ARM templates.

Azure Portal

1. Go to **App Services**

2. Click **+ Create**

3. Select the **subscription** and **resource group**

4. Choose the **App Service Plan** (or create a new one)

5. Pick your **pricing tier**

6. Deploy your app

Azure CLI Example

```
az appservice plan create \
  --name MyAppServicePlan \
  --resource-group MyResourceGroup \
  --sku S1 \
  --is-linux \
  --location "East US"
```

This command creates a Standard tier (S1) Linux-based App Service Plan.

Hosting Options Within App Service

Azure supports various app types under the App Service umbrella:

Web Apps

- Host web applications built using .NET, Java, Python, PHP, Node.js, and more.

- Supports container-based deployments.

- Scalable and resilient.

API Apps

- Build and deploy RESTful APIs.

- Swagger integration for API documentation.

- Authentication and rate limiting features.

Mobile Apps

- Backend support for mobile clients.

- Push notifications, offline sync.

- SDKs for iOS, Android, and Xamarin.

Function Apps

- Serverless compute.

- Event-driven and auto-scaling.

- Can share the App Service Plan with Web Apps for cost efficiency.

Deployment Slots

Deployment slots are a feature of Standard and above tiers that allow you to create **staging environments** within your App Service.

- Create multiple slots (e.g., dev, staging, production)

- Swap slots to promote new code without downtime

- Maintain separate configuration per slot

Example: Swap Deployment Slot with Azure CLI

```
az webapp deployment slot swap \
  --resource-group MyResourceGroup \
  --name MyWebApp \
  --slot staging \
  --target-slot production
```

This enables zero-downtime deployments and testing in production-like environments.

Autoscaling and Manual Scaling

Azure App Service supports both **manual** and **automatic** scaling based on rules and metrics.

Manual Scaling

Scale out (increase instances) or scale up (move to higher tier) from the portal.

Auto-Scale Based on Metrics

1. Go to **App Service > Scale out**

2. Add a **custom rule**, e.g.:

   - CPU usage > 70% for 10 minutes → Increase instance count

   - CPU usage < 30% for 10 minutes → Decrease instance count

Azure CLI Auto-Scale Example

```
az monitor autoscale create \
  --resource-group MyResourceGroup \
  --resource MyAppServicePlan \
  --resource-type Microsoft.Web/serverfarms \
  --name autoscale-settings \
  --min-count 1 \
  --max-count 5 \
  --count 2
```

VNET Integration and Security

From the Standard tier upward, App Services can integrate with **Virtual Networks** for secure communication with internal services.

Benefits:

- Secure access to on-premise or private services

- Private DNS resolution

- IP restrictions and service endpoints

Use **Regional VNET Integration** or **Private Endpoint** depending on your use case.

Custom Domains and SSL

Custom domains and SSL certificates are supported in Basic and higher tiers.

Adding a Custom Domain

1. Go to **App Service > Custom domains**

2. Add domain (e.g., www.contoso.com)

3. Verify DNS settings (CNAME or A record)

4. Bind to the app

SSL Binding

- Upload a certificate (.pfx)

- Add a TLS/SSL binding

- Optionally use **App Service Managed Certificate**

Azure CLI Example for Binding SSL

```
az webapp config ssl bind \
  --name MyWebApp \
  --resource-group MyResourceGroup \
```

```
--certificate-thumbprint ABC1234567890DEF \
--ssl-type SNI
```

Backup and Restore

App Services in Standard and higher tiers support **automated backups**.

- Configure backup schedule

- Store backups in Azure Storage Account

- Restore entire app, or just content or database

Backup Configuration Steps

1. Go to **App Service > Backups**

2. Select **Storage Account**

3. Set schedule (daily, weekly, etc.)

4. Include databases if needed

Logging and Monitoring

Built-in features include:

- **App Service Logs**: HTTP logs, detailed error messages

- **Application Insights**: Performance, request, and exception tracking

- **Azure Monitor**: Metrics and custom alerts

Enable from **App Service > Monitoring > Diagnostic settings**.

Choosing the Right Plan

Choosing the correct App Service Plan depends on your application needs:

- **Development**: Use Free or Shared tiers

- **Startup MVP**: Basic or Standard

- **Production Web App**: Standard or Premium

- **Enterprise**: Premium v3 or Isolated with VNET integration

Factors to consider:

- Uptime requirements

- Anticipated traffic

- Security needs

- Budget constraints

- Integration with other services

Summary

Azure App Service Plans offer a scalable, reliable, and secure environment for deploying modern web applications. By understanding the different hosting options and how to configure your App Service Plan effectively, you can optimize performance, reduce costs, and streamline your deployment workflow.

Whether you're building an API backend, an e-commerce website, or a microservices-based architecture, Azure App Service provides the foundation to run your workloads with minimal overhead and maximum agility. The flexibility of deployment slots, autoscaling, VNET integration, and tier selection ensures that you're ready for any stage of growth.

Deploying Web Apps with GitHub and DevOps Pipelines

Modern application development and deployment demand speed, consistency, and reliability. Azure provides a variety of tools to automate deployments and integrate with common development workflows, notably **GitHub Actions** and **Azure DevOps Pipelines**. Both solutions support continuous integration (CI) and continuous deployment (CD), ensuring that every code change can be tested, built, and deployed automatically and predictably.

In this section, we will explore how to set up CI/CD for your web applications using GitHub and Azure DevOps. We'll cover key concepts, configuration examples, workflows, and best practices that will help you implement robust pipelines for deploying to Azure App Service and beyond.

Overview of CI/CD for Azure Web Apps

Continuous Integration (CI): Automatically builds and tests your application whenever code is pushed to a repository.

Continuous Deployment (CD): Automatically deploys the built application to a target environment (e.g., Azure App Service) after a successful CI run.

Azure enables full support for CI/CD workflows through:

- **GitHub Actions** (integrated natively with GitHub repositories)

- **Azure DevOps Pipelines** (part of Azure DevOps Services)

- **Third-party tools** like Jenkins, CircleCI, and GitLab CI

GitHub Actions for Azure

GitHub Actions is a powerful, YAML-based workflow automation tool built into GitHub. It supports:

- Building, testing, and deploying code directly from your repo

- Event-driven triggers (e.g., push, pull request, release)

- Marketplace actions for Azure App Service, Functions, and more

Setting Up GitHub Actions with Azure

1. **Create an Azure Web App**

If you haven't already:

```
az webapp create \
  --resource-group MyResourceGroup \
  --plan MyAppServicePlan \
  --name mywebapp123 \
```

```
--runtime "NODE|18-lts"
```

2. **Generate a Deployment Profile**

```
az webapp deployment list-publishing-profiles \
  --name mywebapp123 \
  --resource-group MyResourceGroup \
  --output yaml
```

Use these credentials for GitHub secrets.

3. **Add GitHub Secrets**

In your GitHub repository:

- Navigate to **Settings > Secrets**

- Add:

    ○ `AZURE_WEBAPP_PUBLISH_PROFILE` (full XML from above command)

    ○ `AZURE_WEBAPP_NAME` (e.g., `mywebapp123`)

4. **Create** `.github/workflows/deploy.yml`

```
name: Build and Deploy to Azure Web App

on:
  push:
    branches:
      - main

jobs:
  build-and-deploy:
    runs-on: ubuntu-latest

    steps:
      - name: Checkout code
        uses: actions/checkout@v3
```

```
- name: Setup Node.js
  uses: actions/setup-node@v3
  with:
    node-version: '18'

- name: Install dependencies
  run: npm install

- name: Build project
  run: npm run build

- name: Deploy to Azure Web App
  uses: azure/webapps-deploy@v2
  with:
    app-name: ${{ secrets.AZURE_WEBAPP_NAME }}
    publish-profile: ${{ secrets.AZURE_WEBAPP_PUBLISH_PROFILE
}}
    package.: .
```

This workflow checks out code, installs dependencies, builds your app, and deploys it to Azure whenever code is pushed to main.

Azure DevOps Pipelines

Azure DevOps Pipelines is a cloud-based CI/CD platform that supports:

- Multi-stage pipelines

- YAML and visual designer workflows

- Integration with GitHub, Azure Repos, Bitbucket, and more

- Built-in tasks for Azure deployments

Creating a Pipeline

1. **Create an Azure DevOps Project**

Visit https://dev.azure.com and create a new project.

2. **Connect Your GitHub Repo**

- Go to **Pipelines > New Pipeline**

- Select **GitHub** and authorize the connection

- Choose your repository

3. **Define `azure-pipelines.yml` in the repo**

```yaml
trigger:
  branches:
    include:
      - main

pool:
  vmImage: 'ubuntu-latest'

variables:
  appName: 'mywebapp123'
  resourceGroup: 'MyResourceGroup'
  packagePath: '$(System.DefaultWorkingDirectory)'

steps:
  - task: NodeTool@0
    inputs:
      versionSpec: '18.x'
    displayName: 'Install Node.js'

  - script: |
      npm install
      npm run build
    displayName: 'Install dependencies and build'

  - task: ArchiveFiles@2
    inputs:
      rootFolderOrFile: '$(Build.SourcesDirectory)'
      includeRootFolder: false
      archiveType: 'zip'
      archiveFile: '$(Build.ArtifactStagingDirectory)/webapp.zip'
      replaceExistingArchive: true
```

```
- task: AzureWebApp@1
  inputs:
    azureSubscription: 'My Azure Connection'
    appType: 'webApp'
    appName: '$(appName)'
    package: '$(Build.ArtifactStagingDirectory)/webapp.zip'
```

You can set up `My Azure Connection` in **Project Settings > Service Connections**, and authenticate using a service principal or managed identity.

Multi-Stage Deployment Pipelines

For enterprise environments, deploying directly to production is not ideal. Instead, use **multi-stage pipelines** with:

- **Dev**

- **Staging**

- **Production**

Each stage can include validations, approvals, and manual interventions.

YAML Multi-Stage Example

```
stages:
- stage: Build
  jobs:
    - job: BuildApp
      steps:
        - checkout: self
        - script: npm install && npm run build

- stage: Deploy_Dev
  dependsOn: Build
  jobs:
    - deployment: DeployWeb
      environment: 'dev'
      strategy:
        runOnce:
          deploy:
            steps:
```

```
          - task: AzureWebApp@1
            inputs:
              azureSubscription: 'My Azure Connection'
              appName: 'mywebapp-dev'
              package: '$(Pipeline.Workspace)/drop/webapp.zip'

- stage: Deploy_Prod
  dependsOn: Deploy_Dev
  condition: succeeded()
  jobs:
    - deployment: DeployWeb
      environment: 'production'
      strategy:
        runOnce:
          deploy:
            steps:
              - task: AzureWebApp@1
                inputs:
                  azureSubscription: 'My Azure Connection'
                  appName: 'mywebapp-prod'
                  package: '$(Pipeline.Workspace)/drop/webapp.zip'
```

You can enforce **approvals** before progressing to `Deploy_Prod`.

Monitoring and Rollbacks

After deploying, it's essential to monitor and, if needed, roll back to a stable version.

Application Insights

- Add telemetry and performance monitoring with Application Insights.

- View performance, failure rates, user metrics.

Rollbacks with Deployment Slots

- Use **staging slot** for testing.

- Promote to production only after successful validation.

- Swap back in case of issues (instant rollback).

```
az webapp deployment slot swap \
  --name mywebapp \
  --resource-group MyResourceGroup \
  --slot staging \
  --target-slot production
```

Security and Best Practices

- **Use secrets**: Never hardcode credentials or tokens. Use GitHub Secrets or Azure Key Vault.

- **Isolate environments**: Dev, staging, and production should use different App Services or slots.

- **Monitor pipelines**: Set alerts for build failures or unusual deployment activity.

- **Test before deploy**: Include unit tests, linting, and security scans in the CI step.

- **Tag builds**: Use versioning or commit hashes to track deployments.

Summary

CI/CD pipelines are critical for delivering software efficiently and reliably. Azure integrates deeply with both GitHub Actions and Azure DevOps Pipelines, offering flexible and scalable deployment strategies for modern web apps.

By automating build, test, and deployment processes, you eliminate manual errors, speed up development cycles, and deliver better software. Whether you're deploying a static site, a complex Node.js app, or a multi-service API backend, these tools ensure your deployments are repeatable, secure, and fast. With proper monitoring and rollback mechanisms, you can maintain uptime and user satisfaction throughout your release cycles.

Scaling and Load Balancing

As web applications grow and user traffic increases, maintaining performance, availability, and reliability becomes critical. Azure provides a rich set of features for **scaling** and **load balancing** applications hosted on App Service. Whether you're expecting seasonal traffic spikes or consistent growth, Azure allows you to scale proactively and efficiently without overprovisioning.

In this section, we will dive deep into the concepts and implementation of scaling and load balancing in Azure App Service. You will learn how to configure autoscaling, manual scaling, regional redundancy, load balancing with Azure Front Door and Application Gateway, and how to monitor your scaling strategy for performance and cost efficiency.

What is Scaling?

Scaling refers to the process of increasing or decreasing the **capacity** of your application based on load. There are two primary scaling strategies:

- **Vertical Scaling (Scaling Up)**: Increase the size of the instance (CPU, memory, etc.)

- **Horizontal Scaling (Scaling Out)**: Increase the number of instances handling the load

Azure App Service supports both, depending on the pricing tier of your App Service Plan.

Vertical Scaling (Scale Up)

Scaling up means moving to a higher pricing tier with more resources. This is a quick way to improve performance without changing the number of instances.

Steps to Scale Up

1. Go to **App Service > Scale Up (App Service Plan)**

2. Select a higher tier (e.g., from S1 to P1v2)

3. Click **Apply**

Vertical scaling is best for applications bound by compute, memory, or storage requirements that are not parallelizable across instances.

Horizontal Scaling (Scale Out)

Scaling out adds more instances to handle increased traffic. Azure App Service supports **manual** and **automatic** scaling.

Manual Scaling

1. Go to **App Service > Scale Out (App Service Plan)**

2. Choose **Manual scale**

3. Set the **instance count** (e.g., 1–20)

4. Save the settings

Manual scaling is suitable when you anticipate fixed traffic levels (e.g., for an event or campaign).

Autoscaling

Autoscaling allows Azure to dynamically adjust instance count based on resource metrics such as:

- CPU percentage

- Memory usage

- HTTP queue length

- Custom metrics (via Application Insights)

Setting Up Autoscaling

1. Go to **App Service > Scale Out (App Service Plan)**

2. Select **Custom autoscale**

3. Define:

   ◦ **Minimum** and **maximum** instance count

   ◦ **Default** instance count

   ◦ **Rules** for scale-out and scale-in

Example Rule

- If CPU usage > 70% for 10 minutes → Increase by 1 instance

- If CPU usage < 30% for 10 minutes → Decrease by 1 instance

Azure CLI Example

```
az monitor autoscale create \
  --resource-group MyResourceGroup \
  --resource MyAppServicePlan \
  --resource-type Microsoft.Web/serverfarms \
  --name autoscale-rule \
  --min-count 2 \
  --max-count 10 \
  --count 3
```

Add a condition:

```
az monitor autoscale rule create \
  --autoscale-name autoscale-rule \
  --resource-group MyResourceGroup \
  --condition "Percentage CPU > 75 avg 5m" \
  --scale out 1
```

Monitoring and Metrics for Scaling

Use **Azure Monitor** and **Application Insights** to track metrics relevant to scaling:

- **Percentage CPU**

- **Memory Working Set**

- **Requests per second**

- **Failed requests**

- **Response time**

These metrics help refine your scaling rules and ensure optimal performance.

Load Balancing in Azure App Service

When scaling out to multiple instances or deploying across regions, load balancing ensures traffic is distributed evenly and efficiently.

Azure provides multiple load balancing options:

1. Built-In Load Balancer (App Service)

Azure App Service automatically load balances HTTP(S) traffic across all instances in the same App Service Plan. No additional configuration is needed.

Features:

- Round-robin traffic distribution

- Session affinity (ARR) support

- Integration with autoscaling

2. Azure Front Door

Azure Front Door is a global, layer 7 load balancer that provides:

- Global HTTP/HTTPS traffic distribution

- SSL termination

- URL-based routing

- WAF (Web Application Firewall)

- Automatic failover between regions

Use Case Example

Deploy your app in:

- **East US**

- **West Europe**

Front Door routes users to the closest and healthiest region.

Configuration Example

```
az network front-door create \
  --resource-group MyResourceGroup \
  --name MyFrontDoor \
```

```
--backend-address mywebapp-east.azurewebsites.net \
--frontend-endpoints defaultFrontendEndpoint \
--accepted-protocols Http Https \
--backend-host-header mywebapp-east.azurewebsites.net
```

Add second region backend:

```
az network front-door backend-pool backend add \
  --resource-group MyResourceGroup \
  --front-door-name MyFrontDoor \
  --pool-name defaultBackendPool \
  --address mywebapp-west.azurewebsites.net
```

3. Azure Application Gateway

An **Application Gateway** is a regional, layer 7 load balancer with features like:

- Path-based routing

- SSL termination

- WAF integration

- Rewrite rules

It's ideal for apps hosted in a virtual network (e.g., App Service Environment).

Scaling Across Regions

To achieve global resilience and performance:

1. Deploy the app to multiple regions

2. Enable geo-replication for backend services (e.g., databases)

3. Use **Traffic Manager** or **Front Door** for routing

Azure Traffic Manager

- DNS-based load balancer

- Supports:

    - Priority routing

    - Performance routing

    - Weighted routing

Example: Route US traffic to `myapp-us` and EU traffic to `myapp-eu`.

Azure CLI Traffic Manager Profile

```
az network traffic-manager profile create \
  --name MyTrafficProfile \
  --resource-group MyResourceGroup \
  --routing-method Performance \
  --unique-dns-name myappglobal \
  --ttl 30 \
  --protocol HTTP \
  --port 80 \
  --path "/"
```

Ensuring High Availability

Scaling and load balancing contribute to **high availability (HA)**. Key recommendations include:

- **Use multiple instances** to eliminate single points of failure

- **Leverage deployment slots** for zero-downtime releases

- **Use geo-distribution** to ensure global coverage

- **Enable health probes** for backend status checks

- **Implement retry logic and circuit breakers** in application code

Azure provides a **99.95% SLA** for two or more instances in a Standard App Service Plan.

Cost Optimization with Scaling

Autoscaling helps reduce costs by running only what's needed.

Best Practices:

- Define **off-hours scale-in rules**

- Use **different App Service Plans** for dev/test vs production

- Monitor instance utilization trends

- Use **Premium plans** for better scaling granularity

Autoscaling saves money during low-traffic periods and ensures capacity during peak loads.

Common Pitfalls and How to Avoid Them

Pitfall	Solution
Over-provisioning resources	Use autoscaling to adapt to actual load
Unbalanced backend deployments	Use health probes and regional routing
Latency during scaling events	Use proactive scaling or scheduled scaling
No monitoring of scale effectiveness	Monitor performance before and after scaling actions

Summary

Scaling and load balancing are at the heart of delivering performant, reliable, and globally accessible applications on Azure. Azure App Service simplifies horizontal and vertical scaling, while Azure Front Door, Application Gateway, and Traffic Manager offer powerful load balancing options suited to a range of use cases.

By combining intelligent autoscaling with global traffic distribution, you can ensure your applications remain responsive and available, no matter the demand. Monitoring, automation, and careful planning are key to achieving a seamless scaling and load balancing strategy that aligns with both your performance goals and budget.

Integrating with Azure CDN and Traffic Manager

When building web applications on Azure, delivering fast, reliable, and globally distributed user experiences becomes a top priority—especially as user bases span continents. To address this, Azure provides **Azure Content Delivery Network (CDN)** and **Azure Traffic**

Manager, two complementary services designed to improve application performance, scalability, and availability.

Azure CDN offloads static content delivery and accelerates dynamic content caching, while Azure Traffic Manager intelligently routes traffic based on performance, geographic location, or failover logic. Together, they ensure your application is performant and accessible at all times, from anywhere in the world.

What is Azure CDN?

Azure Content Delivery Network (CDN) is a distributed network of servers that deliver web content to users based on their geographic location. It reduces latency, improves load times, and minimizes bandwidth consumption by caching content at strategically placed edge nodes across the globe.

Key Features:

- Global reach with low-latency delivery

- Static content caching (images, JavaScript, CSS)

- Custom domain and HTTPS support

- Geo-filtering and access rules

- Rules Engine for advanced behavior control

Use Cases for Azure CDN

- **Accelerating static content** such as media, images, and scripts

- **Reducing load on origin servers** by offloading traffic

- **Improving page load speed**, especially for global audiences

- **Delivering software downloads** or large files

- **Enhancing video streaming experiences**

Creating an Azure CDN Profile and Endpoint

1. Go to the **Azure Portal**

2. Search for **CDN profiles**

3. Click **+ Create**

4. Fill out:

    o **Resource Group**

    o **Name**

    o **Pricing Tier** (Standard Microsoft, Standard Akamai, Standard Verizon, or Premium)

5. Create a new **CDN endpoint**:

    o **Name**

    o **Origin type** (e.g., Web App)

    o **Origin hostname** (e.g., myapp.azurewebsites.net)

    o **Origin host header** (same as origin hostname)

Once deployed, the CDN endpoint URL (e.g., mycdn.azureedge.net) can be used to serve your application's content.

Enabling CDN for an Azure Web App

Azure Web Apps can serve static and dynamic content. Integrating Azure CDN offloads static asset delivery.

1. Deploy your web app to App Service

2. Configure your CDN endpoint with the web app as origin

3. Use the CDN URL or custom domain with HTTPS to serve your site

Optional: Add Custom Domain and HTTPS

1. Go to your CDN endpoint > **Custom domains**

2. Add your domain (e.g., `cdn.myapp.com`)

3. Create necessary DNS records (CNAME to Azure CDN URL)

4. Enable HTTPS (free certificate via Azure-managed certificate)

Using Azure CLI to Create a CDN Endpoint

```
az cdn profile create \
  --name MyCdnProfile \
  --resource-group MyResourceGroup \
  --sku Standard_Microsoft

az cdn endpoint create \
  --name mycdnendpoint \
  --profile-name MyCdnProfile \
  --resource-group MyResourceGroup \
  --origin mywebapp.azurewebsites.net
```

Azure CDN Rules Engine

The Rules Engine allows fine-grained control over CDN behavior using match conditions and actions.

Example Scenarios:

- Redirect all HTTP traffic to HTTPS

- Set cache expiration headers

- Restrict access by IP or country

- Add custom response headers

Rules can be added in **Azure Portal > CDN Endpoint > Rules Engine**.

Monitoring and Caching Behavior

You can monitor CDN usage via:

- **Azure Monitor**

- **CDN Analytics** (traffic, cache hit ratio, request volume)

To verify content caching:

1. Use browser developer tools (check response headers like `X-Cache`)

2. A `HIT` indicates cached content; `MISS` indicates origin fetch

Set cache rules using response headers or the Rules Engine.

```
Cache-Control: public, max-age=86400
```

What is Azure Traffic Manager?

Azure Traffic Manager is a **DNS-based** global traffic routing service that distributes client requests to the most appropriate endpoint based on the selected routing method.

Unlike Azure Load Balancer (which works at Layer 4), Traffic Manager operates at the DNS level (Layer 7), making it ideal for global redundancy and performance optimization.

Traffic Manager Routing Methods

- **Performance**: Routes to the closest endpoint with lowest latency

- **Priority**: Routes to primary endpoint unless it's down, then to fallback

- **Weighted**: Routes traffic based on defined weights

- **Geographic**: Routes users based on geographic location

- **Multivalue**: Returns multiple healthy endpoints

- **Subnet**: Routes based on client IP address

Example Scenario: Global Web App with Traffic Manager

Let's say your application is deployed in:

- East US (`myapp-east.azurewebsites.net`)

- West Europe (`myapp-eu.azurewebsites.net`)

You want users in the US to connect to East US and users in Europe to connect to West Europe.

Steps:

1. Create a Traffic Manager profile

2. Add endpoints for both web apps

3. Set routing method to **Performance**

Creating a Traffic Manager Profile

Using Azure Portal

1. Go to **Traffic Manager Profiles**

2. Click **+ Create**

3. Choose:

   - **Name** (e.g., `myapp-tm`)

   - **Routing method**: Performance

   - **DNS name**: e.g., `myapp.trafficmanager.net`

4. Add endpoints:

   - Type: Azure Endpoint

   - Target Resource: Your App Service

   - Priority/weight/region based on routing method

Using Azure CLI

```
az network traffic-manager profile create \
  --name MyTrafficProfile \
  --resource-group MyResourceGroup \
```

```
--routing-method Performance \
--unique-dns-name myappglobal \
--ttl 30 \
--protocol HTTP \
--port 80 \
--path "/"
```

Add endpoints:

```
az network traffic-manager endpoint create \
  --name EastUS \
  --profile-name MyTrafficProfile \
  --resource-group MyResourceGroup \
  --type azureEndpoints \
  --target-resource-id "/subscriptions/<sub-
id>/resourceGroups/MyRG/providers/Microsoft.Web/sites/myapp-east"
```

Repeat for West Europe.

Integrating CDN with Traffic Manager

You can combine CDN and Traffic Manager for both performance and availability:

1. **CDN Endpoint Origin**: Use App Services from multiple regions

2. **Traffic Manager**: Route users to nearest region

3. **CDN**: Accelerate content from regional origin

Or reverse:

1. **Traffic Manager** routes user to closest CDN endpoint

2. CDN fetches from shared origin (App Service)

Monitoring Health and Failover

Traffic Manager monitors endpoint health using:

- HTTP/HTTPS probe

- Custom probe paths (e.g., `/health`)

If a region goes down, Traffic Manager automatically fails over to another healthy region.

Health probe example:

```
az network traffic-manager profile update \
  --name MyTrafficProfile \
  --resource-group MyResourceGroup \
  --protocol HTTPS \
  --path "/health"
```

Best Practices for CDN and Traffic Manager Integration

- **Use CDN for all static assets** (CSS, JS, images)

- **Host dynamic and API content via Traffic Manager**

- **Implement health probes on all endpoints**

- **Use HTTPS on both CDN and App Service**

- **Monitor cache hit ratios** and fine-tune headers

- **Leverage geo-filtering** if content must be region-specific

- **Ensure custom domains are secured with certificates**

Summary

Integrating Azure CDN and Traffic Manager into your web application architecture significantly enhances performance, reliability, and user experience. The CDN reduces latency and server load by caching static content at global edge locations, while Traffic Manager intelligently routes users to the optimal backend based on routing policies and health checks.

Whether you're building a high-traffic enterprise platform or a geo-distributed SaaS product, these services allow your app to scale and adapt dynamically to global demand. Properly configured, they create a resilient, fast, and globally accessible web presence—critical for modern cloud-native applications.

Chapter 8: Azure for Developers

Azure SDKs and APIs

Azure provides a vast ecosystem of SDKs and APIs that empower developers to build robust, scalable, and cloud-native applications. Whether you are building web apps, mobile apps, microservices, or data-driven solutions, Azure offers development tools in a variety of programming languages that abstract the complexity of cloud interactions and streamline integration with services like Azure Storage, Azure Cosmos DB, Azure Key Vault, and more.

In this section, we will explore the breadth and depth of Azure SDKs and REST APIs, how to use them in real-world development workflows, how to authenticate securely, and how to follow best practices for building cloud-integrated apps using modern development frameworks and tools.

Overview of Azure SDKs

Azure SDKs are available for multiple programming languages and frameworks, including:

- **.NET**

- **Java**

- **Python**

- **JavaScript/TypeScript**

- **Go**

- **C++**

- **Ruby**

- **PHP**

These SDKs are open-source and maintained by Microsoft, often available as packages in public repositories like NuGet, PyPI, npm, and Maven Central.

Key SDK Categories

1. **Management SDKs**

- For provisioning and managing Azure resources (e.g., ARM templates, resource groups)

- Used in DevOps, automation scripts, or admin tools

2. **Client SDKs**

- For interacting with Azure services like Blob Storage, Key Vault, Cosmos DB, etc.

- Embedded in business applications

Installing Azure SDKs

.NET Example

Install Azure Storage Blob client:

```
dotnet add package Azure.Storage.Blobs
```

JavaScript (Node.js) Example

```
npm install @azure/storage-blob
```

Python Example

```
pip install azure-storage-blob
```

All Azure SDKs follow a consistent design and naming convention, with built-in support for diagnostics, retry policies, authentication, and logging.

Using Azure SDK: Blob Storage Example

.NET (C#)

```
using Azure.Storage.Blobs;

var connectionString = "<your-connection-string>";
var containerName = "my-container";

var blobServiceClient = new BlobServiceClient(connectionString);
```

```
var containerClient =
blobServiceClient.GetBlobContainerClient(containerName);

await containerClient.CreateIfNotExistsAsync();
```

Python
```
from azure.storage.blob import BlobServiceClient

conn_str = "<your-connection-string>"
container_name = "my-container"

blob_service_client =
BlobServiceClient.from_connection_string(conn_str)
container_client =
blob_service_client.get_container_client(container_name)

container_client.create_container()
```

These SDKs allow you to upload, download, list, and manage blobs programmatically with built-in security and error handling.

Azure REST APIs

In addition to SDKs, Azure exposes every service via REST APIs, allowing platform-agnostic interaction over HTTP/HTTPS.

API reference: https://learn.microsoft.com/rest/api/azure/

Structure of Azure REST API
```
https://management.azure.com/subscriptions/{subscriptionId}/resource
Groups/{resourceGroupName}/providers/{resourceProvider}/{resourceTyp
e}/{resourceName}?api-version=2021-04-01
```

You must authenticate using Azure Active Directory (OAuth 2.0) and pass a **Bearer token** in the Authorization header.

Example: Create Resource Group via REST API
```
PUT
https://management.azure.com/subscriptions/{subscriptionId}/resource
groups/myResourceGroup?api-version=2021-04-01
```

```
Authorization: Bearer <access_token>
Content-Type: application/json

{
  "location": "eastus"
}
```

Use tools like **Postman**, **curl**, or programmatic HTTP clients to interact with Azure APIs.

Authentication and Identity

Azure SDKs support multiple authentication mechanisms:

- **Connection strings** (for dev/test)

- **Azure Identity SDK** (recommended for production)

- **Managed Identity** (best for cloud-hosted apps)

- **Service Principals** (for CI/CD automation)

Azure Identity SDK

Install (e.g., .NET):

```
dotnet add package Azure.Identity
```

Then use `DefaultAzureCredential`:

```
using Azure.Identity;
using Azure.Storage.Blobs;

var credential = new DefaultAzureCredential();
var blobClient = new BlobServiceClient(new
Uri("https://<account>.blob.core.windows.net"), credential);
```

`DefaultAzureCredential` checks multiple sources in order:

1. Environment variables

2. Managed Identity

3. Visual Studio / CLI login

Working with Key Vault

Azure Key Vault is a service for storing secrets, certificates, and encryption keys.

JavaScript Example: Retrieving a Secret

```javascript
const { DefaultAzureCredential } = require("@azure/identity");
const { SecretClient } = require("@azure/keyvault-secrets");

const credential = new DefaultAzureCredential();
const url = "https://myvault.vault.azure.net";
const client = new SecretClient(url, credential);

const secret = await client.getSecret("MySecretName");
console.log(secret.value);
```

This approach avoids hardcoding secrets and enables secure, centralized secret management.

Event-Driven Development

SDKs are essential when building apps that respond to Azure events via:

- **Azure Event Grid**

- **Service Bus**

- **Event Hubs**

You can write event handlers that consume messages from queues or topics, process telemetry, or trigger business logic.

Example: Receiving Messages from Azure Service Bus (Python)

```python
from azure.servicebus import ServiceBusClient

conn_str = "<your-connection-string>"
queue_name = "myqueue"
```

```
with ServiceBusClient.from_connection_string(conn_str) as client:
    receiver = client.get_queue_receiver(queue_name)
    with receiver:
        for msg in receiver:
            print("Received:", msg)
            receiver.complete_message(msg)
```

Developer Tools and Extensions

Microsoft provides several tools that enhance the Azure development experience:

- **Visual Studio / VS Code Azure Extensions**

- **Azure CLI** for scripting

- **Azure SDK Trackers** for updates

- **Azure Functions Core Tools**

- **Azure Developer CLI (**azd**)**

These tools help with local development, emulation, deployment, and testing.

SDK Design Principles

The Azure SDK team follows specific guidelines for SDK usability:

- **Idiomatic** for each language

- **Consistent** across services

- **Secure** by default

- **Production-ready** with retries, logging, diagnostics

All new SDKs are released under the Azure.* namespace and versioned semantically (v1, v2, etc.).

Building Cloud-Native Apps

When using SDKs and APIs, follow these design patterns:

1. **Dependency Injection** for client services

2. **Retry Policies** for transient faults

3. **Centralized Configuration** using App Configuration or Key Vault

4. **Monitoring and Telemetry** via Application Insights

5. **Asynchronous Programming** for non-blocking I/O

Example: Retry with Exponential Backoff (Python)

```python
from azure.core.pipeline.policies import RetryPolicy
from azure.storage.blob import BlobServiceClient

retry = RetryPolicy(total_retries=5, backoff_factor=1.5)
client = BlobServiceClient.from_connection_string(conn_str,
retry_policy=retry)
```

Common Scenarios for Developers

- Uploading files to Blob Storage

- Reading and writing secrets to Key Vault

- Querying Cosmos DB with LINQ or SQL

- Pushing telemetry to Application Insights

- Triggering Azure Functions via queues

- Deploying resources via Bicep templates and SDKs

- Building admin panels using Azure APIs

Summary

Azure SDKs and APIs are foundational tools for any developer building on Microsoft Azure. They simplify integration, promote secure practices, and enable automation at every layer of your application.

By using official SDKs, you gain access to powerful abstractions that accelerate development while maintaining control over scalability, security, and performance. Coupled with modern development practices and tools, they allow you to confidently build cloud-native applications ready for production.

Working with Azure Functions and Event Grid

Modern cloud applications often need to respond to events dynamically and scale elastically without the need to provision or manage infrastructure. Azure Functions and Azure Event Grid enable developers to build highly scalable, event-driven, serverless applications that respond to triggers from various sources, such as HTTP requests, queue messages, file uploads, database updates, and more.

Azure Functions provides the compute layer, enabling you to execute code on-demand in response to events, while Azure Event Grid acts as the eventing backbone, allowing different services to communicate through lightweight, scalable event distribution.

In this section, we'll explore how to build, deploy, and integrate Azure Functions and Event Grid into your applications. We'll cover the architecture, use cases, supported triggers and bindings, programming models, monitoring, and best practices.

Azure Functions Overview

Azure Functions is a serverless compute service that lets you run small pieces of code, or "functions", without worrying about infrastructure. Functions can be triggered by events such as HTTP requests, timers, queue messages, database changes, and more.

Key Features:

- Event-driven execution model

- Supports multiple languages (C#, JavaScript, Python, Java, PowerShell)

- Built-in triggers and bindings

- Automatic scaling

- Pay-per-execution pricing

- Local development with CLI tools

Azure Functions Triggers and Bindings

Azure Functions relies on **triggers** to start execution and **bindings** to interact with external systems. A function can have one trigger and multiple input/output bindings.

Common Triggers:

- HTTP Trigger

- Timer Trigger

- Queue Storage Trigger

- Blob Trigger

- Event Hub Trigger

- Event Grid Trigger

- Cosmos DB Trigger

Common Bindings:

- Azure Storage (Blob, Queue, Table)

- Azure Service Bus

- Azure Cosmos DB

- SignalR

- Twilio, SendGrid (via extensions)

Creating an Azure Function

You can create Azure Functions using the Azure Portal, Visual Studio Code, Azure CLI, or ARM/Bicep templates.

Using Azure CLI

```
az functionapp create \
  --resource-group MyResourceGroup \
  --consumption-plan-location westus \
```

```
--runtime node \
--functions-version 4 \
--name myserverlessapp \
--storage-account mystorageaccount
```

This creates a Node.js function app using the Consumption plan.

Sample Function: HTTP Trigger (JavaScript)

```
module.exports = async function (context, req) {
  context.log('HTTP trigger function processed a request.');
  const name = req.query.name || (req.body && req.body.name);
  context.res = {
    body: name ? `Hello, ${name}` : 'Please pass a name on the query
string or in the request body'
  };
};
```

Deploy this using VS Code or the Azure CLI with `az functionapp deployment`.

Azure Event Grid Overview

Azure Event Grid is a fully managed event routing service that allows applications and services to communicate through events. It follows the **publish-subscribe** model and can deliver messages from multiple sources to multiple subscribers.

Event Sources:

- Azure Blob Storage

- Azure Resource Manager

- Azure Media Services

- Azure IoT Hub

- Custom Topics (user-defined apps)

Event Handlers (Destinations):

- Azure Functions

- Azure Logic Apps

- Azure Event Hubs

- Webhooks

- Azure Automation

Event Grid ensures reliable event delivery, low-latency routing, and high throughput.

Event Grid Architecture

1. **Event Source**: Generates an event (e.g., file uploaded to Blob Storage).

2. **Event Grid Topic**: A logical grouping of events.

3. **Event Subscription**: Defines the endpoint to receive the events.

4. **Event Handler**: Azure Function or other service that processes the event.

Connecting Event Grid to Azure Functions

Azure Functions supports native triggers for Event Grid. You can create a function that automatically runs when an event is fired.

Example: Function Triggered by Blob Upload via Event Grid (C#)

```csharp
public static class BlobCreatedFunction
{
    [FunctionName("BlobCreatedFunction")]
    public static void Run([EventGridTrigger] EventGridEvent
eventGridEvent, ILogger log)
    {
        log.LogInformation($"Event received:
{eventGridEvent.Data.ToString()}");
    }
}
```

This function responds to a `Microsoft.Storage.BlobCreated` event.

Creating Event Grid Subscriptions

Using Azure CLI

```
az eventgrid event-subscription create \
  --name BlobUploadSubscription \
  --source-resource-id /subscriptions/{sub-
id}/resourceGroups/{rg}/providers/Microsoft.Storage/storageAccounts/
{account-name} \
  --endpoint-type azurefunction \
  --endpoint /subscriptions/{sub-
id}/resourceGroups/{rg}/providers/Microsoft.Web/sites/{functionapp}/
functions/{function-name}
```

Developing Locally with Azure Functions Core Tools

Install tools:

```
npm install -g azure-functions-core-tools@4 --unsafe-perm true
```

Create a new function:

```
func init my-function-app --javascript
cd my-function-app
func new --template "HTTP trigger"
```

Run locally:

```
func start
```

You can debug and test your function before deploying to the cloud.

Best Practices for Azure Functions

1. **Use Dependency Injection** for better maintainability.

2. **Avoid long-running functions**; use Durable Functions for orchestrations.

3. **Secure HTTP endpoints** using API keys or Azure AD.

4. **Use Application Insights** for logging and monitoring.

5. **Implement retries and error handling** with built-in policies.

6. **Leverage async programming** to improve performance.

7. **Use environment variables and Key Vault** for secrets.

Durable Functions

Durable Functions is an extension of Azure Functions for writing **stateful workflows** in code.

Key patterns:

- **Function chaining**

- **Fan-out/fan-in**

- **Async HTTP APIs**

- **Human interaction workflows**

- **Monitoring workflows**

Example: Orchestrator Function (JavaScript)

```javascript
const df = require("durable-functions");

module.exports = df.orchestrator(function* (context) {
    const output1 = yield context.df.callActivity("Activity1",
"Tokyo");
    const output2 = yield context.df.callActivity("Activity2",
"Seattle");
    const output3 = yield context.df.callActivity("Activity3",
"London");

    return [output1, output2, output3];
});
```

This orchestrator coordinates three activity functions.

Monitoring and Observability

Use **Application Insights** with Azure Functions for:

- Telemetry (requests, dependencies, exceptions)

- Live metrics stream

- Distributed tracing

- Custom events and logging

Enable via Azure Portal or add SDK manually:

```
npm install applicationinsights

const appInsights = require("applicationinsights");
appInsights.setup().start();
```

Pricing Model

Azure Functions offers:

- **Consumption Plan**: Pay-per-execution with auto-scaling

- **Premium Plan**: Enhanced performance, VNET support, no cold starts

- **Dedicated (App Service Plan)**: Fixed resources, for enterprise use

Common Use Cases

- Respond to Blob uploads (e.g., image processing)

- Process messages from Service Bus or Event Hubs

- Execute scheduled tasks (Timer Trigger)

- Build APIs with HTTP triggers

- Real-time file or data ingestion with Event Grid

- Serverless orchestration with Durable Functions

Summary

Azure Functions and Event Grid together offer a powerful, scalable, and flexible platform for event-driven application development. Azure Functions reduces operational overhead by abstracting infrastructure concerns, while Event Grid provides seamless and reliable event routing across Azure services and custom applications.

By mastering these tools, developers can build responsive, resilient systems that scale effortlessly and integrate deeply into the Azure ecosystem. Whether you're handling real-time data streams, reacting to changes in storage, or orchestrating long-running workflows, this serverless approach delivers both agility and cost efficiency.

Serverless Architectures

Serverless computing has transformed the way developers build and deploy applications by abstracting away the complexity of managing servers and infrastructure. In a serverless model, developers write code in small, modular functions that are executed in response to events or HTTP requests, and the cloud provider automatically handles scaling, high availability, and resource provisioning. On Azure, serverless architectures are primarily built using **Azure Functions**, **Azure Logic Apps**, **Azure Event Grid**, and **Azure Durable Functions**, often combined with managed services like **Azure Cosmos DB**, **Azure Blob Storage**, and **Service Bus**.

In this section, we will explore the core components of a serverless architecture on Azure, patterns and practices for building reliable and scalable serverless solutions, integration strategies, monitoring considerations, and cost optimization techniques. Whether you're building a real-time API, an event-driven data pipeline, or a background job processor, serverless computing offers unmatched agility and efficiency.

Core Characteristics of Serverless Architectures

Serverless doesn't mean "no servers"—it means **developers don't manage servers**. The cloud provider handles all infrastructure concerns.

Key Benefits:

- **Event-driven execution**: Code runs in response to triggers like HTTP requests, file uploads, or messages.

- **Automatic scaling**: No need to manually provision instances.

- **Micro-billing**: Pay only for the execution time and resources consumed.

- **Built-in high availability**: Azure provides reliability and redundancy out of the box.

- **Rapid development and deployment**: Focus on business logic, not infrastructure.

Azure Serverless Ecosystem

Azure Functions

- Stateless compute

- Supports many languages

- Triggers include HTTP, Timer, Queue, Blob, Event Grid, etc.

Azure Logic Apps

- No-code/low-code orchestration

- Integrates with 600+ connectors (e.g., Office 365, Salesforce)

- Best suited for workflow automation and enterprise integrations

Azure Event Grid

- Event routing backbone

- Push-based, near real-time event distribution

- Native integration with Azure services and custom event sources

Azure Durable Functions

- State management extension for Azure Functions

- Implements long-running workflows, retries, and parallel tasks

Serverless Architecture Patterns

Azure supports various architectural patterns that are optimized for serverless solutions.

1. Event-Driven Ingestion

- Use Blob Storage + Event Grid + Azure Functions to process files.

- Example: Upload a CSV file → trigger function → parse and store in Cosmos DB.

2. Serverless APIs

- Use HTTP-triggered Azure Functions as endpoints.

- Secure with Azure AD or API Management.

- Add caching or throttling as needed.

3. Scheduled Processing

- Timer-triggered functions run jobs at fixed intervals.

- Ideal for nightly reports, billing runs, or cleanup scripts.

4. Data Transformation Pipelines

- Event Hub → Function → Cosmos DB or Data Lake.

- Real-time or batch data processing with built-in scaling.

5. Orchestrated Workflows

- Use Durable Functions or Logic Apps for business processes.

- Example: Order processing → inventory check → payment → notification.

Example: Serverless Image Processing Pipeline

Use case: Automatically process images uploaded by users.

Architecture:

1. User uploads image to **Blob Storage**

2. **Event Grid** fires a `BlobCreated` event

3. **Azure Function** is triggered

4. Function compresses image and stores it in another blob container

5. Metadata is saved to **Cosmos DB**

6. Notification sent via **SendGrid** or **SignalR**

Sample Function Code (JavaScript)

```javascript
module.exports = async function (context, eventGridEvent) {
    const blobUrl = eventGridEvent.data.url;
    context.log(`Processing blob at ${blobUrl}`);

    // ...Download, compress, upload logic here...

    context.log('Image processing complete.');
};
```

Designing Stateless Functions

To benefit fully from serverless, design functions to be:

- **Idempotent**: Can run multiple times without side effects.

- **Short-lived**: Avoid long blocking operations (>5 minutes).

- **Stateless**: Use external storage (Blob, Cosmos DB, Redis) for state persistence.

Avoid assumptions about:

- Instance affinity

- Local file system persistence

- Memory persistence between executions

Serverless Authentication and Security

Security is critical, even in a serverless world.

Azure Functions Security:

- **API keys** for trigger-level protection

- **Function-level authorization** (`Anonymous`, `Function`, `Admin`)

- **App Service Authentication** with Azure AD, Google, Facebook, etc.

- **CORS** for cross-origin API calls

Logic Apps Security:

- OAuth 2.0, Azure AD for connector authentication

- Access Control via Resource Manager roles

- IP restrictions and managed identities

Use **Managed Identity** to securely access Azure resources without secrets.

Observability and Monitoring

Use **Application Insights** and **Azure Monitor** to track:

- Execution duration

- Success/failure rate

- Cold starts

- Dependency performance

- Custom events and metrics

Enable Application Insights (JavaScript Example)

```
const appInsights = require('applicationinsights');
appInsights.setup().start();
```

This provides end-to-end tracing, making it easy to identify bottlenecks and failures.

Scaling and Performance Considerations

Azure automatically scales functions based on the incoming load. However, understanding scaling behavior helps optimize performance.

Key Factors:

- **Cold Start**: Initial delay for function startup (minimized in Premium Plan)

- **Concurrency Limits**: Adjust as needed for CPU/memory-intensive workloads

- **Connection Limits**: Watch for socket exhaustion with high outbound traffic

- **Throughput Bottlenecks**: Tune storage or database backends

Use **Azure Premium Functions** for:

- No cold starts

- VNET integration

- Longer execution times

- Increased CPU/memory

Cost Optimization in Serverless

Serverless can be very cost-efficient when architected properly.

Strategies:

- **Use Consumption Plan** for sporadic workloads

- **Use Durable Functions** for long-running operations to avoid polling

- **Set maximum instance count** to avoid runaway scaling

- **Batch work** where possible to reduce executions

- **Monitor usage** in Cost Management

Azure Functions pricing:

- 1 million executions/month free

- After that, priced per execution + resource consumption

Logic Apps pricing:

- Based on number of action executions and connector type (standard or enterprise)

DevOps and Deployment

Serverless apps support full CI/CD workflows.

Deployment Options:

- **Azure CLI** and `az functionapp deployment`

- **Visual Studio Code Azure Tools**

- **GitHub Actions**

- **Azure DevOps Pipelines**

- **Bicep/ARM templates**

Sample GitHub Actions Workflow

```
name: Deploy Azure Function

on:
  push:
    branches:
      - main

jobs:
  deploy:
    runs-on: ubuntu-latest
    steps:
      - uses: actions/checkout@v3
      - uses: Azure/functions-action@v1
        with:
          app-name: 'my-function-app'
          package: '.'
```

```
publish-profile: ${{ secrets.AZURE_PUBLISH_PROFILE }}
```

This automates build and deployment on each push to `main`.

Real-World Scenarios

1. **Real-Time Analytics**
   IoT sensor data processed in real-time with Event Hub + Function + Cosmos DB.

2. **Webhook Listener**
   HTTP-triggered Function processes Stripe or GitHub events.

3. **Daily Data Sync**
   Timer-triggered Function synchronizes SaaS data into internal systems.

4. **Form Submissions**
   Form data sent to Logic App → Approval Workflow → Email notification.

5. **Order Fulfillment**
   Durable Functions orchestrate multi-step order processing pipeline.

Summary

Serverless architectures in Azure empower developers to focus on delivering value rather than managing infrastructure. By leveraging Azure Functions, Event Grid, Logic Apps, and related services, you can build scalable, resilient, and cost-effective applications that respond in real-time to a wide range of events and data changes.

Designing serverless applications requires a mindset shift toward statelessness, event-driven flows, and modular logic. When done right, serverless unlocks unparalleled developer productivity, operational agility, and scalability—making it an essential part of the modern cloud-native development toolkit.

Debugging and Troubleshooting in the Cloud

Building applications in the cloud comes with many advantages—scalability, resilience, and speed of deployment—but it also introduces complexity, especially when diagnosing issues across distributed services. Debugging and troubleshooting in Azure requires a shift from traditional on-premises approaches to one that embraces observability, proactive diagnostics, and integration with cloud-native tools.

This section covers the end-to-end lifecycle of identifying, diagnosing, and resolving issues in cloud-native applications hosted on Azure. We will explore best practices for logging, distributed tracing, real-time monitoring, capturing telemetry, handling failures, integrating Application Insights and Azure Monitor, and leveraging tools such as Azure Diagnostics, Kusto Query Language (KQL), and live debugging in production-like environments.

Observability in Azure Applications

Modern applications require **observability**—the ability to understand the internal state of a system based on external outputs. This includes:

- **Logging**: Capturing events and diagnostics from application code.

- **Metrics**: Numeric indicators like CPU usage, response time, or request counts.

- **Tracing**: Following a request through its lifecycle across services and components.

- **Alerts**: Detecting anomalies and triggering notifications.

Azure provides robust built-in tools for collecting and analyzing these signals.

Application Insights: Core Tool for Debugging

Application Insights is an extensible Application Performance Management (APM) service for developers and DevOps professionals. It monitors applications live, detects anomalies, and provides powerful analytics tools.

Key Features:

- Request and dependency tracking

- Exception logging

- Performance metrics (response times, failures, etc.)

- Live metrics stream

- Custom events and metrics

- Distributed tracing (with correlation IDs)

Setting Up Application Insights

.NET Core Example

```
public void ConfigureServices(IServiceCollection services)
{

services.AddApplicationInsightsTelemetry(Configuration["APPINSIGHTS_
INSTRUMENTATIONKEY"]);
}
```

JavaScript/Node.js Example

```
const appInsights = require("applicationinsights");
appInsights.setup("<instrumentation-key>").start();
```

Once configured, telemetry data will start flowing to your Application Insights instance.

Common Telemetry You Should Track

- **Requests**: Track the number of HTTP requests, response time, and success rates.

- **Dependencies**: Log outgoing calls to databases, storage, and external services.

- **Exceptions**: Capture handled and unhandled exceptions with stack traces.

- **Availability Tests**: Monitor uptime with synthetic ping tests.

- **Custom Events and Metrics**: Add domain-specific signals (e.g., user registration count, queue length).

Custom Event Example (C#)

```
TelemetryClient telemetry = new TelemetryClient();
telemetry.TrackEvent("UserRegistered", new Dictionary<string,
string> { { "UserId", "123" } });
```

Debugging HTTP and Dependency Failures

Use Application Insights' **Failures** blade to:

- Identify endpoints returning high failure rates

- View exception types and messages

- Drill into specific operation IDs

- Filter by client IP, user agent, or custom dimensions

Example Filters

- `operation_Name == "GET /api/products"`

- `response_Code == "500"`

- `cloud_RoleName == "ProductService"`

Use this data to detect broken endpoints, unresponsive services, or unhandled errors.

Diagnosing Performance Bottlenecks

Azure helps you identify what's slowing down your application:

- Use **Performance** view to analyze average and percentile response times

- Break down slow operations by:

    - Web requests

    - Dependencies

    - Database calls

    - External APIs

Example: View slow SQL queries
```
dependencies
| where target contains "sql"
| sort by duration desc
```

Distributed Tracing with Correlation

When you have a microservices architecture or distributed systems, tracking a request end-to-end is essential.

- Use **Operation Id** and **Parent Id** to correlate requests

- Enable distributed tracing headers (e.g., `Request-Id`, `traceparent`)

- Supported in ASP.NET Core, Node.js, Java, Python with minimal setup

Correlation Flow Example:

1. Frontend sends request to `api-gateway`

2. API gateway calls `orders-service`

3. Orders service queries `inventory-service`

Each step shares the same correlation ID, enabling a complete trace of the request's path.

Live Metrics Stream

Live Metrics allows real-time visibility into your application's behavior:

- Requests/sec

- Failures/sec

- CPU and memory usage

- Dependency call rate

- Live trace samples

Ideal for:

- Watching deployments

- Investigating active incidents

- Monitoring sudden traffic spikes

Enable Live Metrics in the Application Insights blade and start observing metrics as they come in.

Kusto Query Language (KQL) for Deep Analysis

KQL powers the Azure Monitor Logs query engine. It allows you to slice and dice telemetry data interactively.

Common Queries

```
requests
| where resultCode == "500"
| summarize count() by operation_Name

exceptions
| summarize count() by type, outerMessage
```

These queries help diagnose which endpoints are failing and what exceptions are being thrown.

Azure Monitor for Infrastructure Troubleshooting

While Application Insights focuses on application-level monitoring, **Azure Monitor** provides resource-level insights.

Use it to:

- Analyze VM CPU/memory/disk usage

- Track App Service plan utilization

- Investigate slow query logs from Azure SQL

- Correlate platform metrics with application performance

Enable diagnostic settings to route logs to Log Analytics.

Diagnostic Logs and Crash Dumps

For deeper debugging:

- Enable **detailed error messages** and **failed request tracing** in App Service.

- Download **crash dumps** and **memory dumps** for advanced debugging.

- Use **Kudu Console** (App Service SCM) for file system access and process inspection.

Enable Diagnostic Logs in Azure Portal

1. Go to App Service > Monitoring > Diagnostics settings

2. Enable:

   - Application Logging

   - Web Server Logging

   - Detailed Error Messages

   - Failed Request Tracing

Handling Transient Faults and Retrying

In the cloud, transient faults are expected. Use retry policies for:

- HTTP calls

- SQL queries

- Queue operations

- Storage access

Example: Polly Retry Policy (C#)

```
Policy
  .Handle<HttpRequestException>()
  .WaitAndRetry(3, retryAttempt => TimeSpan.FromSeconds(Math.Pow(2,
retryAttempt)));
```

Avoid retry storms by implementing **circuit breakers**, **timeouts**, and **fallback strategies**.

Debugging Locally vs. Cloud

Use **Azure Functions Core Tools**, **Storage Emulator**, or **Azurite** to simulate cloud environments locally.

Benefits:

- Faster iteration cycle

- No cost for test executions

- Offline testing of logic and integration

Use **Azure Developer CLI (azd)** for full-stack cloud-native development lifecycle, including provisioning, deployment, and debugging.

Post-Mortem Analysis

After an incident or outage, conduct a blameless post-mortem using:

- Azure Activity Log: Changes and deployments

- Application Insights Analytics: Timeline of requests and failures

- Alerts and Dashboards: When and how issues were detected

- Root cause: Code issues, service outages, network failures

Document lessons learned and mitigation plans.

Alerting and Notifications

Set up alerts to proactively catch issues before users report them:

- CPU > 80% for 5 mins

- 5xx response rate > 5%

- Dependency failure rate > 10%

- Application Insights anomalies

Configure alerts to send:

- Emails

- SMS

- Webhooks

- Teams/Slack messages

- Logic Apps or Azure Functions

Summary

Debugging and troubleshooting in Azure is a multifaceted process that requires a combination of logging, metrics, tracing, real-time monitoring, and post-incident analysis. With powerful tools like Application Insights, Azure Monitor, and KQL, developers and operations teams can gain deep visibility into their applications and quickly resolve issues.

By adopting best practices in observability, leveraging built-in diagnostics, and implementing robust retry and error-handling logic, teams can dramatically reduce downtime, improve reliability, and maintain confidence in their cloud-native applications—no matter how complex or distributed.

Chapter 9: Real-World Scenarios and Use Cases

Migrating On-Premise to Azure

Migrating on-premise infrastructure and applications to Microsoft Azure is a strategic move that organizations around the world are making to achieve better scalability, cost-efficiency, and modernization. In this section, we will delve deep into the processes, tools, strategies, and considerations involved in transitioning from traditional on-premise data centers to the Azure cloud environment.

Understanding the Need for Migration

Organizations choose to migrate to Azure for a variety of reasons:

- **Scalability**: On-prem systems often struggle with handling spikes in demand. Azure's scalable architecture enables businesses to scale resources up or down on demand.

- **Cost Optimization**: Azure allows for an OpEx (Operational Expense) model compared to the CapEx (Capital Expense) of maintaining physical infrastructure.

- **Disaster Recovery and Business Continuity**: Azure provides built-in solutions for high availability and backup, reducing the need for complex on-premise disaster recovery systems.

- **Security and Compliance**: With a wide array of compliance certifications and advanced security capabilities, Azure offers a robust environment for sensitive data.

- **Innovation Enablement**: Access to modern tools such as AI, ML, big data, and IoT services fosters innovation and agility.

Migration Strategies

Microsoft outlines several high-level migration strategies, often referred to as the "Five Rs":

1. **Rehost (Lift-and-Shift)**
   Moving applications without redesigning them. Fastest migration method, often done using tools like Azure Migrate.
   Example: Moving a virtual machine from VMware to Azure Virtual Machine.

2. **Refactor**
   Modifying the application slightly to leverage cloud capabilities like containers or

managed services (e.g., replacing a local database with Azure SQL Database).

3. **Rearchitect**
   Redesigning the application to be cloud-native, often to take advantage of microservices or serverless architectures.

4. **Rebuild**
   Rewriting the application from scratch using Azure PaaS services such as Azure App Services or Azure Functions.

5. **Replace**
   Replacing legacy applications with SaaS solutions like Microsoft Dynamics 365 or Microsoft 365.

Discovery and Assessment Phase

The first step in a successful migration is understanding the current environment.

- **Inventory of Assets**: Document all hardware, software, services, and dependencies.

- **Performance Profiling**: Use tools such as Azure Migrate to gather utilization metrics.

- **Compliance Requirements**: Identify legal or industry requirements that may influence data location, encryption, or backup policies.

Using Azure Migrate

Azure Migrate provides a central hub for tools to start, execute, and track your migration journey.

Steps:

1. **Create a project** in Azure Migrate from the Azure Portal.

2. **Download the Azure Migrate appliance** and install it on a VMware/Hyper-V host or physical server.

3. **Start discovery** to gather performance data over time.

4. **Run assessments** to evaluate readiness and estimate cost.

```
# Sample PowerShell script to register Azure Migrate project
Install-Module -Name Az -AllowClobber -Scope CurrentUser
Connect-AzAccount
```

```
New-AzMigrateProject -ResourceGroupName "Migration-RG" -ProjectName
"CorpMigrate" -Location "East US"
```

Planning Phase

Once assessment data is available, use it to plan:

- **Sizing**: Use performance data to recommend VM sizes in Azure.

- **Cost Estimation**: Use the Azure Pricing Calculator and TCO calculator.

- **Downtime Windows**: Determine acceptable downtime for services.

- **Dependencies**: Map and plan for interdependent services to migrate together.

Azure provides **Azure Advisor** and **Azure Cost Management** to help make these decisions effectively.

Execution Phase

Rehosting Example with Azure Migrate and Azure Site Recovery

You can use Azure Site Recovery (ASR) for lift-and-shift migrations.

Process:

1. **Replicate your VMs** using ASR.

2. **Perform test failovers** to ensure the application functions as expected.

3. **Schedule the final cutover** and switch production over to Azure.

```
# Azure CLI snippet to enable replication
az backup protection enable-for-vm \
  --resource-group MyResourceGroup \
  --vault-name MyRecoveryServicesVault \
  --vm MyVM \
  --policy-name DefaultPolicy
```

Refactoring Example

Imagine moving an on-premise application that uses SQL Server and IIS.

- Migrate SQL Server to **Azure SQL Database** or **SQL Managed Instance**.

- Deploy the application on **App Service** using containers or code deployment.

- Replace SMTP services with **SendGrid on Azure Marketplace**.

This approach improves scalability and reduces administrative overhead.

Rearchitecting and Rebuilding

Some legacy applications may not function well in the cloud or are nearing end-of-life. These are ideal candidates for rebuilding:

- Rebuild into **microservices** using **Azure Kubernetes Service (AKS)**.

- Use **Azure API Management** to expose services securely.

- Integrate **Azure DevOps** for CI/CD pipelines.

```
# Azure DevOps YAML pipeline for a .NET Core app
trigger:
- main

pool:
  vmImage: 'ubuntu-latest'

steps:
- task: UseDotNet@2
  inputs:
    packageType: 'sdk'
    version: '6.0.x'

- script: dotnet build
  displayName: 'Build project'

- script: dotnet publish -c Release -o publish
  displayName: 'Publish app'
```

Post-Migration Optimization

After a successful migration, organizations must focus on:

- **Monitoring and Alerting**: Configure Azure Monitor, Application Insights, and Log Analytics.

- **Backup and DR**: Set up Azure Backup and geo-redundant storage.

- **Security**: Audit permissions using Azure Active Directory, set up Just-In-Time (JIT) access, and configure Azure Defender.

- **Scaling**: Use auto-scaling for compute and databases based on load.

- **Cost Optimization**: Analyze with Cost Management + Billing. Consider Reserved Instances (RIs) or Spot VMs for predictable workloads.

Common Challenges and Solutions

Challenge	Solution
Application downtime	Use phased migrations and test failovers
Data loss risk	Enable backup and verify replication before cutover
Compliance gaps	Use Compliance Manager and choose appropriate Azure regions
Performance issues	Use Performance Recommendations from Azure Advisor

Conclusion

Migrating from on-premise to Azure is not a one-size-fits-all approach. It requires careful assessment, planning, and execution. Whether using a simple lift-and-shift or rearchitecting your applications for maximum agility, Azure offers the tools and services necessary for a successful transition. By adopting a structured approach and leveraging native Azure tools like Azure Migrate, Azure Site Recovery, and Azure DevOps, organizations can modernize their IT infrastructure while minimizing risk and maximizing return on investment.

Designing for High Availability and Resilience

Designing systems for high availability and resilience in Microsoft Azure is a crucial part of modern cloud architecture. It ensures that applications remain accessible and recoverable even during failures, maintenance, or peak traffic conditions. In this section, we will explore best practices, design patterns, Azure-native services, and example configurations to help architects and developers build systems that withstand failures and deliver seamless user experiences.

Key Concepts

Before diving into implementation, it's important to define some foundational terms:

- **High Availability (HA)**: The ability of a system to remain operational and accessible for the maximum possible time. This typically involves redundancy and failover mechanisms.

- **Resilience**: The ability of a system to recover from failures and continue operating with minimal disruption.

- **Fault Tolerance**: A system's capability to operate properly even when one or more of its components fail.

- **Disaster Recovery (DR)**: Strategies and services used to recover data and restore applications after a catastrophic failure.

These goals are achieved using architectural strategies and Azure services that support distributed and fault-tolerant designs.

Architectural Principles

Designing for high availability and resilience requires adherence to several architectural principles:

- **Redundancy**: Duplicate critical components across availability zones or regions.

- **Load Balancing**: Distribute incoming traffic to ensure no single component is overwhelmed.

- **Auto-Scaling**: Automatically increase or decrease resources based on demand.

- **Failover Mechanisms**: Automatically redirect traffic to healthy resources in case of failure.

- **Monitoring and Alerting**: Detect issues before they become critical using tools like Azure Monitor and Application Insights.

- **Loose Coupling**: Decouple components to prevent cascading failures.

Azure Services for High Availability

Availability Sets

An Availability Set is a logical grouping of VMs that allows Azure to understand how your application is built to provide redundancy and availability.

- **Fault Domains (FDs)**: Represent the physical separation of hardware.

- **Update Domains (UDs)**: Represent groups of VMs that can be updated at the same time.

```
New-AzAvailabilitySet `
  -Location "East US" `
  -Name "AppAvailabilitySet" `
  -ResourceGroupName "MyResourceGroup" `
  -Sku aligned `
  -PlatformFaultDomainCount 2 `
  -PlatformUpdateDomainCount 5
```

Availability Zones

Availability Zones are unique physical locations within an Azure region. They offer higher availability than Availability Sets by ensuring physical and logical separation of services.

Use them with:

- Virtual Machines

- Managed Disks

- Load Balancers

- Azure Kubernetes Service (AKS)

Azure Load Balancer

Used to distribute network traffic across multiple VMs. Supports both internal and external load balancing.

Azure Traffic Manager

A DNS-based traffic load balancer that enables you to distribute traffic optimally to services across global Azure regions.

- **Priority Routing** for failover scenarios

- **Weighted Routing** for load testing

- **Geographic Routing** for location-specific traffic

```json
{
  "type": "Microsoft.Network/trafficManagerProfiles",
  "name": "myTrafficManager",
  "properties": {
    "trafficRoutingMethod": "Priority",
    "dnsConfig": {
      "relativeName": "myapp",
      "ttl": 30
    },
    "monitorConfig": {
      "protocol": "HTTPS",
      "port": 443,
      "path": "/health"
    }
  }
}
```

Designing a Multi-Region Architecture

Active-Active vs. Active-Passive

- **Active-Active**: Multiple regions serve traffic concurrently. Requires data replication and synchronization.

- **Active-Passive**: One region handles traffic while the other is on standby.

Example Scenario

An e-commerce application using:

- Azure App Service in two regions

- Azure SQL with geo-replication

- Traffic Manager with Priority routing

Traffic is routed to Region A by default. In case of failure, Traffic Manager detects health probe failure and routes traffic to Region B.

Azure Front Door

Offers global HTTP/HTTPS load balancing with instant failover.

Features:

- SSL Offloading

- Application acceleration

- URL-based routing

- Web Application Firewall (WAF)

Data Resilience and Replication

Storage Accounts

Azure Storage provides several replication options:

- **LRS (Locally Redundant Storage)**: 3 copies within a single data center.

- **ZRS (Zone-Redundant Storage)**: 3 copies across availability zones.

- **GRS (Geo-Redundant Storage)**: Copies in a secondary region.

- **RA-GRS (Read-Access GRS)**: Read access to secondary copies.

Azure SQL Database

Use **Active Geo-Replication** to create readable secondary replicas in different regions.

```
-- Enable Geo-Replication
ALTER DATABASE MyDatabase
ADD SECONDARY ON SERVER SecondaryServerName;
```

Cosmos DB

Cosmos DB provides multi-region writes, automatic failover, and five consistency models for globally distributed applications.

Monitoring and Self-Healing

Azure Monitor

Tracks metrics, logs, and telemetry. Can integrate with Action Groups for alert-based remediation.

Application Insights

Offers deep diagnostics for application-level issues.

Azure Automation

Combine with runbooks for automated responses.

```
# Runbook example to restart a VM on alert
Start-AzVM -Name "AppVM01" -ResourceGroupName "MyResourceGroup"
```

Auto-Scaling

Enable Auto-Scaling on:

- App Services

- Virtual Machine Scale Sets

- AKS Node Pools

Scale conditions can be based on CPU, memory, queue length, or custom metrics.

```
{
  "rules": [
    {
      "metricTrigger": {
        "metricName": "CpuPercentage",
        "operator": "GreaterThan",
        "threshold": 70
      },
      "scaleAction": {
        "direction": "Increase",
        "type": "ChangeCount",
        "value": "1",
        "cooldown": "PT5M"
      }
    }
  ]
}
```

Testing for Availability and Resilience

It is critical to test systems for failure scenarios before they occur in production.

Chaos Engineering

- Inject faults intentionally

- Validate recovery and observability

- Tools: Azure Chaos Studio

Load Testing

Use Azure Load Testing service to simulate peak usage.

- Simulate hundreds to thousands of users

- Measure latency, throughput, failure rates

Disaster Recovery Drills

Simulate a failover event and validate recovery time (RTO) and data loss (RPO) against SLAs.

Real-World Patterns

Pattern: Queue-Based Load Leveling

Use **Azure Storage Queues** or **Service Bus** to decouple load-generating front ends from back-end processing components.

Pattern: Circuit Breaker

Wrap critical services with logic to short-circuit calls during outages to prevent cascading failures.

Pattern: Retry with Exponential Backoff

For transient errors, implement retry logic with increasing delays.

```
async function retryOperation(operation, retries = 5) {
  for (let i = 0; i < retries; i++) {
    try {
      return await operation();
    } catch (err) {
      await new Promise(res => setTimeout(res, Math.pow(2, i) *
100));
    }
  }
  throw new Error("Operation failed after retries");
}
```

Cost Considerations

High availability comes with trade-offs:

- More regions and redundancy increase cost

- Evaluate the business impact of downtime

- Use Azure Pricing Calculator to estimate

Balance the architecture between cost, complexity, and SLA requirements.

Conclusion

Designing for high availability and resilience is essential for ensuring that applications meet modern expectations for uptime, performance, and reliability. Azure offers a broad ecosystem of services to support highly available architectures—from availability sets and zones to global load balancing and multi-region data replication. Successful designs take a proactive, layered approach: introducing redundancy, automating recovery, decoupling components, and continuously monitoring for anomalies.

By understanding and applying these principles using Azure-native tools, organizations can confidently build cloud solutions that not only recover gracefully from disruptions but also scale reliably in response to user demand.

Building Multi-Tier Applications

A multi-tier application, also known as a n-tier application, separates various aspects of an application into logical and physical layers to enhance scalability, maintainability, and flexibility. In Azure, this architectural approach can be implemented using a wide variety of services and strategies that align with best practices in cloud computing.

This section explores how to design, build, and manage multi-tier applications on Microsoft Azure. We'll break down the different tiers, examine how services map to each, and provide examples and configurations to help you implement this architecture efficiently.

Overview of Multi-Tier Architecture

A typical multi-tier application is divided into three main layers:

- **Presentation Tier**: The user interface, typically a web or mobile frontend.

- **Application Tier**: The business logic layer, handling the core processing.

- **Data Tier**: The storage layer, responsible for database interactions.

Each tier is independently scalable and can be hosted on separate services or resources.

Benefits of Multi-Tier Design

- **Separation of Concerns**: Isolates business logic from UI and data.

- **Independent Scaling**: Scale each tier based on its workload.

- **Improved Security**: Restrict access between tiers with NSGs, subnets, and identity roles.

- **Reusability**: Components in the application tier can be reused across multiple frontends.

Designing the Presentation Tier

The presentation layer is responsible for rendering the user interface and interacting with backend APIs. Azure provides several options:

- **Azure App Service**: Host web applications using frameworks like .NET, Node.js, or Python.

- **Static Web Apps**: Serve static content (HTML, CSS, JS) with integrated API support.

- **Azure Front Door or Azure CDN**: Improve performance and availability by caching and routing content globally.

Example: Hosting a React Frontend on Azure Static Web Apps

1. Push your code to GitHub.

2. Link repository in the Azure Static Web Apps creation wizard.

3. Azure automatically builds and deploys the app on push.

```
# staticwebapp.config.json
{
  "routes": [
    {
      "route": "/*",
      "serve": "/index.html"
```

```
      }
    ]
}
```

Add authentication using built-in identity providers like Azure AD B2C.

Designing the Application Tier

This tier hosts the core business logic and APIs. Azure provides several powerful options:

- **App Service (Web Apps)**: Great for monolithic or microservice APIs.

- **Azure Functions**: Event-driven, serverless compute ideal for light logic or glue code.

- **Azure Kubernetes Service (AKS)**: Best for containerized workloads or microservices at scale.

- **Container Apps**: Lightweight Kubernetes alternative with scaling and event integration.

Example: ASP.NET Core Web API on App Service

Deploy your API as a .NET Core application, connect it to Azure SQL Database, and secure it with Azure AD.

```
[Authorize]
[ApiController]
[Route("[controller]")]
public class ProductsController : ControllerBase
{
    private readonly AppDbContext _context;

    public ProductsController(AppDbContext context)
    {
        _context = context;
    }

    [HttpGet]
    public async Task<IActionResult> Get() =>
        Ok(await _context.Products.ToListAsync());
}
```

Add middleware to enforce authentication using
`Microsoft.AspNetCore.Authentication.AzureAD.UI`.

Designing the Data Tier

The data layer stores and retrieves application data. Azure offers multiple managed options:

- **Azure SQL Database**: Fully managed relational database.

- **Azure Cosmos DB**: Globally distributed NoSQL database.

- **Azure Table Storage**: Simple key-value storage for structured data.

- **Azure Blob Storage**: For unstructured data like files, images, or videos.

Example: Connecting Web API to Azure SQL Database

Connection string from Azure Portal:

```
Server=tcp:myserver.database.windows.net,1433;Initial
Catalog=mydb;Persist Security Info=False;User
ID=admin;Password=myPassword;MultipleActiveResultSets=False;Encrypt=
True;TrustServerCertificate=False;Connection Timeout=30;
```

Entity Framework Core is used for ORM:

```
dotnet ef dbcontext scaffold "<connection_string>"
Microsoft.EntityFrameworkCore.SqlServer -o Models
```

Integrating the Tiers

Use secure, scalable communication methods between tiers:

- **HTTPS and Authentication**: Secure API endpoints using OAuth2 with Azure AD.

- **API Management**: Publish, secure, and monitor APIs.

- **Service Bus**: Decouple tiers via message queues and topics.

- **Private Endpoints**: Use VNet integration for internal communication.

Example: Azure API Management Setup

1. Create an API Management instance.

2. Import API from App Service.

3. Apply policies such as rate limiting, authentication, and logging.

```
<inbound>
    <base />
    <rate-limit calls="100" renewal-period="60" />
    <set-header name="X-Secure" exists-action="override">
        <value>true</value>
    </set-header>
</inbound>
```

Securing Each Tier

Security is vital in a multi-tier architecture:

- **Network Security Groups (NSGs)**: Control traffic between subnets.

- **Azure Application Gateway with WAF**: Protect web apps from common attacks.

- **Azure Key Vault**: Store secrets, connection strings, and certificates securely.

- **Managed Identities**: Allow Azure services to authenticate without hardcoded credentials.

Example: Restrict Backend API Access

Only allow frontend App Service to call backend API using VNet Integration and IP restrictions.

```
{
  "ipSecurityRestrictions": [
    {
      "ipAddress": "52.164.10.10",
      "action": "Allow",
      "priority": 100,
      "name": "FrontendApp"
    }
  ]
}
```

CI/CD for Multi-Tier Applications

Automate deployment using Azure DevOps or GitHub Actions:

- Build and test each tier independently.

- Deploy using Infrastructure as Code (Bicep, ARM, Terraform).

- Ensure rollout is consistent and versioned.

GitHub Actions Workflow

```
name: Deploy Web API

on:
  push:
    branches: [ main ]

jobs:
  build-and-deploy:
    runs-on: ubuntu-latest
    steps:
    - uses: actions/checkout@v2
    - name: Setup .NET
      uses: actions/setup-dotnet@v1
      with:
        dotnet-version: '6.0.x'
    - run: dotnet publish -c Release -o output
    - uses: azure/webapps-deploy@v2
      with:
        app-name: 'my-api-app'
        publish-profile: ${{ secrets.AZURE_WEBAPP_PUBLISH_PROFILE }}
        package: './output'
```

Monitoring and Logging

Use the following tools to monitor health and performance:

- **Azure Monitor**: Aggregates metrics across tiers.

- **Application Insights**: Tracks requests, dependencies, and exceptions.

- **Log Analytics**: Centralized querying and visualization.

- **Azure Dashboards**: Custom monitoring boards for quick insights.

Set up alerts for failures, latency issues, or usage spikes across all tiers.

Scaling the Application

Each tier can scale independently:

- **Frontend**: Scale App Service Plans or Static Web Apps with CDN.

- **Backend**: Use autoscaling rules for App Service, AKS, or Functions.

- **Data Layer**: Use elastic pools for Azure SQL, autoscale for Cosmos DB.

Set autoscale based on:

- CPU/memory usage

- Request count

- Custom metrics (queue length, latency)

Real-World Example: E-Commerce Application

- **Presentation Tier**: Static Web App (React), served via Azure CDN.

- **Application Tier**: .NET Core API in App Service, Azure Functions for scheduled tasks.

- **Data Tier**: Azure SQL for product data, Cosmos DB for user sessions, Blob Storage for media.

- **Integration**: Azure API Management and Azure Service Bus.

- **Security**: Azure AD B2C for identity, Application Gateway WAF for protection.

Benefits achieved:

- Seamless scaling during holiday sales

- Near-zero downtime with regional failover

- Independent development and deployment of tiers

Conclusion

Building multi-tier applications on Azure provides a robust, scalable, and secure approach to cloud development. By decoupling layers and leveraging specialized Azure services, teams can improve reliability, enforce best practices, and streamline maintenance. Each tier can evolve independently, enabling agile feature delivery and efficient resource utilization.

With clear architectural boundaries and automation in place, organizations can focus on delivering value rather than managing infrastructure. From startups to enterprises, multi-tier designs on Azure offer the flexibility and resilience needed to support mission-critical applications in the cloud.

Case Studies from Industry

Exploring real-world case studies provides valuable insights into how enterprises leverage Microsoft Azure to transform their businesses. This section dives into diverse scenarios across different industries to highlight the practical application of Azure services in delivering innovation, cost savings, high availability, and operational efficiency. From retail to healthcare and finance to manufacturing, each example offers architectural blueprints, challenges faced, implementation strategies, and the outcomes achieved.

Case Study 1: Retail Giant Scales Globally with Azure

Company Overview

A multinational retail chain with operations in over 40 countries faced challenges with scaling its e-commerce infrastructure during seasonal sales. Their legacy systems couldn't handle traffic spikes, and downtime was causing significant revenue losses.

Challenges

- Frequent outages during high-traffic events like Black Friday.

- Delayed updates and deployments due to monolithic architecture.

- Limited insight into user behavior and application performance.

Azure Implementation

Architecture Highlights:

- **Frontend**: Hosted on Azure Static Web Apps for global distribution.

- **Backend APIs**: Rewritten into microservices using Azure Kubernetes Service (AKS).

- **Data Layer**: Azure SQL Database for transactions, Cosmos DB for session state.

- **Cache**: Azure Redis Cache for product and cart data.

- **CDN**: Azure Front Door and Azure CDN for edge caching.

CI/CD Pipelines:

- Azure DevOps pipelines deployed microservices independently.

- Canary releases implemented via Azure Traffic Manager and Kubernetes Ingress.

```
# Azure DevOps release pipeline for AKS
trigger:
  branches:
    include:
      - main

stages:
  - stage: Deploy
    jobs:
      - job: DeployAKS
        pool:
          vmImage: 'ubuntu-latest'
        steps:
          - task: KubectlInstaller@0
            inputs:
              kubectlVersion: 'latest'
          - script: |
              kubectl apply -f k8s/deployment.yaml
```

Monitoring and Insights:

- Azure Monitor and Application Insights were integrated for real-time performance tracking.

- Azure Log Analytics dashboards used for central logging and troubleshooting.

Outcomes

- 99.99% uptime during peak seasons.

- 5x faster deployment velocity.

- 30% increase in sales due to improved performance and reduced cart abandonment.

Case Study 2: Healthcare Provider Modernizes Data Infrastructure

Organization Background

A national healthcare provider needed to modernize its legacy data warehouse to support research, patient care, and compliance reporting.

Challenges

- On-premise SQL Server databases were expensive and nearing capacity.

- Data silos made real-time analytics nearly impossible.

- Stringent compliance requirements (HIPAA, GDPR).

Azure Implementation

Data Platform Modernization:

- Data migrated to **Azure Synapse Analytics** for large-scale analytics.

- **Azure Data Factory** used to orchestrate data movement from over 50 data sources.

- **Azure Data Lake Storage Gen2** for unstructured data.

- **Power BI Embedded** for visualization and dashboards.

Security and Compliance:

- All data encrypted at rest and in transit.

- Azure Policy and Azure Blueprints enforced HIPAA compliance.

- Azure Purview introduced for data governance and lineage.

```
// Example Azure Policy definition snippet
{
  "if": {
    "field": "location",
    "notIn": ["East US", "West US"]
  },
```

```
  "then": {
    "effect": "deny"
  }
}
```

Machine Learning:

- Azure Machine Learning services used to build models predicting patient readmissions and optimizing care pathways.

Outcomes

- Reduced data query times from hours to seconds.

- 20% reduction in patient readmission rates.

- Achieved full HIPAA compliance through automated policy enforcement.

Case Study 3: Financial Institution Embraces DevSecOps

Company Overview

A mid-sized investment firm needed to move away from waterfall development and adopt a DevSecOps culture while migrating to the cloud.

Challenges

- Long release cycles (months).

- Manual testing and security reviews led to delays.

- Need for regulatory compliance with SOX and PCI DSS.

Azure Implementation

DevSecOps Transformation:

- Adopted **Azure DevOps** for build and release pipelines.

- Integrated **GitHub Advanced Security** and **Microsoft Defender for DevOps**.

- Shift-left approach with embedded security scanning in every pull request.

Infrastructure Automation:

- Entire infrastructure defined using **Terraform** and stored in GitHub repos.

- Deployed to **Azure Resource Manager (ARM)** using GitHub Actions.

```
# Terraform for Azure Key Vault
resource "azurerm_key_vault" "example" {
  name                    = "kv-example"
  location                = "East US"
  resource_group_name     = azurerm_resource_group.example.name
  tenant_id               =
data.azurerm_client_config.current.tenant_id
  sku_name                = "standard"
}
```

Microsegmentation and RBAC:

- Used Azure Network Security Groups (NSGs) and Azure Firewall to isolate workloads.

- Role-Based Access Control (RBAC) implemented at the resource group and subscription level.

Outcomes

- Release frequency increased to multiple times per week.

- 40% reduction in critical security vulnerabilities.

- Streamlined compliance audits with centralized governance tools.

Case Study 4: Manufacturing Firm Implements IoT with Azure

Company Background

A large-scale manufacturing company sought to improve predictive maintenance, reduce downtime, and digitize factory operations.

Challenges

- Legacy machines lacked connectivity.

- Data was being manually collected and analyzed, leading to delays.

- Frequent equipment failures led to production loss.

Azure Implementation

IoT Platform Buildout:

- Machines retrofitted with sensors sending telemetry data to **Azure IoT Hub**.

- Data ingested in real time via **Azure Stream Analytics**.

- Stored in **Azure Data Explorer** for fast querying and visualization.

Edge Computing:

- **Azure IoT Edge** deployed on factory floor devices for real-time anomaly detection.

- Models trained in Azure ML and deployed as Docker containers to edge devices.

Visualization and Control:

- Custom dashboards built with **Power BI**.

- Alerts configured with Azure Monitor and Logic Apps to notify maintenance teams.

```
// Stream Analytics example query
SELECT
    DeviceId,
    AVG(Temperature) AS AvgTemp,
    System.Timestamp AS TimeWindow
INTO
    output
FROM
    input TIMESTAMP BY EventEnqueuedUtcTime
GROUP BY
    TumblingWindow(minute, 5), DeviceId
```

Outcomes

- Predictive maintenance reduced machine failures by 35%.

- Real-time analytics shortened decision-making from days to minutes.

- Achieved 24/7 monitoring across global factory locations.

Case Study 5: SaaS Startup Launches Global Application

Company Profile

A fast-growing SaaS startup offering a productivity platform needed to go global while ensuring data locality and performance.

Challenges

- Required low latency access from APAC, EU, and US.

- Customers demanded data residency compliance (e.g., GDPR).

- Needed scalability without a large ops team.

Azure Implementation

Cloud-Native Architecture:

- Built on **Azure App Services**, **Azure SQL**, and **Cosmos DB** with multi-region writes.

- **Azure Front Door** used for geo-routing and SSL termination.

- All deployments automated using **GitHub Actions** and **Bicep templates**.

Tenant Isolation and Scaling:

- Used resource tagging and naming conventions to isolate tenants logically.

- Cosmos DB partitioning used for tenant-based data sharding.

Observability:

- Custom telemetry sent to **Application Insights** for usage tracking and debugging.

- Alerts integrated with Microsoft Teams for engineering triage.

```
resource app 'Microsoft.Web/sites@2021-02-01' = {
  name: 'prod-app-${tenantId}'
  location: 'West Europe'
  properties: {
    serverFarmId: appServicePlan.id
    siteConfig: {
      appSettings: [
        {
          name: 'TENANT_ID'
          value: tenantId
        }
      ]
    }
  }
}
```

Outcomes

- 3-week time-to-market for new regions.

- Met GDPR, CCPA, and ISO 27001 compliance from day one.

- Achieved 99.999% availability and zero downtime deployments.

Conclusion

These case studies reflect how organizations of different sizes and across diverse industries have successfully adopted Azure to solve complex challenges. From global scalability in retail and SaaS to data modernization in healthcare and IoT in manufacturing, Azure's comprehensive ecosystem empowers businesses to transform, innovate, and thrive.

By leveraging services such as AKS, Cosmos DB, Azure DevOps, and IoT Hub, and incorporating best practices in architecture, governance, and security, these organizations have not only addressed their immediate problems but also laid strong foundations for future growth. These examples serve as practical blueprints and inspiration for building your own enterprise-grade solutions on Azure.

Chapter 10: Certification and Career Paths

Overview of Azure Certifications

Microsoft Azure certifications are among the most sought-after credentials in the cloud computing industry. They validate your expertise in cloud concepts, solution architecture, development, security, administration, and more. Whether you are new to cloud technology or an experienced professional aiming to validate and enhance your skills, Azure certifications provide structured learning paths and global recognition that can significantly boost your career.

This section provides a comprehensive overview of Microsoft Azure certifications, the structure of the certification paths, exam formats, study resources, and career benefits associated with achieving these credentials. We will also explore how certifications align with different job roles, tips for preparation, and long-term growth strategies.

Why Get Azure Certified?

Azure certifications serve multiple purposes:

- **Career Advancement**: Certifications can qualify you for higher-paying roles and better job prospects.

- **Skill Validation**: They offer third-party validation of your cloud knowledge and experience.

- **Employer Trust**: Many employers require or prefer certified candidates to reduce onboarding time and training costs.

- **Community and Networking**: Microsoft Certified Professionals (MCPs) gain access to exclusive events, groups, and continued education.

The Certification Structure

Microsoft certifications are role-based and organized into three levels:

- **Fundamentals**: Introductory certifications suitable for beginners.

- **Associate**: For professionals with some experience in Azure or IT.

- **Expert**: Advanced certifications targeting specialized roles.

There are also **Specialty certifications** that focus on niche areas such as IoT, SAP on Azure, or virtual desktop management.

Here is a breakdown of the key certifications at each level.

Fundamentals

1. **AZ-900: Microsoft Azure Fundamentals**

   - Audience: Beginners and non-technical professionals.

   - Covers: Cloud concepts, core Azure services, pricing, SLAs, compliance, and governance.

   - Format: 40–60 questions, multiple-choice and drag-and-drop.

2. **AI-900: Microsoft Azure AI Fundamentals**

   - Covers: AI workloads and considerations, Azure AI services.

3. **DP-900: Microsoft Azure Data Fundamentals**

   - Covers: Core data concepts, relational and non-relational data in Azure.

Associate Level

1. **AZ-104: Microsoft Azure Administrator Associate**

   - Covers: Managing Azure identities, governance, storage, compute, virtual networking, and monitoring.

   - Role: Azure Administrators who manage cloud services spanning storage, networking, and compute.

2. **AZ-204: Microsoft Azure Developer Associate**

   - Covers: Designing, building, testing, and maintaining cloud applications and services on Azure.

   - Role: Cloud developers with 1–2 years of professional experience.

3. **DP-203: Data Engineering on Microsoft Azure**

   - Covers: Designing and implementing data solutions with Azure Synapse, Data Lake, and Data Factory.

4. **AI-102: Designing and Implementing an Azure AI Solution**

   - Role: AI Engineers working with Cognitive Services, Azure Bot Service, and machine learning.

Expert Level

1. **AZ-305: Microsoft Azure Solutions Architect Expert**

   - Requires: AZ-104 as a prerequisite.

   - Focus: Designing cloud and hybrid solutions including compute, network, storage, monitoring, and security.

2. **AZ-400: Microsoft DevOps Engineer Expert**

   - Requires: AZ-104 or AZ-204.

   - Covers: DevOps strategy, CI/CD, infrastructure as code, monitoring, and feedback loops.

Specialty Certifications

- **SC-100: Microsoft Cybersecurity Architect**

- **AZ-600: Azure Stack Hub Operator**

- **MB-500: Dynamics 365 Finance and Operations Apps Developer**

These are ideal for individuals in highly specific technical roles.

Choosing the Right Certification

The right certification depends on your current role and career aspirations. Here are some typical paths:

- **Beginner or Transitioning into Cloud**: Start with AZ-900 to learn fundamentals.

- **System Administrator or IT Pro**: AZ-104 is a strong entry point.

- **Developer**: AZ-204 followed by AZ-400 if you want to enter DevOps.

- **Architect**: AZ-305 (after AZ-104 or AZ-204) for a comprehensive view of Azure architecture.

- **Data Professional**: DP-900 → DP-203 for data engineering.

- **Security Professional**: SC-900 → SC-200 → SC-300 or SC-100.

Certification Exam Details

- **Exam Format**: Includes multiple-choice, drag-and-drop, case studies, and active screen scenarios.

- **Duration**: Most exams take 100–120 minutes.

- **Scoring**: Pass mark is typically 700 out of 1000.

- **Language**: Available in multiple languages including English, Japanese, Spanish, German, and more.

You can schedule your exam via Pearson VUE or take it from home with an online proctor.

Preparing for an Azure Certification

Learning Resources

- **Microsoft Learn**: Free, official platform with interactive tutorials and learning paths.

- **Pluralsight & LinkedIn Learning**: Paid platforms with in-depth video tutorials and hands-on labs.

- **Exam Ref Books**: Official Microsoft Press books aligned with exam objectives.

- **GitHub Repos**: Many instructors and contributors have sample labs and notes.

Practice Exams

Use practice tests to simulate exam scenarios and assess your readiness. Whizlabs, MeasureUp, and Tutorials Dojo are reputable providers.

Study Plan Template

```
**4-Week AZ-104 Study Plan**

**Week 1**
- Identity and Access Management
- Azure Active Directory
- Role-Based Access Control (RBAC)
```

```
**Week 2**
- Virtual Networks
- Load Balancers
- VPN and ExpressRoute

**Week 3**
- Storage Accounts
- Azure Files, Blob, and Disks
- Backup and Site Recovery

**Week 4**
- Monitoring and Alerts
- Practice Exams
- Review Weak Areas
```

Exam Tips

- Read the questions carefully—look for keywords like "most cost-effective", "high availability", "minimum configuration".

- Use the "mark for review" feature to revisit tricky questions at the end.

- Eliminate clearly incorrect options to narrow down choices.

- Use logic based on Azure's capabilities—don't overthink or assume.

Certification Renewal

Certifications are valid for **one year**. Microsoft offers **free online renewals** through open-book, non-proctored assessments on Microsoft Learn. This encourages professionals to stay current with evolving technologies.

Community and Events

Joining the Azure community can accelerate your learning:

- **Microsoft Tech Community**

- **Reddit's r/Azure**

- **Meetups and User Groups**

- **Microsoft Ignite and Build conferences**

Career Impact

Professionals who are Azure certified often report:

- **Higher Salaries**: Azure-certified roles can command up to 20% more.

- **Job Mobility**: Certifications open doors to remote and international opportunities.

- **Recognition**: Employers value candidates who show initiative and verified skills.

- **Consulting and Freelance Opportunities**: Certified professionals can build a brand around their credentials.

Conclusion

Earning an Azure certification is not just about passing an exam—it's about mastering concepts that drive real-world cloud transformation. With a structured certification framework, high-quality study resources, and strong community support, Microsoft makes it accessible for professionals at any stage to validate their skills and grow their careers.

Whether you're an aspiring cloud engineer, seasoned developer, or enterprise architect, there's a certification path tailored to your ambitions. Embrace the journey, stay consistent with learning, and let Azure certifications be your launchpad to success in the ever-evolving tech landscape.

Choosing the Right Path: Admin, Developer, Architect

Choosing the right certification and career path in Azure is a strategic decision that impacts your professional trajectory. Microsoft Azure offers a wide range of role-based certifications tailored for different job functions. Understanding each path—Administrator, Developer, and Architect—helps you align your learning efforts with your career goals, technical interests, and long-term aspirations.

In this section, we'll explore the differences between these roles, their typical responsibilities, the required skills, certification pathways, and example career scenarios. By the end, you'll be equipped with the insight needed to make informed decisions about your Azure journey.

Role Comparison Overview

Role	Focus Area	Key Certifications	Ideal For

Administrator	Infrastructure, networking, access control	AZ-104	IT pros, sysadmins
Developer	Application development and integration	AZ-204	Software developers
Architect	Solution design, performance, cost, resilience	AZ-305 (after AZ-104 or AZ-204)	Experienced cloud professionals

Each path can also branch into specialties such as DevOps, Security, or Data, depending on your interests.

Azure Administrator Path

Overview

Azure Administrators manage and monitor Azure resources. They ensure workloads are configured securely, perform optimally, and scale appropriately. These professionals play a pivotal role in hybrid and cloud-native infrastructure environments.

Key Responsibilities

- Provisioning and managing VMs, storage, and networking.

- Implementing identity and access control using Azure AD and RBAC.

- Monitoring resources and setting up alerts.

- Ensuring backup and disaster recovery policies are in place.

Certification Path

1. **Start with AZ-900** (Optional for beginners)

2. **Take AZ-104: Azure Administrator Associate**

3. **Advance to AZ-305: Azure Solutions Architect Expert** (Optional)

Example Career Titles

- Cloud Administrator

- Systems Engineer

- Infrastructure Engineer

- Azure Support Engineer

Sample Task

Creating a VM with a secure NSG in Azure using CLI:

```
az group create --name WebAppGroup --location eastus

az vm create \
  --resource-group WebAppGroup \
  --name WebServer01 \
  --image UbuntuLTS \
  --admin-username azureuser \
  --generate-ssh-keys

az network nsg rule create \
  --resource-group WebAppGroup \
  --nsg-name myNSG \
  --name allow-ssh \
  --priority 1000 \
  --direction Inbound \
  --access Allow \
  --protocol Tcp \
  --destination-port-range 22
```

Skills Required

- Networking fundamentals (VNet, NSG, Load Balancer)

- Storage types and access control

- Azure CLI, PowerShell, and ARM templates

- Monitoring and security baselines

Azure Developer Path

Overview

Azure Developers design and build applications that run in the cloud. They use platform-as-a-service (PaaS) offerings, integrate services, and follow modern DevOps practices. Developers are essential in creating scalable, maintainable, and efficient software solutions.

Key Responsibilities

- Writing and deploying code to Azure services (App Services, Functions, AKS).

- Integrating with Azure services like Cosmos DB, Event Grid, and Logic Apps.

- Implementing APIs and SDKs.

- Writing automated deployment pipelines.

Certification Path

1. **Start with AZ-900** (Optional)

2. **Take AZ-204: Azure Developer Associate**

3. **Advance to AZ-400: DevOps Engineer Expert**

Example Career Titles

- Cloud Developer

- Software Engineer

- Backend Developer

- Full-Stack Developer (Azure-focused)

Sample Code: Azure Function Triggered by Blob Upload

```
public static class ProcessImage
{
    [FunctionName("ProcessImage")]
    public static void Run(
        [BlobTrigger("images/{name}", Connection =
"AzureWebJobsStorage")] Stream myBlob,
        string name, ILogger log)
    {
```

```
        log.LogInformation($"C# Blob trigger function processed
blob\n Name:{name} \n Size: {myBlob.Length} Bytes");
    }
}
```

Skills Required

- Proficiency in programming (C#, Python, JavaScript, etc.)

- REST APIs and microservices

- Event-driven architectures

- CI/CD with GitHub Actions or Azure DevOps

- Serverless and container-based deployments

Azure Architect Path

Overview

Azure Architects design end-to-end solutions that are secure, scalable, reliable, and cost-optimized. They combine in-depth technical knowledge with strategic thinking to translate business requirements into cloud designs.

Key Responsibilities

- Designing architectures for web apps, data platforms, and enterprise solutions.

- Making decisions about storage, compute, security, and cost trade-offs.

- Leading cloud migration projects and hybrid setups.

- Communicating with both technical and non-technical stakeholders.

Certification Path

1. **AZ-104 or AZ-204** (either satisfies prerequisite)

2. **AZ-305: Azure Solutions Architect Expert**

Example Career Titles

- Cloud Solutions Architect

- Enterprise Architect

- Cloud Consultant

- Technical Lead

Sample Architecture Scenario

Designing a global e-commerce solution:

- Use **Azure Front Door** for global load balancing and SSL offloading.

- Deploy APIs via **App Service Environment (ASE)** for secure VNet integration.

- Store data in **Cosmos DB with multi-region writes**.

- Use **Azure Key Vault** for managing secrets.

- Build monitoring into every layer using **Azure Monitor and Log Analytics**.

Skills Required

- Deep understanding of cloud infrastructure and platform services

- Experience with hybrid and multi-cloud architectures

- Knowledge of security, compliance, and governance

- Familiarity with business continuity and disaster recovery (BCDR)

Choosing Based on Career Goals

I Want to Manage Systems and Infrastructure

- **Go with Azure Administrator (AZ-104)**

- Eventually branch into security (SC-200, SC-300) or architecture (AZ-305)

I Love Writing Code and Building Applications

- **Start with Azure Developer (AZ-204)**

- Progress into DevOps (AZ-400) or Architect roles

I Enjoy Strategic Thinking and Solution Design

- **Target Azure Architect (AZ-305)**

- Combine with AZ-104 or AZ-204 based on prior experience

I'm a Beginner Exploring Options

- Start with **AZ-900** to explore all paths

- Use Microsoft Learn's learning paths to experiment with tasks from different roles

---

Combining Paths

Azure professionals often blend responsibilities over time:

- **Admin + Developer**: DevOps Engineer (AZ-400)

- **Developer + Architect**: Lead Engineer or Solutions Architect

- **Admin + Security**: Cloud Security Engineer (SC-200/SC-300)

You can pivot your career based on evolving interests. Azure's role-based certification model supports lateral and upward movement between disciplines.

Career Progression Examples

Example 1: Infrastructure to Architect

- AZ-104 → AZ-305 → SC-100

- Role: Senior Architect overseeing infrastructure modernization

Example 2: Developer to DevOps Lead

- AZ-204 → AZ-400 → SC-200

- Role: Engineering Manager automating secure deployments

Example 3: New Graduate to Cloud Consultant

- AZ-900 → AZ-104 + AZ-204 → AZ-305

- Role: Consultant designing hybrid cloud systems

Conclusion

Choosing the right path in Azure is a personal and professional decision that should align with your current skills, future goals, and the kind of work you enjoy doing. Whether you're an infrastructure guru, a coding enthusiast, or a big-picture thinker, Azure offers a tailored path to help you grow and specialize.

Start small, validate your skills, and then build upward or pivot as needed. Each certification not only improves your technical expertise but also signals to employers and peers that you're serious about your cloud career. The Administrator, Developer, and Architect roles each offer rewarding opportunities—choose your starting point and embrace the journey.

Preparing for the AZ-900 and Beyond

The AZ-900: Microsoft Azure Fundamentals certification is the gateway to the Azure ecosystem. It's designed for individuals who are new to cloud computing or Azure and provides a solid foundation of cloud concepts, Azure services, pricing models, and governance. This section provides an in-depth guide to preparing for the AZ-900 exam and progressing beyond it into role-based certifications like AZ-104 (Administrator), AZ-204 (Developer), and AZ-305 (Architect).

Whether you're pursuing Azure to kickstart a new career, enhance your current role, or validate your knowledge, the AZ-900 is a strategic first step. This section covers the exam blueprint, learning strategies, recommended resources, practical labs, and a roadmap for moving beyond the fundamentals.

Who Should Take AZ-900?

AZ-900 is suitable for:

- Absolute beginners with no technical background

- Business decision-makers, sales professionals, or marketers working with cloud-based products

- Aspiring cloud administrators, developers, or architects

- Students exploring careers in cloud computing

You do not need prior experience with Azure to take this exam, but an understanding of general IT concepts (like networking, databases, compute, and storage) can help.

Exam Objectives and Domains

The AZ-900 exam is structured around five main domains:

1. **Describe Cloud Concepts (25–30%)**

   - Benefits of cloud computing (CapEx vs. OpEx, elasticity, scalability)

   - Cloud service models (IaaS, PaaS, SaaS)

   - Public, Private, and Hybrid cloud models

2. **Describe Core Azure Services (15–20%)**

   - Core architecture components: regions, availability zones, resource groups

   - Core services: compute (VMs, App Services), networking, storage, databases

3. **Describe Core Solutions and Management Tools on Azure (10–15%)**

   - Solutions like IoT, Azure Machine Learning, Azure Synapse, and DevOps

   - Tools like Azure Portal, Azure CLI, Cloud Shell, and ARM templates

4. **Describe General Security and Network Security Features (10–15%)**

   - Azure Security Center, Key Vault, Azure DDoS Protection, NSGs

5. **Describe Identity, Governance, Privacy, and Compliance Features (20–25%)**

   - Azure Active Directory, RBAC, subscriptions, management groups, policies

6. **Describe Azure Pricing, SLA, and Lifecycle (10–15%)**

   - Azure cost management tools

- Service Level Agreements (SLAs)

- Azure Free Tier and pricing calculator

Study Strategy for AZ-900

Step 1: Set a Timeline

Allocate 2–4 weeks of focused study depending on your background. Here's a sample plan:

Week 1: Cloud Concepts + Core Azure Services
Week 2: Azure Solutions + Security + Identity and Governance
Week 3: Pricing, SLA, and Practice Exams
Week 4: Review and Hands-on Labs

Step 2: Use Microsoft Learn

Microsoft Learn provides a **free, official learning path**:

- Azure Fundamentals Learning Path

- Interactive modules with quizzes and sandboxed labs

- No subscription or Azure setup required

Step 3: Watch Video Courses

Recommended platforms:

- **YouTube** – John Savill's AZ-900 Master Class (Free)

- **Udemy** – AZ-900 courses by Scott Duffy or Alan Rodrigues

- **LinkedIn Learning** – Beginner-friendly explanations and quizzes

Step 4: Read the Documentation

Focus on:

- Azure global infrastructure

- Azure Pricing Calculator

- Azure Compliance Offerings

Step 5: Hands-On Labs

Even though AZ-900 doesn't test hands-on tasks, practical knowledge reinforces concepts.

Use the **Azure Free Account**:

```
# Create a resource group
az group create --name LearnGroup --location "East US"

# Create a storage account
az storage account create \
  --name mystorage900 \
  --resource-group LearnGroup \
  --location "East US" \
  --sku Standard_LRS
```

Other labs to try:

- Create a VM and explore NSGs

- Configure a storage account and upload files

- Use Azure Pricing Calculator to estimate costs

Step 6: Take Practice Tests

Practice exams help you understand the format and assess your readiness.

Trusted sources:

- Whizlabs (AZ-900 practice exams)

- MeasureUp (Microsoft Official Provider)

- Tutorials Dojo or ExamTopics (community-sourced questions)

Exam Format and Tips

- **Time**: 85 minutes

- **Questions**: 40–60

- **Types**: Multiple choice, drag-and-drop, hot area, case studies

- **Passing Score**: 700/1000

Tips:

- Read each question carefully—identify keywords (e.g., "cost-effective", "minimize downtime").

- Don't second-guess; go with your first logical answer.

- Use the "Mark for Review" feature for difficult questions.

After the Exam: What's Next?

Passing AZ-900 is just the beginning. Depending on your interests, here's how you can move forward:

If You Enjoy Infrastructure and Management:

- **AZ-104: Azure Administrator**

  - Learn about VM scaling, identity, networking, and automation

  - Requires practical experience with the Azure portal and CLI

If You Love Building Apps:

- **AZ-204: Azure Developer**

  - Focuses on creating and integrating APIs, Azure Functions, and App Services

If You Think Like a Designer or Strategist:

- **AZ-305: Solutions Architect**

  - Emphasizes designing secure, scalable, and cost-efficient systems

If You're a Security Enthusiast:

- **SC-900 → SC-200 or SC-300**

  - Learn about securing Azure environments and managing identity

If You Want to Explore Data:

- **DP-900 → DP-203**

○ Data engineering and analysis using Synapse, Data Lake, and Databricks

Building a Long-Term Azure Career

1. **Continue Learning**: Azure evolves fast—subscribe to blogs, follow GitHub repos, and join Microsoft Learn's Cloud Skills Challenge.

2. **Hands-On Projects**: Start with small projects like building a resume website or setting up a WordPress blog using Azure App Service and MySQL.

3. **Join the Community**: Attend Azure meetups, join forums like Tech Community, and follow Azure engineers on Twitter and LinkedIn.

4. **Earn More Certs**: Stack your credentials to become a subject matter expert (SME) in a specialized area.

5. **Showcase Your Skills**: Use platforms like GitHub, Dev.to, or Medium to write about your learning journey.

Career Outcomes with AZ-900 and Beyond

Certification	Common Job Titles	Avg. Salary (USD)
AZ-900	Cloud Intern, Sales Engineer	$55,000–$75,000
AZ-104	Azure Admin, Support Engineer	$75,000–$100,000
AZ-204	Developer, Backend Engineer	$85,000–$110,000
AZ-305	Architect, Consultant	$120,000–$160,000

AZ-900 alone won't make you a cloud expert, but it opens the door to interviews and proves your commitment to learning.

Conclusion

Preparing for the AZ-900 exam is an achievable and rewarding first step into the world of Azure. With a strategic approach, curated resources, and consistent study habits, you can earn your certification in under a month—even with no prior experience. Beyond the exam, the journey continues with more advanced certifications tailored to your goals—whether you're aiming for admin, dev, security, data, or architecture roles.

The cloud is growing exponentially, and now is the perfect time to start. Earn your AZ-900, and you'll be well on your way to building a cloud-first career that's both future-proof and fulfilling.

Resume Tips and Interview Preparation for Azure Roles

Securing a role in the Azure ecosystem involves more than just earning certifications—it's about effectively presenting your skills, experience, and mindset to prospective employers. This section is dedicated to helping you create a standout resume tailored for Azure roles and prepare thoroughly for technical and behavioral interviews. Whether you're targeting roles in administration, development, architecture, DevOps, or data, this guide will give you practical steps, templates, and strategies to increase your chances of landing the job.

Resume Strategy for Azure Roles

Your resume is the first impression you make. In the competitive cloud job market, it needs to be clear, concise, and aligned with the job you're applying for.

Key Sections to Include

1. **Contact Information**

   - Full name, location, email, phone, and optionally, LinkedIn and GitHub links.

2. **Professional Summary**

   - A 2–3 sentence snapshot highlighting your experience, focus areas, and Azure competencies.

   - Example: *"Certified Azure Administrator with 3+ years of experience managing cloud infrastructure, implementing security protocols, and automating deployments using Azure DevOps and Terraform."*

3. **Certifications**

   - Place this high on the resume if you're early in your cloud career.

   - Include the certification name, issuing body (Microsoft), and year.

   - Example:

     - Microsoft Certified: Azure Fundamentals (AZ-900), 2024

     - Microsoft Certified: Azure Administrator Associate (AZ-104), 2025

4. **Technical Skills**

   - Group by category: Cloud Platforms, DevOps Tools, Scripting Languages, Monitoring Tools, etc.

   - Example:

     - **Cloud**: Azure App Service, Azure Functions, AKS, Cosmos DB

     - **DevOps**: Azure DevOps, GitHub Actions, Terraform, Bicep

     - **Languages**: PowerShell, Python, C#, Bash

5. **Professional Experience**

   - Use bullet points with the STAR method (Situation, Task, Action, Result).

   - Start each bullet with an action verb.

   - Focus on achievements and metrics, not just responsibilities.

   - Example:

     - *Deployed and managed 20+ Azure Virtual Machines across production and staging environments, improving app uptime by 15% using Availability Sets and Azure Monitor.*

6. **Projects**

   - Especially valuable if you're early in your career or transitioning into cloud.

   - Include GitHub links if available.

   - Example:

     - *Built a serverless API using Azure Functions and Cosmos DB for a task management app. Automated CI/CD using GitHub Actions.*

7. **Education**

   - List degrees and relevant coursework if applicable.

Tailoring Your Resume for Job Descriptions

Use keywords from the job description. Many companies use Applicant Tracking Systems (ATS) to filter resumes.

- Look for repeating terms like "RBAC", "ARM templates", "Azure DevOps", or "PaaS".

- Mirror the phrasing in your resume where applicable without keyword stuffing.

- Example: If the JD mentions "cost optimization", update your experience with:

    - *"Optimized cloud spending by 25% through right-sizing Azure VMs and implementing Reserved Instances."*

Use tools like **Jobscan** or **Resumatch** to score your resume against job postings.

Azure-Specific Action Verbs and Phrases

Use action verbs specific to cloud projects:

- Deployed, Automated, Configured, Secured, Integrated, Monitored, Orchestrated, Migrated, Scaled, Refactored, Containerized

Examples:

- *"Automated infrastructure deployment using Bicep templates and Azure DevOps pipelines."*

- *"Migrated legacy apps to Azure App Service with zero downtime."*

Portfolio and GitHub Tips

Having a portfolio is a huge plus. Include:

- Repositories of projects (e.g., Azure Functions, Terraform IaC, Logic Apps).

- README files with clear project overviews, architecture diagrams (if applicable), and deployment instructions.

- A link to a personal website showcasing certifications, blogs, and projects.

Example README.md snippet for an Azure DevOps project:

```
# Azure DevOps CI/CD Pipeline for Node.js API

This project demonstrates a CI/CD pipeline setup using Azure DevOps
for deploying a Node.js API to Azure App Service.

## Tools Used
- Azure DevOps
- App Service
- Bicep for IaC

## Pipeline Stages
- Build and test
- Deploy to staging
- Approval and deploy to production
```

Interview Preparation Strategy

Prepare for a blend of technical and behavioral questions. Most Azure roles require demonstrating not only technical proficiency but also problem-solving and communication skills.

Common Technical Topics

For Azure Administrator Roles (AZ-104 Level):

- Azure AD and RBAC

- Virtual Networks and NSGs

- Azure Monitor, Alerts, and Log Analytics

- Backup and Site Recovery

- ARM Templates or Bicep

- Cost Management

For Azure Developer Roles (AZ-204 Level):

- Azure Functions and Logic Apps

- App Service configuration and deployment

- Cosmos DB and Table Storage

- Authentication with Azure AD

- CI/CD pipelines (GitHub Actions, Azure DevOps)

For Architect Roles (AZ-305 Level):

- Designing for high availability and scalability

- Disaster recovery (RTO/RPO)

- Multi-region architecture

- Application security and identity architecture

- Azure Front Door vs Traffic Manager

Example Technical Questions

- *What's the difference between Azure AD and Active Directory on-prem?*

- *How would you secure access to an Azure Storage account?*

- *Explain the components of an Azure Virtual Network.*

- *What tools would you use to automate infrastructure deployment?*

- *How do you ensure cost optimization in Azure?*

Prepare to whiteboard or describe your architecture for a solution like this:

Prompt: "Design a scalable web app with secure data access, multi-region failover, and automated deployment."

Expected Response Outline:

- Frontend via Azure Static Web Apps or App Service

- Backend APIs with Azure Functions or AKS

- Cosmos DB with multi-region writes

- Azure Front Door for global routing

- Azure DevOps for pipeline deployment

- Key Vault for secrets management

- Monitor and Application Insights for telemetry

Behavioral and Soft Skills Questions

Use the STAR method (Situation, Task, Action, Result) to structure responses.

Sample questions:

- *Tell me about a time you solved a performance issue in production.*

- *How do you prioritize tasks when managing multiple cloud projects?*

- *Describe a time you failed and how you handled it.*

- *How do you ensure collaboration across teams when working on cloud projects?*

Example Answer (STAR Method):

Situation: Our team's production API started timing out frequently.
Task: I had to identify the root cause and implement a fix with minimal downtime.
Action: I used Azure Monitor and Application Insights to identify a memory leak in the backend service. I then implemented a rolling restart strategy using Azure DevOps and set up auto-healing rules.
Result: API response time improved by 40%, and we avoided further outages.

Mock Interview Practice

Simulate interviews with peers or use platforms like:

- **Pramp**

- **Interviewing.io**

- **TechMockInterview**

- **LeetCode (for coding challenges if applicable)**

Record yourself answering questions and refine your responses for clarity and confidence.

Final Checklist Before Applying

- Resume tailored to job description

- Certifications prominently listed

- GitHub with at least 2–3 public Azure-related projects

- Azure portal hands-on practice completed

- Mock interviews or technical question rehearsals

- LinkedIn profile updated with Azure skills and certifications

Conclusion

Breaking into or advancing within an Azure-focused role requires more than just technical knowledge. It's about positioning yourself correctly on paper, demonstrating hands-on experience, and effectively communicating your value during interviews.

Tailor your resume to reflect real Azure skills, build a portfolio that proves your capabilities, and practice both technical and behavioral questions with structured responses. With this comprehensive preparation, you'll significantly increase your chances of landing that coveted Azure role—whether it's your first job in tech or your next step into senior leadership. The cloud job market is growing rapidly, and your path to success starts with preparation, clarity, and confidence.

Chapter 11: Appendices

Glossary of Terms

Understanding the terminology used throughout the Azure ecosystem is essential for mastering the platform and effectively communicating in cloud-centric roles. The following glossary covers core Azure-specific concepts, general cloud computing vocabulary, and frequently used acronyms. This section serves as a long-form reference guide, useful for beginners and seasoned professionals alike.

A

Azure Active Directory (Azure AD)
A cloud-based identity and access management service that enables employees to sign in and access resources. It supports Single Sign-On (SSO), multi-factor authentication, and integration with on-premises AD.

Availability Set
A configuration that ensures VM redundancy by distributing them across multiple fault and update domains within a single data center.

Availability Zone
Physically separate data center locations within an Azure region. Using multiple zones increases application availability and fault tolerance.

ARM (Azure Resource Manager)
The deployment and management service for Azure. It provides a consistent management layer that enables you to create, update, and delete resources via templates, CLI, or API.

B

Bicep
A domain-specific language (DSL) used to declaratively deploy Azure resources. It simplifies authoring and improves readability over traditional JSON ARM templates.

```
resource storage 'Microsoft.Storage/storageAccounts@2022-09-01' = {
  name: 'myuniquestorageacct'
  location: 'eastus'
  sku: {
    name: 'Standard_LRS'
  }
  kind: 'StorageV2'
```

}

Blob Storage
An object storage solution in Azure optimized for storing massive amounts of unstructured data like images, videos, and documents.

Backup Vault
A storage entity in Azure used for backing up and restoring data, including files, virtual machines, and databases.

C

Cloud Shell
An interactive, browser-accessible shell for managing Azure resources using either Bash or PowerShell, preconfigured with Azure CLI, Git, and other tools.

Cosmos DB
A globally distributed, multi-model database service designed for low-latency and high-availability access to data.

Content Delivery Network (CDN)
A distributed network of servers used to cache and deliver content like websites, images, and videos to users based on their geographic location.

Container Instance (ACI)
An Azure service that allows users to run Docker containers without managing any infrastructure.

CI/CD (Continuous Integration/Continuous Deployment)
Development practices that automate the process of code integration, testing, and deployment into production.

D

DevOps
A combination of cultural philosophies, practices, and tools that integrates software development and IT operations, improving delivery and reliability.

Data Lake
A centralized repository for storing structured and unstructured data at scale. Azure Data Lake is used for big data analytics.

DDoS Protection
A security feature that protects Azure resources from Distributed Denial-of-Service attacks.

Data Factory
A cloud-based ETL (Extract, Transform, Load) and data integration service that automates data movement and transformation.

E

Event Grid
A fully managed event routing service that allows developers to react to events in near real-time from Azure resources or custom sources.

Elasticity
The ability to dynamically allocate or deallocate resources based on workload demand.

ExpressRoute
A dedicated, private connection between an on-premises environment and Azure, bypassing the public internet for improved reliability and performance.

F

Function App / Azure Functions
A serverless compute service that allows users to run event-driven code without provisioning or managing servers.

Failover
The process of automatically switching to a redundant system or component upon failure of the original system.

Firewall (Azure Firewall)
A managed, cloud-based network security service that protects Azure Virtual Network resources.

G

Geo-Redundancy
The practice of replicating data and services across multiple geographic regions to ensure high availability and disaster recovery.

GitHub Actions
An automation platform that can be used to build CI/CD pipelines directly from GitHub repositories and integrate with Azure.

General Availability (GA)
The stage in the release lifecycle when a product or feature is considered stable and available for all users.

H

Hybrid Cloud
A cloud computing environment that combines on-premises infrastructure (or private cloud) with public cloud services.

Hot Path / Cold Path
Terms used in data architecture; the hot path refers to real-time data processing, while the cold path deals with batch processing of large datasets.

I

Infrastructure as Code (IaC)
The process of managing and provisioning computing infrastructure using machine-readable definition files rather than physical hardware configuration.

Identity Provider (IdP)
A system that authenticates user identities and issues access tokens—Azure AD is a common IdP.

IoT Hub
Azure's central messaging hub for bi-directional communication between IoT applications and the devices it manages.

J

JSON (JavaScript Object Notation)
A lightweight data-interchange format commonly used for ARM templates and API responses.

K

Key Vault
A service for securely storing and accessing secrets like API keys, passwords, certificates, and cryptographic keys.

Kubernetes Service (AKS)
Azure's managed Kubernetes service that simplifies deploying, managing, and operating containerized applications.

L

Load Balancer
A Layer 4 (TCP, UDP) service that distributes incoming network traffic across multiple targets (VMs, containers, etc.).

Logic App
A cloud-based service that enables you to create and run automated workflows that integrate services, applications, and data.

M

Managed Identity
Provides an automatically managed identity in Azure AD for applications to use when connecting to resources that support Azure AD authentication.

Marketplace (Azure Marketplace)
An online store for buying and selling cloud solutions that are certified and optimized to run on Azure.

Monitoring
Azure Monitor provides a full-stack monitoring experience including metrics, logs, and alerts across applications and infrastructure.

N

Network Security Group (NSG)
A set of rules that control inbound and outbound traffic to network interfaces, VMs, and subnets.

NoSQL
A type of database that stores and retrieves data without requiring predefined schemas—Azure Cosmos DB is a NoSQL solution.

O

Operating Expense (OpEx)
An accounting category for ongoing costs for running a business or system—cloud services are usually considered OpEx.

Object Storage
Storage architecture that manages data as objects rather than files or blocks. Azure Blob Storage is a form of object storage.

P

Platform as a Service (PaaS)
A cloud computing model that provides hardware and software tools over the internet, often for application development.

Private Endpoint
Allows secure access to Azure services over a private IP address from within your virtual network.

Q

Queue Storage
Part of Azure Storage used for storing large numbers of messages. Useful for decoupling components in a cloud application.

R

Resource Group
A container that holds related Azure resources, allowing unified management, billing, and access control.

Role-Based Access Control (RBAC)
A system that provides fine-grained access management of Azure resources based on user roles.

Reserved Instances (RI)
Discounted Azure VM pricing based on a long-term commitment (1 or 3 years).

S

Storage Account
An Azure resource that provides namespace and access control for storing blobs, files, queues, and tables.

Scalability
The ability of a system to handle increased load by adding resources, either vertically (scale-up) or horizontally (scale-out).

Service Bus
A fully managed enterprise message broker used for decoupling applications and services.

SLA (Service Level Agreement)
A contract that defines the guaranteed uptime and performance standards between Azure and the customer.

T

Terraform
An open-source tool for building, changing, and versioning infrastructure safely and efficiently. It's cloud-agnostic and often used with Azure.

Traffic Manager
A DNS-based load balancer that distributes traffic across multiple Azure endpoints.

U

Update Domain
A logical unit in Azure Availability Sets that allows for updates without affecting the availability of other instances.

Usage Metering
Azure provides detailed usage reports and analytics for cost tracking and forecasting.

V

Virtual Machine (VM)
A software-based simulation of a physical computer. In Azure, VMs are used to run workloads without managing hardware.

VNet (Virtual Network)
Azure's foundational networking component that allows isolated, secure communication between resources.

W

Web App (App Service)
A PaaS offering in Azure used to build and host web apps in various languages like .NET, Java, Node.js, and Python.

Workload
A specific application, service, or capability that runs on a cloud platform.

Y

YAML (YAML Ain't Markup Language)
A human-readable data serialization standard commonly used for defining infrastructure (e.g., CI/CD pipelines).

Z

Zone Redundant Storage (ZRS)
A storage option that replicates data across three availability zones within a region for enhanced durability.

Conclusion

This glossary provides a foundation for understanding the terminology and acronyms you'll encounter in Azure documentation, exams, and daily work. As you grow in your Azure journey, revisiting and expanding your vocabulary will enhance your communication skills, accelerate your learning, and improve your technical precision when designing and discussing solutions. Refer to this section often as a living reference throughout your cloud career.

Resources for Further Learning

Continuing your Azure education beyond this book is essential to stay current in a fast-moving cloud environment. Microsoft Azure evolves rapidly with new features, services, pricing models, and architectural best practices being introduced on a regular basis. This section provides a comprehensive and structured collection of learning resources—official and community-driven—that will help you deepen your knowledge, gain hands-on experience, and stay ahead in your Azure career.

Whether you're preparing for certifications, diving deeper into specific services, or looking for community interaction, these resources are curated to guide your journey as a cloud practitioner.

Microsoft Learn

Microsoft Learn is the most authoritative and comprehensive platform for free, self-paced Azure learning. It includes guided learning paths, interactive labs, and sandbox environments.

Key Benefits:

- Role-based modules (e.g., Administrator, Developer, Architect)

- Real-time sandboxes (no Azure subscription required)

- Integrated certification paths

- Badges and achievements for progress tracking

Recommended Learning Paths:

- Azure Fundamentals

- Administer Azure Resources

- Develop for Azure

- Architecting Microsoft Azure Solutions

You can use this sample PowerShell script to launch a Cloud Shell session from the Learn environment:

```
# Start Cloud Shell session

az login

az group create --name LearnGroup --location eastus

az vm create --name LearnVM --resource-group LearnGroup --image
UbuntuLTS --generate-ssh-keys
```

Documentation and Reference Guides

Microsoft's official documentation is extensive, covering every Azure service in detail. It includes how-tos, reference guides, SDK documentation, API reference, and pricing info.

Must-Bookmark Sections:

- Azure Documentation Home

- Azure Architecture Center

- Azure CLI Reference

- ARM Template Reference

- REST API Reference

You can also subscribe to the Azure Updates page to track feature releases and announcements.

Online Courses and Bootcamps

For structured learning, video-based training is a popular and effective approach.

Udemy

- Inexpensive, lifetime-access courses

- Popular instructors: Scott Duffy (AZ-104, AZ-900), Alan Rodrigues (AZ-204, AZ-400)

- Offers hands-on labs and practice tests

Pluralsight

- Subscription-based

- Offers "Skill IQ" assessments and learning paths

- Deep dive topics in Azure DevOps, AI, Infrastructure, and Architecture

LinkedIn Learning

- Includes business-focused Azure content

- Offers beginner to advanced paths

Cloud Academy / A Cloud Guru

- Real-world labs with Azure console access

- Scenario-based challenges

- Team plans available for corporate training

Hands-On Practice Labs

Azure is best learned by doing. These platforms offer guided labs with live Azure environments.

Microsoft Learn Sandbox

- Included in Learn modules

- Fully managed environment, no credit card required

GitHub Repositories

- Search for "Azure Labs", "Azure Bicep Projects", or "Azure Functions Examples"

- Example: Azure Quickstart Templates

Katacoda (Retired, replaced by Instruqt)

- Scenario-based learning in browser

- Cloud-specific lab exercises

Instruqt

- Sandbox-style platform for teams

- Offers Azure tracks with real-world projects

Example GitHub Project for Practicing Bicep:

```
param location string = 'eastus'
```

```
param appName string = 'mywebapp'


resource appServicePlan 'Microsoft.Web/serverfarms@2022-03-01' = {

  name: '${appName}-plan'

  location: location

  sku: {

    name: 'B1'

    tier: 'Basic'

  }

}


resource webApp 'Microsoft.Web/sites@2022-03-01' = {

  name: appName

  location: location

  properties: {

    serverFarmId: appServicePlan.id

  }

}
```

Books

Books offer in-depth explorations of concepts and are especially useful for structured exam preparation and enterprise architecture understanding.

Recommended Titles:

- *Exam Ref AZ-104 Microsoft Azure Administrator* by Harshul Patel

- *Microsoft Azure Architecture Best Practices* by Ritesh Modi

- *Azure for Architects* by Mustafa Toroman and Shahid Shaikh

- *The Azure Cloud Native Architecture Mapbook* by Stephane Eyskens

Many titles are available as eBooks through Microsoft Press Store, O'Reilly, or Packt.

Azure Blogs and Newsletters

To stay updated, follow these regularly:

- **Azure Blog**: https://azure.microsoft.com/en-us/blog/

- **Microsoft Tech Community**: https://techcommunity.microsoft.com

- **The Azure Weekly Newsletter**: https://azureweekly.info

- **Build5Nines**: https://build5nines.com

- **Thomas Maurer's Blog** (Microsoft MVP): https://www.thomasmaurer.ch

YouTube Channels

YouTube provides free, often up-to-date video tutorials, walkthroughs, and cloud news.

Recommended Channels:

- **Microsoft Azure** (official)

- **John Savill's Technical Training**

- **Cloud Advocate Team**

- **ExamPro**

- **The Azure Academy**

Playlists often include demos, certifications, architecture deep dives, and Azure news recaps.

Community Forums and Groups

Participating in communities helps with Q&A, problem-solving, and finding new learning opportunities.

Top Platforms:

- **Reddit** – r/AZURE, r/devops, r/learnprogramming

- **Stack Overflow** – Tag questions with [azure]

- **Microsoft Q&A** – https://learn.microsoft.com/en-us/answers/

- **Discord Servers** – Many cloud certification and dev communities

You can also join local or virtual **Meetups** and **Microsoft Reactor** events to connect with Azure professionals and attend workshops.

Podcasts and Audio Learning

Perfect for learning on the go, these podcasts cover Azure news, best practices, and real-world experiences.

Popular Azure Podcasts:

- **Azure Friday** – Short, digestible episodes by Microsoft engineers

- **The Azure Podcast** – Weekly discussions from the Azure product team

- **CloudSkills.fm** – Career-focused interviews with cloud professionals

- **Architecting the Cloud** – Covers hybrid and enterprise Azure strategies

---

Certification and Exam Practice Resources

For exam-focused preparation, mock tests and flashcards help reinforce knowledge.

Practice Test Providers:

- Whizlabs (AZ-900 to AZ-305)

- MeasureUp (Microsoft's official partner)

- Tutorials Dojo

- ExamTopics (Community-contributed questions)

Flashcards:

- Anki Decks for AZ-900, AZ-104, and others

- Quizlet decks by certified professionals

Exam Strategy Tip:

Use spaced repetition to retain core facts. Try reviewing the same set of questions over several days to reinforce memory.

GitHub, Code Samples, and Projects

Building real projects not only solidifies learning but also builds a public portfolio.

Ideas to Start With:

- Deploy a personal portfolio website with Azure Static Web Apps and GitHub Actions

- Create a serverless backend using Azure Functions, Logic Apps, and Cosmos DB

- Automate infrastructure deployment using Bicep or Terraform

Example Repo Structure:

```
azure-projects/

├── static-site-deployment/

│   ├── bicep/

│   └── GitHubActions/

├── serverless-api/

│   ├── functions/

│   ├── arm-templates/
```

├── vm-provisioning/

│   └── terraform/

Continuous Learning Strategy

Here's a long-term roadmap to guide your continued Azure education:

Quarter 1: Foundations

- Complete AZ-900 and related Microsoft Learn paths

- Explore Azure CLI, Portal, and core services

- Deploy a sample web app

Quarter 2: Role-Based Certification

- Choose a specialization (Admin, Dev, Architect)

- Study for AZ-104 or AZ-204

- Complete at least 2–3 projects on GitHub

Quarter 3: Advanced Practice

- Implement CI/CD pipelines

- Explore Infrastructure as Code with Bicep/Terraform

- Contribute to open-source or community blogs

Quarter 4: Real-World Integration

- Practice enterprise patterns (e.g., high availability, cost optimization)

- Study for AZ-305 or DevOps Expert (AZ-400)

- Attend at least one live event or conference

Conclusion

The Azure ecosystem is expansive, but so are the resources available to help you master it. Whether you're learning from Microsoft Learn, deploying your first project, or preparing for an expert-level exam, there's a wealth of tutorials, tools, and communities to guide your journey.

Bookmark, revisit, and update your learning toolkit regularly. Embrace continuous learning not just as a strategy for certifications, but as an approach to long-term cloud success. The more you engage with Azure hands-on, the faster you'll gain the confidence and depth needed to design, build, and scale impactful cloud solutions.

Sample Projects and Code Snippets

One of the most effective ways to solidify your Azure knowledge is by applying it in real-world projects. This section provides a curated collection of hands-on sample projects along with code snippets, deployment strategies, architectural guidance, and explanations of why each project matters. Whether you're a beginner looking for a guided experience or an intermediate learner seeking to build a portfolio, these projects will give you confidence, credibility, and competence in Microsoft Azure.

Project 1: Deploying a Static Website Using Azure Storage

Overview

This project demonstrates how to host a static website (HTML, CSS, JS) using Azure Blob Storage.

Use Cases

- Personal portfolio

- Documentation site

- Landing pages

Steps

1. Create a storage account:

```
az storage account create \
  --name mystaticsite \
```

```
    --resource-group WebRG \

    --location eastus \

    --sku Standard_LRS \

    --kind StorageV2 \

    --access-tier Hot
```

2. Enable static website hosting:

```
az storage blob service-properties update \

    --account-name mystaticsite \

    --static-website \

    --index-document index.html \

    --error-document 404.html
```

3. Upload content to the $web container:

```
az storage blob upload-batch \

    --account-name mystaticsite \

    --destination \$web \

    --source ./site-content
```

4. Visit the provided endpoint to access your site.

Key Concepts

- Blob Storage

- Azure CLI

- Static Web Hosting

Project 2: Serverless API with Azure Functions and Cosmos DB

Overview

This project builds an HTTP-triggered Azure Function that reads/writes data to Cosmos DB, creating a basic serverless API.

Use Cases

- Microservices

- APIs for mobile/web apps

- Event-driven systems

Architecture

- Azure Functions (HTTP trigger)

- Azure Cosmos DB (NoSQL)

- Azure Application Insights (monitoring)

Code Snippet (C#)

```
public static class CreateNote

{

    [FunctionName("CreateNote")]

    public static async Task<IActionResult> Run(

        [HttpTrigger(AuthorizationLevel.Function, "post", Route =
null)] HttpRequest req,

        [CosmosDB(

            databaseName: "NotesDb",

            containerName: "Notes",
```

```
            Connection = "CosmosDbConnection")]
IAsyncCollector<Note> notesOut,

        ILogger log)

    {

        string requestBody = await new
StreamReader(req.Body).ReadToEndAsync();

        var input =
JsonConvert.DeserializeObject<Note>(requestBody);

        await notesOut.AddAsync(input);

        return new OkObjectResult(input);

    }

}
```

Deployment

Use Azure CLI or VS Code Azure Functions extension.

```
func azure functionapp publish my-function-api
```

Project 3: Infrastructure as Code with Bicep

Overview

This project demonstrates using Bicep to provision an App Service and a SQL Database.

Use Cases

- Automating cloud deployments

- Reproducible environments

- CI/CD integration

Bicep Template

```
param location string = resourceGroup().location

param appName string

param sqlServerName string

param sqlAdmin string

param sqlPassword string


resource appServicePlan 'Microsoft.Web/serverfarms@2022-03-01' = {

  name: '${appName}-plan'

  location: location

  sku: {

    name: 'F1'

    tier: 'Free'

  }

}


resource appService 'Microsoft.Web/sites@2022-03-01' = {

  name: appName

  location: location

  properties: {

    serverFarmId: appServicePlan.id

  }

}


resource sqlServer 'Microsoft.Sql/servers@2022-02-01-preview' = {
```

```
  name: sqlServerName

  location: location

  properties: {

    administratorLogin: sqlAdmin

    administratorLoginPassword: sqlPassword

  }

}


resource sqlDb 'Microsoft.Sql/servers/databases@2022-02-01-preview'
= {

  name: '${sqlServer.name}/myappdb'

  properties: {

    readScale: 'Disabled'

  }

}
```

Deployment

```
az deployment group create \

  --resource-group MyRG \

  --template-file main.bicep \

  --parameters appName=myapp sqlServerName=sqlserver123
sqlAdmin=adminuser sqlPassword=P@ssword123
```

Project 4: Multi-Tier Web Application with CI/CD

Overview

Deploy a frontend, backend, and database with automated pipelines using Azure DevOps or GitHub Actions.

Architecture

- Frontend: React app in Azure Static Web Apps

- Backend: .NET Core API in Azure App Service

- Database: Azure SQL

- CI/CD: GitHub Actions

GitHub Actions Workflow (for Backend)

```
name: Deploy API


on:
  push:
    branches: [main]


jobs:
  build-and-deploy:
    runs-on: ubuntu-latest
    steps:
      - uses: actions/checkout@v2
      - name: Setup .NET
        uses: actions/setup-dotnet@v1
        with:
          dotnet-version: '6.0.x'
      - name: Build
```

```
      run: dotnet build

    - name: Publish

      run: dotnet publish -c Release -o ./publish

    - name: Deploy to Azure

      uses: azure/webapps-deploy@v2

      with:

        app-name: 'my-api-app'

        publish-profile: ${{ secrets.AZURE_PUBLISH_PROFILE }}

        package: ./publish
```

Project 5: IoT Data Ingestion with Event Hub and Stream Analytics

Overview

Build a system that ingests sensor data and writes to a dashboard-ready data store.

Components

- Azure IoT Hub

- Azure Event Hub

- Azure Stream Analytics

- Azure Blob Storage or Azure SQL

Stream Analytics Query Example

```
SELECT

  DeviceId,

  AVG(Temperature) AS AvgTemp,

  System.Timestamp AS TimeWindow
```

```
INTO

  [output]

FROM

  [input]

TIMESTAMP BY EventEnqueuedUtcTime

GROUP BY

  TumblingWindow(minute, 1), DeviceId
```

Project 6: Azure DevOps Pipeline for Terraform

Overview

Deploy resources using Terraform through Azure DevOps pipeline.

Pipeline YAML

```yaml
trigger:

  branches:

    include:

      - main


pool:

  vmImage: 'ubuntu-latest'


steps:

- checkout: self

- task: TerraformInstaller@0

  inputs:
```

```
    terraformVersion: '1.4.0'

- script: terraform init

- script: terraform plan -out tfplan

- script: terraform apply tfplan
```

Project 7: Secure Web App with Key Vault Integration

Overview

Build a web app that retrieves secrets from Azure Key Vault securely using a managed identity.

Backend Code (C#)

```csharp
var kvUri = "https://myvault.vault.azure.net/";

var client = new SecretClient(new Uri(kvUri), new
DefaultAzureCredential());

KeyVaultSecret secret = await
client.GetSecretAsync("DbConnectionString");

string dbConnStr = secret.Value;
```

Key Concepts

- Managed Identity

- Key Vault access policies

- Secure coding practices

Project 8: Cost Optimization Dashboard

Overview

Create a dashboard that visualizes Azure costs using Cost Management APIs and Power BI.

Components

- Azure Cost Management + Billing API

- Azure Functions or Logic App to fetch data

- Power BI for dashboard visualization

API Sample Request

```
GET
https://management.azure.com/subscriptions/{subscriptionId}/provider
s/Microsoft.CostManagement/query?api-version=2023-03-01

Content-Type: application/json


{

  "type": "Usage",

  "timeframe": "MonthToDate",

  "dataset": {

    "granularity": "Daily",

    "aggregation": {

      "totalCost": {

        "name": "PreTaxCost",

        "function": "Sum"

      }

    }

  }

}
```

Building and Showcasing Your Portfolio

Once you've built multiple projects, organize them in a portfolio repository or website.

Tips:

- Use GitHub READMEs with architecture diagrams, tech stacks, and deployment instructions.

- Deploy your portfolio using Azure Static Web Apps.

- Include links to your LinkedIn and certifications.

Example Repo Layout:

```
azure-portfolio/
├── static-website/
├── serverless-api/
├── bicep-infra/
├── devops-terraform/
├── dashboard-powerbi/
└── README.md
```

Conclusion

These sample projects and code snippets demonstrate a range of Azure services and patterns—from static hosting to complex multi-tier applications, automation, DevOps pipelines, serverless computing, and cost monitoring. Each project reinforces concepts in a practical way and offers real value to your learning journey and professional portfolio.

By building and refining these projects, you gain not just technical know-how but also the ability to think critically, solve real-world problems, and communicate your solutions effectively to peers and employers. Keep experimenting, keep coding, and keep deploying— your next Azure opportunity might come from a project you build today.

API Reference Guide

Understanding Azure APIs and how to interact with them is essential for developers, DevOps engineers, automation specialists, and architects. Microsoft Azure offers a wide range of REST APIs, SDKs, and service-specific endpoints that enable automation, integration, and customization of cloud operations. This section serves as a practical reference guide for working with Azure APIs—covering the REST architecture, authentication, common endpoints, SDK usage, and sample implementations.

Introduction to Azure REST APIs

Azure provides REST APIs to manage every resource within its ecosystem, including compute, storage, networking, identity, and more. REST (Representational State Transfer) is an architectural style that uses HTTP methods for communication.

Common HTTP methods:

- **GET** – Retrieve resource data

- **POST** – Create a resource

- **PUT** – Replace an existing resource

- **PATCH** – Update part of a resource

- **DELETE** – Remove a resource

Example: Listing all virtual machines in a subscription.

```
GET
https://management.azure.com/subscriptions/{subscriptionId}/provider
s/Microsoft.Compute/virtualMachines?api-version=2022-11-01
```

Authentication with Azure APIs

Before accessing Azure REST APIs, you must authenticate using Azure Active Directory (Azure AD). Authentication is typically performed using OAuth 2.0 and Azure AD tokens.

Steps to Authenticate:

1. Register an app in Azure AD.

2. Get client ID, tenant ID, and client secret.

3. Request a token using the OAuth 2.0 endpoint.

4. Use the token in the Authorization header for subsequent API requests.

Token Request (via cURL):

```
curl -X POST
https://login.microsoftonline.com/{tenantId}/oauth2/token \

  -H "Content-Type: application/x-www-form-urlencoded" \

  -d
"grant_type=client_credentials&client_id={clientId}&client_secret={c
lientSecret}&resource=https://management.azure.com/"
```

Using the Token:

```
GET
https://management.azure.com/subscriptions/{subscriptionId}/resource
groups?api-version=2022-09-01

Authorization: Bearer eyJ0eXAiOiJKV1QiLCJhbGciOiJ...
```

Key Azure API Endpoints

Below are commonly used endpoints categorized by service. Each includes a sample request format and description.

Resource Groups

- **List Resource Groups**

```
GET
https://management.azure.com/subscriptions/{subscriptionId}/resource
groups?api-version=2022-09-01
```

- **Create/Update a Resource Group**

```
PUT
https://management.azure.com/subscriptions/{subscriptionId}/resource
groups/{resourceGroupName}?api-version=2022-09-01

Content-Type: application/json


{

  "location": "eastus"

}
```

- **Delete a Resource Group**

```
DELETE
https://management.azure.com/subscriptions/{subscriptionId}/resource
groups/{resourceGroupName}?api-version=2022-09-01
```

Virtual Machines

- **List VMs**

```
GET
https://management.azure.com/subscriptions/{subscriptionId}/provider
s/Microsoft.Compute/virtualMachines?api-version=2022-11-01
```

- **Start a VM**

```
POST
https://management.azure.com/subscriptions/{subscriptionId}/resource
Groups/{resourceGroupName}/providers/Microsoft.Compute/virtualMachin
es/{vmName}/start?api-version=2022-11-01
```

- **Stop a VM**

```
POST
https://management.azure.com/subscriptions/{subscriptionId}/resource
Groups/{resourceGroupName}/providers/Microsoft.Compute/virtualMachin
es/{vmName}/deallocate?api-version=2022-11-01
```

Storage Accounts

- **List Storage Accounts**

```
GET
https://management.azure.com/subscriptions/{subscriptionId}/provider
s/Microsoft.Storage/storageAccounts?api-version=2022-09-01
```

- **Create Storage Account**

```
PUT
https://management.azure.com/subscriptions/{subscriptionId}/resource
Groups/{resourceGroupName}/providers/Microsoft.Storage/storageAccoun
ts/{accountName}?api-version=2022-09-01

Content-Type: application/json


{

  "location": "eastus",
```

```
  "sku": {

    "name": "Standard_LRS"

  },

  "kind": "StorageV2",

  "properties": {}

}
```

App Services

- **List Web Apps**

```
GET
https://management.azure.com/subscriptions/{subscriptionId}/provider
s/Microsoft.Web/sites?api-version=2022-03-01
```

- **Restart a Web App**

```
POST
https://management.azure.com/subscriptions/{subscriptionId}/resource
Groups/{resourceGroupName}/providers/Microsoft.Web/sites/{appName}/r
estart?api-version=2022-03-01
```

Azure SDKs

While REST APIs offer granular control, SDKs simplify the development process. Microsoft provides SDKs for .NET, Java, Python, JavaScript, Go, and others.

Example: Using Azure SDK for Python to List Resource Groups

```python
from azure.identity import DefaultAzureCredential

from azure.mgmt.resource import ResourceManagementClient
```

```
credential = DefaultAzureCredential()

subscription_id = 'xxxxxxxx-xxxx-xxxx-xxxx-xxxxxxxxxxxx'


client = ResourceManagementClient(credential, subscription_id)


for rg in client.resource_groups.list():
    print(f"Resource Group: {rg.name} - Location: {rg.location}")
```

Installing SDKs

```
pip install azure-mgmt-resource azure-identity
```

Or for .NET:

```
dotnet add package Azure.Identity
dotnet add package Azure.ResourceManager
```

Using Microsoft Graph API with Azure

Microsoft Graph is the gateway to data and intelligence in Microsoft 365 and also interacts with Azure AD.

List Users:

```
GET https://graph.microsoft.com/v1.0/users

Authorization: Bearer {access_token}
```

Create User:

```
POST https://graph.microsoft.com/v1.0/users

Content-Type: application/json


{

  "accountEnabled": true,

  "displayName": "John Doe",

  "mailNickname": "johnd",

  "userPrincipalName": "johnd@example.com",

  "passwordProfile" : {

    "forceChangePasswordNextSignIn": true,

    "password": "Password123!"

  }

}
```

Error Handling

Azure REST APIs return standard HTTP status codes to indicate success or failure.

Status Code	Description
200 OK	Request succeeded
201 Created	Resource created
400 Bad Request	Invalid input or syntax

401 Unauthorized	Missing or invalid token
403 Forbidden	Insufficient permissions
404 Not Found	Resource not found
409 Conflict	Resource already exists
500 Internal Server Error	Azure-side failure

Always log and parse response messages for debugging and use retry logic where appropriate.

Tools for Testing APIs

- **Postman** – Great for sending test requests and visualizing responses.

- **Insomnia** – Lightweight REST client with environment and plugin support.

- **cURL** – CLI-based HTTP client, ideal for automation.

- **PowerShell + Invoke-RestMethod** – Native support for RESTful operations in scripting.

Example using PowerShell:

```
$token = "Bearer eyJ0eXAiOiJKV1QiLC..."

Invoke-RestMethod -Uri
"https://management.azure.com/subscriptions/{subscriptionId}/resourc
egroups?api-version=2022-09-01" `

  -Headers @{ Authorization = $token } `

  -Method Get
```

Best Practices

- Use service principals and managed identities instead of user tokens.

- Always validate input and sanitize parameters.

- Paginate responses when dealing with large datasets.

- Use API versioning to maintain consistency.

- Secure secrets with Azure Key Vault.

- Implement exponential backoff for retry logic.

Conclusion

This API reference guide equips you with the knowledge and tools to programmatically interact with Azure services. Whether through REST endpoints or SDK libraries, mastering Azure APIs enables automation, integration, and greater control over your cloud infrastructure. By using authenticated requests, following best practices, and leveraging tools like Postman and SDKs, you can build scalable, secure, and efficient solutions tailored to your organization's needs.

Make API interaction a core part of your skillset, and you'll unlock the full potential of Azure in both development and operational scenarios.

Frequently Asked Questions

As you progress through your Azure learning and implementation journey, questions will naturally arise. Whether you're preparing for certification, deploying a production workload, exploring new services, or just getting started, this section compiles the most frequently asked questions (FAQs) about Microsoft Azure. These questions are grouped by category to make them easier to navigate and revisit as needed.

General Azure Questions

Q: What is Microsoft Azure?
A: Azure is Microsoft's cloud computing platform, offering over 200 services including compute, storage, networking, databases, artificial intelligence, analytics, DevOps, and Internet of Things (IoT). It enables users to build, deploy, and manage applications globally using Microsoft-managed data centers.

Q: Is Azure only for Windows-based workloads?
 A: No. Azure supports a wide range of operating systems, programming languages, frameworks, and databases—including Linux, Java, Python, PHP, PostgreSQL, and MySQL. Azure is an open cloud and works well for both Microsoft and non-Microsoft stacks.

Q: What's the difference between a region and an availability zone?
 A:

- A **region** is a geographic location with one or more data centers.

- An **availability zone** is a physically separate location within a region, designed for high availability and fault tolerance. Each region may contain multiple zones.

Account and Subscription Management

Q: What's the difference between a subscription and a resource group?
 A:

- A **subscription** defines the billing boundary and container for resources.

- A **resource group** is a logical container that holds related resources for an Azure solution and is used for organizing, managing access, and lifecycle.

Q: Can I have multiple Azure subscriptions under the same account?
 A: Yes. You can create multiple subscriptions under one Azure AD tenant. This is commonly used for separating environments (Dev/Test/Prod), managing cost centers, or assigning different policies.

Q: How can I estimate the cost of using Azure services?
 A: Use the **Azure Pricing Calculator** (https://azure.microsoft.com/en-us/pricing/calculator/) and **Cost Management + Billing** in the portal for real-time cost tracking, forecasting, and optimization.

Azure Resource Management

Q: How do I deploy resources programmatically?
 A: Use Infrastructure as Code (IaC) tools such as:

- **ARM Templates**

- **Bicep**

- Terraform

- Azure CLI / PowerShell

Q: What's the best way to manage access to resources?
A: Use **Role-Based Access Control (RBAC)** to assign roles like Reader, Contributor, or Owner to users, groups, or managed identities at the subscription, resource group, or resource level.

Q: Can I automate the shutdown/startup of VMs?
A: Yes. Use **Azure Automation**, **Logic Apps**, or **Azure Functions** with schedules or event triggers. For example, use this PowerShell runbook to shut down a VM:

```
Stop-AzVM -Name "MyVM" -ResourceGroupName "MyRG" -Force
```

Networking

Q: What is a Virtual Network (VNet)?
A: A VNet is a logically isolated section of the Azure network where you can deploy and manage Azure resources securely. Think of it as the Azure equivalent of an on-premises network.

Q: What are NSGs and how do they work?
A: Network Security Groups (NSGs) contain security rules that allow or deny network traffic to/from resources in a VNet. They can be applied to subnets or NICs.

Q: Can I create a VPN between my on-premises network and Azure?
A: Yes. You can use **Site-to-Site VPN**, **Point-to-Site VPN**, or **Azure ExpressRoute** for private, dedicated connectivity.

Compute

Q: What are my options for running code in Azure?
A:

- **Virtual Machines** (IaaS) for full OS-level control

- **App Services** for web and API hosting (PaaS)

- **Azure Functions** for event-driven serverless compute

- **Container Apps** and **Azure Kubernetes Service (AKS)** for containerized workloads

Q: How do I scale my application?
A: Azure provides multiple options:

- **App Service Plans** with auto-scaling rules

- **Virtual Machine Scale Sets (VMSS)**

- **Azure Functions Premium Plan**

- **Manual or scheduled scale via APIs or scripts**

Storage

Q: What types of storage does Azure offer?
A:

- **Blob Storage** – Object storage for unstructured data

- **File Storage** – Managed file shares

- **Queue Storage** – Message storage for decoupled communication

- **Table Storage** – NoSQL key-value store

- **Disk Storage** – Managed OS and data disks for VMs

Q: How do I secure access to storage accounts?
A: Use:

- **Access keys** (not recommended for production)

- **Shared Access Signatures (SAS)**

- **Azure AD Authentication**

- **Private Endpoints**

- **Firewall rules and VNet integration**

Identity and Security

Q: What is Azure AD and how is it different from on-prem AD?
A: Azure AD is a cloud-based identity service for managing users, groups, roles, and applications. Unlike on-prem Active Directory, Azure AD is built for internet-scale applications and supports OAuth2, OpenID Connect, and SAML.

Q: What is a managed identity?
A: A managed identity allows Azure services to authenticate securely without storing credentials in your code. It integrates directly with Azure AD and can be used to access services like Key Vault, Storage, and Azure SQL.

Q: How do I enforce multi-factor authentication (MFA)?
A: Configure MFA via **Conditional Access Policies** in Azure AD. You can require MFA based on group membership, location, or application.

Monitoring and Troubleshooting

Q: What tools can I use to monitor Azure resources?
A:

- **Azure Monitor** – Metrics and diagnostics

- **Log Analytics** – Queryable centralized logging

- **Application Insights** – APM for apps

- **Alerts and Action Groups** – Customizable responses to metrics/logs

Q: How can I track downtime or performance issues?
A: Use **Availability Tests** in Application Insights, or monitor Service Health in the portal. Set up alerts for CPU usage, response time, disk I/O, etc.

DevOps and Automation

Q: What is Azure DevOps?
A: A suite of services including:

- **Repos** (Git source control)

- **Pipelines** (CI/CD)

- **Boards** (Agile project management)

- **Artifacts** (package management)

- **Test Plans** (manual and exploratory testing)

Q: How do I deploy my app automatically?
 A: Use **Azure Pipelines**, **GitHub Actions**, or **Deployment Center** for App Services.
Example GitHub Actions for .NET:

```
name: Deploy to Azure

on:

  push:

    branches: [ main ]

jobs:

  build-and-deploy:

    runs-on: ubuntu-latest

    steps:

      - uses: actions/checkout@v2

      - name: Setup .NET

        uses: actions/setup-dotnet@v1

        with:

          dotnet-version: '6.0.x'

      - name: Publish

        run: dotnet publish -c Release -o output

      - name: Deploy

        uses: azure/webapps-deploy@v2

        with:
```

```
app-name: my-app

publish-profile: ${{ secrets.AZURE_PUBLISH_PROFILE }}

package: output
```

Databases and Analytics

Q: What database services does Azure offer?
A:

- **Azure SQL Database** – PaaS relational DB

- **SQL Managed Instance** – Lift-and-shift for SQL Server

- **Cosmos DB** – NoSQL multi-model database

- **Azure Database for PostgreSQL/MySQL**

- **Azure Synapse Analytics** – Data warehousing and analytics

Q: How can I monitor database performance?
A: Use **SQL Insights**, **Query Performance Insight**, and **Azure Monitor for databases**.

Certifications and Career

Q: What Azure certification should I start with?
A: Start with **AZ-900: Microsoft Azure Fundamentals**. Then choose:

- **AZ-104** for Administration

- **AZ-204** for Development

- **AZ-305** for Architecture

- **AZ-400** for DevOps

- **SC/D/AI/DP** series for specialties

Q: Do certifications expire?
A: Yes. Most role-based certifications are valid for one year and can be renewed online for free through Microsoft Learn.

Final Notes

Q: How do I stay up to date with Azure changes?
A:

- Subscribe to Azure Updates

- Follow Azure Blog

- Join Microsoft Learn, GitHub, and community forums

- Attend Microsoft Ignite, Build, and virtual events

Q: What's the best way to learn Azure hands-on?
A:

- Use the **Azure Free Tier**

- Complete **Microsoft Learn labs**

- Deploy sample apps via GitHub

- Try services like Functions, Storage, and App Service

- Build a portfolio of real projects

Conclusion

This FAQ section serves as a quick-access repository for common Azure concerns across administration, development, architecture, security, networking, and DevOps. Use it as your go-to checklist for certification prep, project work, and daily cloud operations. If you're ever stuck, chances are the answer is already in here—or just one Microsoft Learn module or API call away. Keep building, keep exploring, and keep asking questions. That's how true cloud fluency is forged.

TABLE OF CONTENTS

INTRODUCTION

Kali Linux is the current Linux distribution from Offensive Security, customized for the unique purposes of carrying out network security audits and forensic examinations. Kali comes totally filled with numerous incorporated tools to perform every element of a penetration test.

Kali Linux-- Backtrack Evolved: A Penetration Tester's Guide helps you to establish beneficial and useful professional abilities in the info security market, while simultaneously delivering the high level of enjoyment and enjoyment that goes hand-in-hand with the world of computer and network hacking.

Cyber-crime is on the rise and information security is becoming more paramount than ever before. A single attack on a business's network infrastructure can frequently result in irreparable damage to a company's possessions and/or credibility.

It is no longer sufficient to simply rely on traditional security steps. In order to ensure the security of vital info possessions, it is vital to end up being knowledgeable about the methods, tactics, and techniques that are utilized by real hackers who look for to compromise your network.

Kali Linux-- Backtrack Evolved: A Penetration Tester's Guide will prepare you to go into the world of expert hacking by making sure that you are well versed with the abilities required and tools utilized to compromise the security of business networks and info systems.

Kali Linux is one of the best security plans of an ethical hacker, including a set of tools divided by the classifications. It is an open source and its main website is https://www.kali.org.

Usually, Kali Linux can be set up in a maker as an Operating System, as a virtual machine which we will discuss in the following section. Setting Up Kali Linux is an useful choice as it offers more options to work and combine the tools.

BackTrack was the old version of Kali Linux circulation. The most recent release is Kali 2016.1 and it is updated really typically.

INSTALLING KALI ON A VM

To install Kali Linux –

We will download the Virtual box and install it.

Later on, we will set up and download Kali Linux distribution.

Download and Install the Virtual Box

A Virtual Box is particularly beneficial when you wish to check something on Kali Linux that you are not sure of. When you want to experiment with unknown bundles or when you want to test a code, running Kali Linux on a Virtual Box is safe.

With the help of a Virtual Box, you can install Kali Linux on your system (not straight in your hard disk) alongside your main OS which can MAC or Windows or another taste of Linux.

Let's understand how you can download and set up the Virtual Box on your system.

Action 1 – To download, go to https://www.virtualbox.org/wiki/Downloads. Depending on your operating system, pick the best package. In this case, it will be the very first one for Windows as shown in the following screenshot.

7

VirtualBox

Download VirtualBox

Here, you will find links to VirtualBox binaries and its source code.

VirtualBox binaries

By downloading, you agree to the terms and conditions of the respective license.

- VirtualBox platform packages. The binaries are released under the terms of the GPL version 2.
  - VirtualBox 5.1.2 for Windows hosts ⇒x86/amd64
  - VirtualBox 5.1.2 for OS X hosts ⇒amd64
  - VirtualBox 5.1.2 for Linux hosts
  - VirtualBox 5.1.2 for Solaris hosts ⇒amd64
- VirtualBox 5.1.2 Oracle VM VirtualBox Extension Pack ⇒All supported platforms
  Support for USB 2.0 and USB 3.0 devices, VirtualBox RDP and PXE boot for Intel cards. See this chapter from the User Manual for an introduct
  Extension Pack binaries are released under the VirtualBox Personal Use and Evaluation License (PUEL).
  Please install the extension pack with the same version as your installed version of VirtualBox:
  If you are using VirtualBox 5.0.26, please download the extension pack ⇒here.
  If you are using VirtualBox 4.3.38, please download the extension pack ⇒here.

Step 2 – Click Next.

Step 3 – The next page will provide you options to select the area where you wish to set up the application. In this case, let us leave it as default and click Next.

Step 4 – Click Next and the following Custom Setup screenshot pops up. Select the functions you wish to be installed and click Next.

8

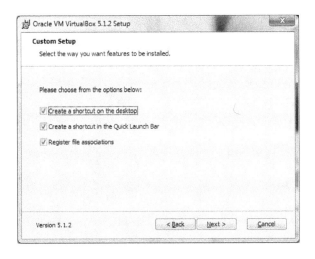

Step 5 – Click Yes to proceed with the setup

Step 6 – The Ready to Install screen turns up. Click Install

Action 7 – Click the Finish button.

The Virtual Box application will now open as displayed in the following screenshot. Now we are ready to set up the rest of the hosts for this manual and this is likewise suggested for expert use.

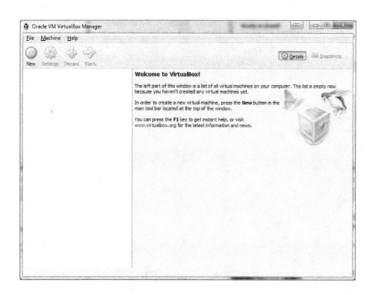

Install Kali Linux

Now that we have effectively installed the Virtual Box, let's proceed to the next step and set up Kali Linux.

Step 1 – Download the Kali Linux bundle from its official website: https://www.kali.org/downloads/

Step 2 – Click VirtualBox → New as shown in the following screenshot.

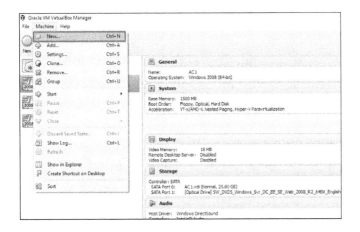

Step 3 − Choose the right virtual hard disk file and click Open.

Step 4 − The following screenshot turns up. Click the Create button.

Step 5 − Start Kali OS. The default username is root and the password is toor.

Update Kali

It is necessary to keep updating Kali Linux and its tools to the brand-new variations, to stay practical. Following are the actions to update Kali.

Action 1 – Go to Application → Terminal. Type "apt-get upgrade" and the upgrade will take location as revealed in the following screenshot.

Step 2 – Now to update the tools, type "apt-get upgrade" and the brand-new bundles will be downloaded.

Step 3 – It will ask if you want to continue. Type "Y" and "Enter".

Step 4 – To update to a newer version of Operating System, type "apt-get distupgrade".

Laboratory Setup

In this section, we will establish another screening maker to perform the tests with the help of tools of Kali Linux.

Action 1 − Download Metasploitable, which is a Linux machine. It can be downloaded from the main website of Rapid7: https://information.rapid7.com/metasploitabledownloa d.html?LS=1631875&CS=web

Step 2 − Register by providing your information. After filling the type, you can download the software application.

Step 3 − Click VirtualBox → New.

Step 4 − Click "Use an existing virtual hard drive file". Browse the file where you have downloaded Metasploitable and click Open.

Step 5 – A screen to create a virtual machine appears. Click "Create".

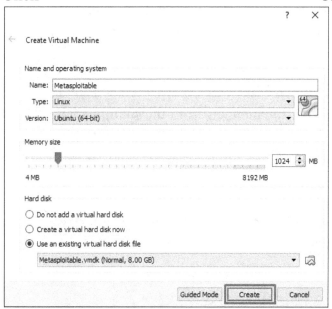

The default username is msfadmin and the password is msfadmin.

THE BEST PRE-INSTALLED TOOLS TO GET YOU STARTED WITH KALI LINUX

Since this is an easy introductory to the Kali Linux distro i will present to you a few of the best pre-installed tools for a beginner hacker.

1. ProxyChains

ProxyChains can cover practically anything you want to do. For instance, i want to use ProxyChains to cover NMAP

The command:

~$ proxychains nmap -sS -O scanme.nmap.org/24

This command releases a stealth SYN scan against each machine that depends on 256 IPs on the class C sized network where Scanme lives, and it gets cover by ProxyChains.

Prior to you utilize ProxyChains, you need to configure it.-- > Configure ProxyChains Tutorial

2. WhoIs

WhoIs is a database handled by regional web registrars, it is an inquiry and response protocol that is commonly used for querying databases that store the signed up users of an Internet resource, such as domain name ot an IP address block, but it is also utilized for a broader series of other individual information about the domain owner.

Here is an easy whois output for duthcode.com.

root@kali:~# whois duthcode.com

Domain: DUTHCODE.COM

Registry Domain ID: 2218163516_DOMAIN_COM-VRSN

Registrar WHOIS Server: whois.papaki.gr

Registrar URL: http://www.papaki.gr

Updated Date: 2019-01-11T19:42:46 Z.

Creation Date: 2018-01-24T21:47:52 Z.

Registry Expiry Date: 2020-01-24T21:47:52 Z.

Registrar: Papaki Ltd

. Registrar IANA ID: 1727.

Registrar Abuse Contact Email: abuse@papaki.gr.

Registrar Abuse Contact Phone: +30 211-800-2275.
Domain Status: clientTransferProhibited https://icann.org/epp#clientTransferProhibited.
Domain Status: clientUpdateProhibited https://icann.org/epp#clientUpdateProhibited. Call Server: NS1.ADOPT-HOST. CLOUD.

Name Server: NS2.ADOPT-HOST. CLOUD.

DNSSEC: unsigned.

URL of the ICANN Whois Inaccuracy Complaint Form: https://www.icann.org/wicf/ ...

3. NMAP.

NMap (Network Mapper) is a totally free and open-source energy utilized for network discovery and security auditing.

NMAP is my individual favorite because it's Flexible, Portable, FREE, Powerful and really ... really Famous, for that reason you can discover a huge selection of various tutorials matching your every need. Visit NMAP Official Page.

NMAP has likewise been included in The Matrix!

Trinity using NMAP.

Here we see Trinity doing an NMAP scan in order to find a vulnerable SSH Server inside the power grid's internal network.

See ran the following command :

nmap -v -sS -O 10.2.2.2

Command Explanation :

-v : increase verbosity Level

-sS : TCP Scan

-O : Enabling Operating System Detection

You can easily get all the available nmap commands by running in your kali Terminal the following command

root@kali:~# nmap -h

Nmap 7.70 (https://nmap.org)

Usage: nmap [Scan Type(s)] [Options] {target specification}

TARGET SPECIFICATION:

Can pass hostnames, IP addresses, networks, etc.

Ex: scanme.nmap.org, microsoft.com/24, 192.168.0.1; 10.0.0-255.1-254

-iL <inputfilename>: Input from list of hosts/networks

-iR <num hosts>: Choose random targets

--exclude <host1[,host2][,host3],...>: Exclude hosts/networks

--excludefile <exclude_file>: Exclude list from file

HOST DISCOVERY:

-sL: List Scan - simply list targets to scan

-sn: Ping Scan - disable port scan

-Pn: Treat all hosts as online -- skip host discovery

-PS/PA/PU/PY[portlist]: TCP SYN/ACK, UDP or SCTP discovery to given ports

-PE/PP/PM: ICMP echo, timestamp, and netmask re□uest discovery probes

-PO[protocol list]: IP Protocol Ping

-n/-R: Never do DNS resolution/Always resolve [default: sometimes]

--dns-servers <serv1[,serv2],...>: Specify custom DNS servers

--system-dns: Use OS's DNS resolver

--traceroute: Trace hop path to each host

SCAN TECHNIQUES:

-sS/sT/sA/sW/sM: TCP SYN/Connect()/ACK/Window/Maimon scans

-sU: UDP Scan

-sN/sF/sX: TCP Null, FIN, and Xmas scans

--scanflags <flags>: Customize TCP scan flags

-sI <zombie host[:probeport]>: Idle scan

-sY/sZ: SCTP INIT/COOKIE-ECHO scans

-sO: IP protocol scan

-b <FTP relay host>: FTP bounce scan

PORT SPECIFICATION AND SCAN ORDER:

-p <port ranges>: Only scan specified ports

Ex: -p22; -p1-65535; -p U:53,111,137,T:21-25,80,139,8080,S:9

--exclude-ports <port ranges>: Exclude the specified ports from scanning

-F: Fast mode - Scan fewer ports than the default scan

-r: Scan ports consecutively - don't randomize

--top-ports <number>: Scan <number> most common ports

--port-ratio <ratio>: Scan ports more common than <ratio>

SERVICE/VERSION DETECTION:

-sV: Probe open ports to determine service/version info

--version-intensity <level>: Set from 0 (light) to 9 (try all probes)

--version-light: Limit to most likely probes (intensity 2)

--version-all: Try every single probe (intensity 9)

--version-trace: Show detailed version scan activity (for debugging)

SCRIPT SCAN:

-sC: e□uivalent to --script=default

--script=<Lua scripts>: <Lua scripts> is a comma separated list of

    directories, script-files or script-categories

--script-args=<n1=v1,[n2=v2,...]>: provide arguments to scripts

--script-args-file=filename: provide NSE script args in a file

--script-trace: Show all data sent and received

--script-updatedb: Update the script database.

--script-help=<Lua scripts>: Show help about scripts.

   <Lua scripts> is a comma-separated list of script-files or

   script-categories.

OS DETECTION:

-O: Enable OS detection

--osscan-limit: Limit OS detection to promising targets

--osscan-guess: Guess OS more aggressively

TIMING AND PERFORMANCE:

Options which take <time> are in seconds, or append 'ms' (milliseconds),

's' (seconds), 'm' (minutes), or 'h' (hours) to the value (e.g. 30m).

-T<0-5>: Set timing template (higher is faster)

--min-hostgroup/max-hostgroup <size>: Parallel host scan group sizes

--min-parallelism/max-parallelism <numprobes>: Probe parallelization

--min-rtt-timeout/max-rtt-timeout/initial-rtt-timeout <time>: Specifies

probe round trip time.

--max-retries <tries>: Caps number of port scan probe retransmissions.

--host-timeout <time>: Give up on target after this long

--scan-delay/--max-scan-delay <time>: Adjust delay between probes

--min-rate <number>: Send packets no slower than <number> per second

--max-rate <number>: Send packets no faster than <number> per second

FIREWALL/IDS EVASION AND SPOOFING:

-f; --mtu <val>: fragment packets (optionally w/given MTU)

-D <decoy1,decoy2[,ME],...>: Cloak a scan with decoys

-S <IP_Address>: Spoof source address

-e <iface>: Use specified interface

-g/--source-port <portnum>: Use given port number

--proxies <url1,[url2],...>: Relay connections through HTTP/SOCKS4 proxies

--data <hex string>: Append a custom payload to sent packets

--data-string <string>: Append a custom ASCII string to sent packets

--data-length <num>: Append random data to sent packets

--ip-options <options>: Send packets with specified ip options

--ttl <val>: Set IP time-to-live field

--spoof-mac <mac address/prefix/vendor name>: Spoof your MAC address

--badsum: Send packets with a bogus TCP/UDP/SCTP checksum

OUTPUT:

-oN/-oX/-oS/-oG <file>: Output scan in normal, XML, s|<rIpt kIddi3,

and Grepable format, respectively, to the given filename.

-oA <basename>: Output in the three major formats at once

-v: Increase verbosity level (use -vv or more for greater effect)

-d: Increase debugging level (use -dd or more for greater effect)

--reason: Display the reason a port is in a particular state

--open: Only show open (or possibly open) ports

--packet-trace: Show all packets sent and received

--iflist: Print host interfaces and routes (for debugging)

--append-output: Append to rather than clobber specified output files

--resume <filename>: Resume an aborted scan

--stylesheet <path/URL>: XSL stylesheet to transform XML output to HTML

--webxml: Reference stylesheet from Nmap.Org for more portable XML

--no-stylesheet: Prevent associating of XSL stylesheet w/XML output

MISC:

-6: Enable IPv6 scanning

-A: Enable OS detection, version detection, script scanning, and traceroute

--datadir <dirname>: Specify custom Nmap data file location

--send-eth/--send-ip: Send using raw ethernet frames or IP packets

--privileged: Assume that the user is fully privileged

--unprivileged: Assume the user lacks raw socket privileges

-V: Print version number

-h: Print this help summary page.

EXAMPLES:

nmap -v -A scanme.nmap.org

nmap -v -sn 192.168.0.0/16 10.0.0.0/8

3. HTTRACK

This tool i love. Httrack is a website cloner, from a penetration screening viewpoint, it is mainly used to develop a phony site and utilize it for some phising purpose. But a tool never has only one use. Just to provide you a concept, you could easily clone the website that pops up whenever you link to free public coffee bar wifi and constract your own captive portal attack. Food for thought.

You can run httrack wizard by simply typing:

~$ httrack

You will then be prompted with a list of command recommendations to get you started using the tool.

4. THC Hydra

Hydra is the fastest network login cracker and it supports many attack procedures.

Basically when you need to brute force fracture a remote authentication service, Hydra is often the tool of option. It can perform fast dictionary attacks versus more than 50 procedures, including telnet, ftp, http(s), smb, a number of databases and far more.

root@kali:~# hydra -h

Hydra v7.6 (c)2013 by van Hauser/THC & David Maciejak - for legal purposes only

Syntax: hydra [[[-l LOGIN|-L FILE] [-p PASS|-P FILE]] | [-C FILE]] [-e nsr] [-o FILE] [-t TASKS] [-M FILE [-T TASKS]] [-w TIME] [-W TIME] [-f] [-s PORT] [-x MIN:MAX:CHARSET] [-SuvV46] [service://server[:PORT][/OPT]]

Options:

-R   restore a previous aborted/crashed session

-S   perform an SSL connect

-s PORT   if the service is on a different default port, define it here

-l LOGIN or -L FILE login with LOGIN name, or load several logins from FILE

-p PASS or -P FILE try password PASS, or load several passwords from FILE

-x MIN:MAX:CHARSET password bruteforce generation, type "-x -h" to get help

-e nsr try "n" null password, "s" login as pass and/or "r" reversed login

-u loop around users, not passwords (effective! implied with -x)

-C FILE colon separated "login:pass" format, instead of -L/-P options

-M FILE list of servers to be attacked in parallel, one entry per line

-o FILE write found login/password pairs to FILE instead of stdout

-f / -F exit when a login/pass pair is found (-M: -f per host, -F global)

-t TASKS run TASKS number of connects in parallel (per host, default: 16)

-w / -W TIME waittime for responses (32s) / between connects per thread

-4 / -6   prefer IPv4 (default) or IPv6 addresses

-v / -V / -d verbose mode / show login+pass for each attempt / debug mode

-U   service module usage details

server   the target server (use either this OR the -M option)

service   the service to crack (see below for supported protocols)

OPT   some service modules support additional input (-U for module help)

Supported services: asterisk afp cisco cisco-enable cvs firebird ftp ftps http[s]-{head|get} http[s]-{get|post}-form http-proxy http-proxy-urlenum ic☐ imap[s] irc ldap2[s] ldap3[-{cram|digest}md5][s] mssql mys☐l ncp nntp oracle-listener oracle-sid pcanywhere pcnfs pop3[s] postgres rdp rexec rlogin rsh s7-300 sip smb smtp[s] smtp-enum snmp socks5 ssh sshkey svn teamspeak telnet[s] vmauthd vnc xmpp

Hydra is a tool to guess/crack valid login/password pairs - usage only allowed for legal purposes. This tool is licensed under AGPL v3.0.

The newest version is always available at http://www.thc.org/thc-hydra

Use HYDRA_PROXY_HTTP or HYDRA_PROXY - and if needed HYDRA_PROXY_AUTH - environment for a proxy setup.

E.g.: % export HYDRA_PROXY=socks5://127.0.0.1:9150 (or socks4:// or connect://)

% export HYDRA_PROXY_HTTP=http://proxy:8080

% export HYDRA_PROXY_AUTH=user:pass

Examples:

hydra -l user -P passlist.txt ftp://192.168.0.1

hydra -L userlist.txt -p defaultpw imap://192.168.0.1/PLAIN

hydra -C defaults.txt -6 pop3s://[fe80::2c:31ff:fe12:ac11]:143/TLS:DIGEST-MD5

5. Aircrack-ng Suite

Aircrack-ng is a total suite of tools to examine WiFi network security.

It concentrates on various areas of WiFi security:

Tracking: Packet capture and export of information to text files for more processing by 3rd party tools.

Assaulting: Replay attacks, deauthentication, phony access points and others via packet injection.

Evaluating: Checking WiFi cards and driver abilities (capture and injection).

Cracking: WEP and WPA/WPA2 PSK.

All tools are command line which permits heavy scripting. A lot of guis have benefited from this feature.

This Suite includes:.

aircrack-ng|Cracks WEP secrets utilizing the FMS attack, PTW attack, and dictionary attacks and WPA/WPA2 PSK utilizing dictionary attacks.

airdecap-ng|Decrypts WEP or WPA encrypted capture files with recognized key.

airmon-ng|Putting various cards in display mode.

aireplay-ng|Packet injector (Linux and Windows with CommView chauffeurs).

airodump-ng|Packet sniffer: Places air traffic into pcap or IVS files and shows details about networks.

airtun-ng|Virtual tunnel user interface developer.

packetforce-ng|Produce encrypted packets for injection.

ivstools|Tools to convert and combine.

airbase-ng|Incorporates techniques for attacking customer, as opposed to Access Points.

airdecloak-ng|Eliminates WEP masking from pcap files.

airolib-ng|Stores and manages ESSID and password lists and compute Pairwise Master Keys.

airserv-ng|Enables to access the wireless card from other computers.

buddy-ng|The assistant server for easside-ng, run on a remote computer system.

easside-ng|A tool for communicating to an access point, without the WEP secret.

tkiptun-ng|WPA/TKIP attack.

wesside-ng|Automatic tool for recovering wep secret.

6. Wireshark.

Wireshark is a preferred, open-source and free network analyzer tool that is mainly used in network security auditing. Wireshark uses display filters for general package filtering. It provides the capability to drill down and check out the contents of each packet and is filtered to fulfill your particular needs.

Show only SMTP (port 25) and ICMP traffic:

port eq 25 or icmp

Show only traffic in the LAN (192.168.x.x), between workstations and servers, offline:

src==192.168.0.0/16 and ip.dist==192.168.0.0/16

TCP buffer full, Source is instructing Destination to stop sending data:

window_size == 0 && tcp.flags.reset !=1

Match HTTP re□uests where the last characters in the uri are the characters "lang=gr":

re□uest.uri matches "lang=gr$"

Filter against particular IP:

addr == 104.193.19.59

Display POST request method, mostly containing user password:

request.method == "POST"

To run wireshark, simply type "wireshark" in the terminal. It will open a graphical user interface. It will ask you to set the network interface that will be utilized.

7. Metasploit Framework

Metasploit is, without a doubt, the most pre-owned pen-testing structure. It is used to make use of vulnerabilities in daemons operating on an open port, in basic words, it runs in the background. It is very effective and is not easy too control. In numerous methods is a tool every hacker must master! Flexible, complimentary and loaded with a shit lots of choices, metasploit is unquestionably the coolest offensive tool of this list! You can ask anyone. The response will always be ... eehhh ... Metasploit ...

Before getting your hands dirty with this incredible tool you firt have to have a concept of these standard meanings:

What is a vulnerability?

What is a make use of?

What is a payload!!!?

Metasploit and all of its exploits are written in Ruby. Metasploit as four main user interfaces:

MsfCli

MsdConsole

MsfGui

Armitage

I Won't be entering much information about Metasploit as i will make a dedicated article about it and how to utilize its basic performances.

To run metasploit in Kali Linux you simply need to open a terminal and run

root@kali~# msfconsole

And you will be prompted with the following window! To have some fun for now type:

msf > banner

And your metasploit banner (little drawing) will change.

Just saying, the metasploit framework is actually something else and it can really co-operate with other tools in an extremely cool method!

LINUX COMMANDS

There have a lot of kali Linux commands specifically for running or dealing with any kind of define files, develop documents, maintaining ranges directory sites or composing script in Linux platform. Some of the basic Kali Linux commands are discussed below:

Command for getting Date: This is one of the typical commands for helping to show normal date with time in the Linux screen. It is also possible to set some of the customized dates which can be dealt with by using this specific command.

date-- set= '17 Jan 2019 12:16'

Performing the above command, constantly offered below outcome as output:

Thu Jan 17 12:18:20 EDT 2019

Command for showing Calendar: One of the essential commands of Kali Linux operating system is cal which really helps for displaying appropriate need calendar in Linux terminal screen where anyone can able to identify the regional date. There has a lot of additional calendar package available in case of Kali Linux command, where people can able to handle the calendar in ranges way, in some cases they can able to provide it vertically or some other crucial features with this extra command. This additional command package call ncal package need to download in your regional Linux device for using those functions.

Whoami and who command: There is two quite helpful and popular command in Kali Linux platform are whoami and who commands. Whoami is one of the key commands which supplied precise efficient username instantly who are involved in performing this particular command. And who is the command where it will offer whole visited user detail info?

This Kali Linux command is mainly using for showing the specific directory where command executer is currently belonged to. PWD is the crucial command for understanding the same.

Ls: This is likewise a very typically utilized command in Kali Linux platform. There have a number of other prolonged commands of Ls which are utilizing for handling the display screen of those files in an appropriate way.

Cd: Cd command is mainly used for changing the directory site in Kali Linux platform.

Mkdir: Mkdir is one of the essential commands for Kali Linux platform. This actually helps for creating one brand-new directory in Kali Linux platform.

Cat: Cat command is frequently utilized for displaying the entire content of one file. It likewise can be utilized for developing or concatenate single or numerous files in Kali Linux platform.

Cp: This Kali Linux command is generally used for copying the image of an existing file or directory site and paste the exact same throughout the Kali Linux platform with the different file name.

Mv: Mv command is also extremely frequently utilized command for moving the files or directory site to another place with the very same name and content.

Intermediate Kali Linux Commands

There are several other popular kali Linux commands which have been used by the developer who are not very standard however dealing with Kali Linux more, those Linux commands are very much needed to carry out. Some of those kinds of needing intermediate Linux commands are pointed out below:

Rm: Rm command is used for primarily deleting or getting rid of the files or several files. Then it will remove the whole directory site, if we utilize this rm command recursively.

Uname: This command is very much helpful for showing the whole existing system details correctly. It helps for displaying Linux system information in Linux environment correct method for comprehending system existing setup.

Uptime: The uptime commands is likewise among the key commands for Kali Linux platform which gives information about the length of time system is running.

Users: This Kali Linux commands are utilized for showing login user name who are presently visited on Linux system.

Less: Less command is quite used for displaying the file without using or opening feline or vi commands. This command is generally among the powerful extension of 'more' command in Linux environment.

Advanced Kali Linux Commands

Still, a few of the important jobs require to be done by the Kali Linux command users frequently. Those tasks also have some advance sort of commands require to be carried out, which generally used by a few of the supervisory individuals for arranging, determining or customizing a particular file, shell scripting writing, job scheduling etc. Those advance sort of Kali Linux commands are listed below:

More: This command is used for showing appropriate output in one page at a time. It is primarily useful for reading one long file by preventing scrolling the same.

Sort: This is for using arranging the material of one particular define file. This is very much helpful for showing a few of the important contents of a huge file in arranged order. If we user including this sort command, then it will give reverse order of the material.

Vi: This is among the key editor available from the very first day onwards in UNIX or Linux platform. It usually provided two kinds of mode, typical and insert.

Free: It is offered details information of complimentary memory or RAM offered in a Linux system.

History: This command is holding the history of all the executed command on the Linux platform.

Other commands

$ man command-name

adduser/addgroup Command

The adduser and addgroup commands are used to add a user and group to the system respectively according to the default configuration specified in /etc/adduser.conf file.

$ sudo adduser tecmint

agetty Command

agetty is a program which manages physical or virtual terminals and is invoked by init. Once it detects a connection, it opens a tty port, asks for a user's login name and calls up the /bin/login command. Agetty is a substitute of Linux getty:

$ agetty -L 9600 ttyS1 vt100

alias Command

alias is a useful shell built-in command for creating aliases (shortcut) to a Linux command on a system. It is helpful for creating new/custom commands from existing Shell/Linux commands (including options):

$ alias home='cd /home/tecmint/public_html'

The above command will create an alias called home for /home/tecmint/public_html directory, so whenever you type home in the terminal prompt, it will put you in the /home/tecmint/public_html directory.

anacron Command

anacron is a Linux facility used to run commands periodically with a fre□uency defined in days, weeks and months.

Unlike its sister cron; it assumes that a system will not run continuously, therefore if a scheduled job is due when the system is off, it's run once the machine is powered on.

apropos Command

apropos command is used to search and display a short man page description of a command/program as follows.

$ apropos adduser

apt Command

apt tool is a relatively new higher-level package manager for Debian/Ubuntu systems:

$ sudo apt update

apt-get Command

apt-get is a powerful and free front-end package manager for Debian/Ubuntu systems. It is used to install new software packages, remove available software packages, upgrade existing software packages as well as upgrade entire operating system.

$ sudo apt-get update

aptitude Command

aptitude is a powerful text-based interface to the Debian GNU/Linux package management system. Like apt-get and apt; it can be used to install, remove or upgrade software packages on a system.

$ sudo aptitude update

arch Command

arch is a simple command for displaying machine architecture or hardware name (similar to uname -m):

$ arch

arp Command

ARP (Address Resolution Protocol) is a protocol that maps IP network addresses of a network neighbor with the hardware (MAC) addresses in an IPv4 network.

You can use it as below to find all alive hosts on a network:

```
$ sudo arp-scan --interface=enp2s0 --localnet
```

at Command

at command is used to schedule tasks to run in a future time. It's an alternative to cron and anacron, however, it runs a task once at a given future time without editing any config files:

For example, to shutdown the system at 23:55 today, run:

```
$ sudo echo "shutdown -h now" | at -m 23:55
```

at□ Command

atq command is used to view jobs in at command □ueue:

```
$ atq
```

atrm Command

atrm command is used to remove/deletes jobs (identified by their job number) from at command ⬚ueue:

$ atrm 2

awk Command

Awk is a powerful programming language created for text processing and generally used as a data extraction and reporting tool.

$ awk '//{print}'/etc/hosts

batch Command

batch is also used to schedule tasks to run a future time, similar to the at command.

basename Command

basename command helps to print the name of a file stripping of directories in the absolute path:

```
$ basename bin/findhosts.sh
```

bc Command

bc is a simple yet powerful and arbitrary precision CLI calculator language which can be used like this:

```
$ echo 20.05 + 15.00 | bc
```

bg Command

bg is a command used to send a process to the background.

```
$ tar -czf home.tar.gz .
```

```
$ bg
```

```
$ jobs
```

bzip2 Command

bzip2 command is used to compress or decompress file(s).

```
$ bzip2 -z filename     #Compress
```

```
$ bzip2 -d filename.bz2 #Decompress
```

cal Command

The cal command print a calendar on the standard output.

$ cal

cat Command

cat command is used to view contents of a file or concatenate files, or data provided on standard input, and display it on the standard output.

$ cat file.txt

chgrp Command

chgrp command is used to change the group ownership of a file. Provide the new group name as its first argument and the name of file as the second argument like this:

$ chgrp tecmint users.txt

chmod Command

chmod command is used to change/update file access permissions like this.

$ chmod +x sysinfo.sh

chown Command

chown command changes/updates the user and group ownership of a file/directory like this.

$ chmod -R www-data:www-data /var/www/html

cksum Command

cksum command is used to display the CRC checksum and byte count of an input file.

$ cksum README.txt

clear Command

clear command lets you clear the terminal screen, simply type.

$ clear

cmp Command

cmp performs a byte-by-byte comparison of two files like this.

$ cmp file1 file2

comm Command

comm command is used to compare two sorted files line-by-line as shown below.

$ comm file1 file2

cp Command

cp command is used for copying files and directories from one location to another.

$ cp /home/tecmint/file1 /home/tecmint/Personal/

date Command

date command displays/sets the system date and time like this.

$ date

$ date --set="8 JUN 2017 13:00:00"

dd Command

dd command is used for copying files, converting and formatting according to flags provided on the command line. It can strip headers, extracting parts of binary files and so on.

The example below shows creating a boot-able USB device:

$ dd if=/home/tecmint/kali-linux-1.0.4-i386.iso of=/dev/sdc1 bs=512M; sync

df Command

df command is used to show file system disk space usage as follows.

$ df -h

diff Command

diff command is used to compare two files line by line. It can also be used to find the difference between two directories in Linux like this:

$ diff file1 file2

dir Command

dir command works like Linux ls command, it lists the contents of a directory.

$ dir

dmidecode Command

dmidecode command is a tool for retrieving hardware information of any Linux system. It dumps a computer's DMI (a.k.a SMBIOS) table contents in a human-readable format for easy retrieval.

To view your system hardware info, you can type:

$ sudo dmidecode --type system

du Command

du command is used to show disk space usage of files present in a directory as well as its sub-directories as follows.

$ du /home/aaronkilik

echo Command

echo command prints a text of line provided to it.

$ echo "This is TecMint - Linux How Tos"

eject Command

eject command is used to eject removable media such as DVD/CD ROM or floppy disk from the system.

$ eject /dev/cdrom

$ eject /mnt/cdrom/

$ eject /dev/sda

env Command

env command lists all the current environment variables and used to set them as well.

$ env

exit Command

exit command is used to exit a shell like so.

$ exit

expr Command

expr command is used to calculate an expression as shown below.

$ expr 20 + 30

factor Command

factor command is used to show the prime factors of a number.

$ factor 10

find Command

find command lets you search for files in a directory as well as its sub-directories. It searches for files by attributes such as permissions, users, groups, file type, date, size and other possible criteria.

$ find /home/tecmint/ -name tecmint.txt

free Command

free command shows the system memory usage (free, used, swapped, cached, etc.) in the system including swap space. Use the -h option to display output in human friendly format.

$ free -h

grep Command

grep command searches for a specified pattern in a file (or files) and displays in output lines containing that pattern as follows.

$ grep 'tecmint' domain-list.txt

groups Command

groups command displays all the names of groups a user is a part of like this.

$ groups

$ groups tecmint

gzip Command

Gzip helps to compress a file, replaces it with one having a .gz extension as shown below:

$ gzip passwds.txt

$ cat file1 file2 | gzip > foo.gz

gunzip Command

gunzip expands or restores files compressed with gzip command like this.

$ gunzip foo.gz

head Command

head command is used to show first lines (10 lines by default) of the specified file or stdin to the screen:

ps -eo pid,ppid,cmd,%mem,%cpu --sort=-%mem | head

history Command

history command is used to show previously used commands or to get info about command executed by a user.

$ history

hostname Command

hostname command is used to print or set system hostname in Linux.

$ hostname

$ hostname NEW_HOSTNAME

hostnamectl Command

hostnamectl command controls the system hostname under systemd. It is used to print or modify the system hostname and any related settings:

$ hostnamectl

$ sudo hostnamectl set-hostname NEW_HOSTNAME

hwclock

hwclock is a tool for managing the system hardware clock; read or set the hardware clock (RTC).

$ sudo hwclock

$ sudo hwclock --set --date 8/06/2017

hwinfo Command

hwinfo is used to probe for the hardware present in a Linux system like this.

$ hwinfo

id Command

id command shows user and group information for the current user or specified username as shown below.

$ id tecmint

ifconfig Command

ifconfig command is used to configure a Linux systems network interfaces. It is used to configure, view and control network interfaces.

$ ifconfig

$ sudo ifconfig eth0 up

$ sudo ifconfig eth0 down

$ sudo ifconfig eth0 172.16.25.125

ionice Command

ionice command is used to set or view process I/O scheduling class and priority of the specified process.

If invoked without any options, it will □uery the current I/O scheduling class and priority for that process:

$ ionice -c 3 rm /var/logs/syslog

iostat Command

iostat is used to show CPU and input/output statistics for devices and partitions. It produces useful reports for updating system configurations to help balance the input/output load between physical disks.

$ iostat

ip Command

ip command is used to display or manage routing, devices, policy routing and tunnels. It also works as a replacement for well known ifconfig command.

This command will assign an IP address to a specific interface (eth1 in this case).

$ sudo ip addr add 192.168.56.10 dev eth1

iptables Command

iptables is a terminal based firewall for managing incoming and outgoing traffic via a set of configurable table rules.

The command below is used to check existing rules on a system (using it may re□uire root privileges).

$ sudo iptables -L -n -v

iw Command

iw command is used to manage wireless devices and their configuration.

$ iw list

iwlist Command

iwlist command displays detailed wireless information from a wireless interface. The command below enables you to get detailed information about the wlp1s0 interface.

$ iwlist wlp1s0 scanning

kill Command

kill command is used to kill a process using its PID by sending a signal to it (default signal for kill is TERM).

$ kill -p 2300

$ kill -SIGTERM -p 2300

killall Command

killall command is used to kill a process by its name.

$ killall firefox

kmod Command

kmod command is used to manage Linux kernel modules. To list all currently loaded modules, type.

$ kmod list

last Command

last command display a listing of last logged in users.

$ last

ln Command

ln command is used to create a soft link between files using the -s flag like this.

$ ln -s /usr/bin/lscpu cpuinfo

locate Command

locate command is used to find a file by name. The locate utility works better and faster than it's find counterpart.

The command below will search for a file by its exact name (not *name*):

$ locate -b '\domain-list.txt'

login Command

login command is used to create a new session with the system. You'll be asked to provide a username and a password to login as below.

$ sudo login

ls Command

ls command is used to list contents of a directory. It works more or less like dir command.

The -l option enables long listing format like this.

$ ls -l file1

lshw Command

lshw command is a minimal tool to get detailed information on the hardware configuration of the machine, invoke it with superuser privileges to get a comprehensive information.

$ sudo lshw

lscpu Command

lscpu command displays system's CPU architecture information (such as number of CPUs, threads, cores, sockets, and more).

$ lscpu

lsof Command

lsof command displays information related to files opened by processes. Files can be of any type, including regular files, directories, block special files, character special files, executing text reference, libraries, and stream/network files.

To view files opened by a specific user's processes, type the command below.

$ lsof -u tecmint

lsusb Command

lsusb command shows information about USB buses in the system and the devices connected to them like this.

$ lsusb

man Command

man command is used to view the on-line reference manual pages for commands/programs like so.

$ man du

$ man df

md5sum Command

md5sum command is used to compute and print the MD5 message digest of a file. If run without arguments, debsums checks every file on your system against the stock md5sum files:

$ sudo debsums

mkdir Command

mkdir command is used to create single or more directories, if they do not already exist (this can be overridden with the -p option).

$ mkdir tecmint-files

OR

$ mkdir -p tecmint-files

more Command

more command enables you to view through relatively lengthy text files one screenful at a time.

$ more file.txt

mv Command

mv command is used to rename files or directories. It also moves a file or directory to another location in the directory structure.

$ mv test.sh sysinfo.sh

nano Command

nano is a popular small, free and friendly text editor for Linux; a clone of Pico, the default editor included in the non-free Pine package.

To open a file using nano, type:

$ nano file.txt

nc/netcat Command

nc (or netcat) is used for performing any operation relating to TCP, UDP, or UNIX-domain sockets. It can handle both IPv4 and IPv6 for opening TCP connections, sending UDP packets, listening on arbitrary TCP and UDP ports, performing port scanning.

The command below will help us see if the port 22 is open on the host 192.168.56.5.

$ nc -zv 192.168.1.5 22

netstat Command

netstat command displays useful information concerning the Linux networking subsystem (network connections, routing tables, interface statistics, mas□uerade connections, and multicast memberships).

This command will display all open ports on the local system:

$ netstat -a | more

nice Command

nice command is used to show or change the nice value of a running program. It runs specified command with an adjusted niceness. When run without any command specified, it prints the current niceness.

The following command starts the process "tar command" setting the "nice" value to 12.

$ nice -12 tar -czf backup.tar.bz2 /home/*

nmap Command

nmap is a popular and powerful open source tool for network scanning and security auditing. It was intended to □uickly scan large networks, but it also works fine against single hosts.

The command below will probe open ports on all live hosts on the specified network.

```
$ nmap -sV 192.168.56.0/24
```

nproc Command

nproc command shows the number of processing units present to the current process. It's output may be less than the number of online processors on a system.

```
$ nproc
```

openssl Command

The openssl is a command line tool for using the different cryptography operations of OpenSSL's crypto library from the shell. The command below will create an archive of all files in the current directory and encrypt the contents of the archive file:

```
$ tar -czf - * | openssl enc -e -aes256 -out backup.tar.gz
```

passwd Command

passwd command is used to create/update passwords for user accounts, it can also change the account or associated password validity period. Note that normal system users may only change the password of their own account, while root may modify the password for any account.

$ passwd tecmint

pidof Command

pidof displays the process ID of a running program/command.

$ pidof init

$ pidof cinnamon

ping Command

ping command is used to determine connectivity between hosts on a network (or the Internet):

$ ping google.com

ps Command

ps shows useful information about active processes running on a system. The example below shows the top running processes by highest memory and CPU usage.

```
# ps -eo pid,ppid,cmd,%mem,%cpu --sort=-%mem |
head
```

pstree Command

pstree displays running processes as a tree which is
rooted at either PID or init if PID is omitted.

```
$ pstree
```

pwd Command

pwd command displays the name of current/working
directory as below.

```
$ pwd
```

rdiff-backup Command

rdiff-backup is a powerful local/remote incremental
backup script written in Python. It works on any
POSIX operating system such as Linux, Mac OS X.

Note that for remote backups, you must install the
same version of rdiff-backup on both the local and
remote machines. Below is an example of a local
backup command:

$ sudo rdiff-backup /etc /media/tecmint/Backup/server_etc.backup

reboot Command

reboot command may be used to halt, power-off or reboot a system as follows.

$ reboot

rename Command

rename command is used to rename many files at once. If you've a collection of files with ".html" extension and you want to rename all of them with ".php" extension, you can type the command below.

$ rename 's/\.html$/\.php/' *.html

rm command

rm command is used to remove files or directories as shown below.

$ rm file1

$ rm -rf my-files

rmdir Command

rmdir command helps to delete/remove empty directories as follows.

$ rmdir /backup/all

scp Command

scp command enables you to securely copy files between hosts on a network, for example.

$ scp ~/names.txt root@192.168.56.10:/root/names.txt

shutdown Command

shutdown command schedules a time for the system to be powered down. It may be used to halt, power-off or reboot the machine like this.

$ shutdown --poweroff

sleep Command

sleep command is used to delay or pause (specifically execution of a command) for a specified amount of time.

$ check.sh; sleep 5; sudo apt update

sort Command

sort command is used to sort lines of text in the specified file(s) or from stdin as shown below

$ cat words.txt

split Command

split as the name suggests, is used to split a large file into small parts.

$ tar -cvjf backup.tar.bz2 /home/tecmint/Documents/*

ssh Command

ssh (SSH client) is an application for remotely accessing and running commands on a remote machine. It is designed to offer a secure encrypted communications between two untrusted hosts over an insecure network such as the Internet.

$ ssh tecmint@192.168.56.10

stat Command

stat is used to show a file or file system status like this (-f is used to specify a filesystem).

$ stat file1

su Command

su command is used to switch to another user ID or become root during a login session. Note that when su is invoked without a username, it defaults to becoming root.

$ su

$ su tecmint

sudo Command

sudo command allows a permitted system user to run a command as root or another user, as defined by the security policy such as sudoers.

In this case, the real (not effective) user ID of the user running sudo is used to determine the user name with which to ☐uery the security policy.

$ sudo apt update

$ sudo useradd tecmint

$ sudo passwd tecmint

sum Command

sum command is used to show the checksum and block counts for each each specified file on the command line.

$ sum output file.txt

tac Command

tac command concatenates and displays files in reverse. It simply prints each file to standard output, showing last line first.

$tac file.txt

tail Command

tail command is used to display the last lines (10 lines by default) of each file to standard output.

If there more than one file, precede each with a header giving the file name. Use it as follow (specify more lines to display using -n option).

$ tail long-file

OR

$ tail -n 15 long-file

talk Command

talk command is used to talk to another system/network user. To talk to a user on the same machine, use their login name, however, to talk to a user on another machine use 'user@host'.

$ talk person [ttyname]

OR

$ talk'user@host' [ttyname]

tar Command

tar command is a most powerful utility for archiving files in Linux.

$ tar -czf home.tar.gz .

tee Command

tee command is used to read from standard input and prints to standard output and files as shown below.

$ echo "Testing how tee command works" | tee file1

tree Command

The tree command is a tiny, cross-platform command-line program used to recursively list or display the content of a directory in a tree-like format.

$ tree

time Command

time command runs programs and summarizes system resource usage.

$ time wc /etc/hosts

top Command

top program displays all processes on a Linux system in regards to memory and CPU usage and provides a dynamic real-time view of a running system.

$ top

touch Command

touch command changes file timestamps, it can also be used to create a file as follows.

$ touch file.txt

tr Command

tr command is a useful utility used to translate (change) or delete characters from stdin, and write the result to stdout or send to a file as follows.

$ cat domain-list.txt | tr [:lower:] [:upper:]

uname Command

uname command displays system information such as operating system, network node hostname kernel name, version and release etc.

Use the -a option to show all the system information:

$ uname

uniq Command

uniq command displays or omits repeated lines from input (or standard input). To indicate the number of occurrences of a line, use the -c option.

$ cat domain-list.txt

uptime Command

uptime command shows how long the system has been running, number of logged on users and the system load averages as follows.

$ uptime

users Command

users command shows the user names of users currently logged in to the current host like this.

$ users

vim/vi Command

vim (Vi Improved) popular text editor on Unix-like operating systems. It can be used to edit all kinds of plain text and program files.

$ vim file

w Command

w command displays system uptime, load averages and information about the users currently on the machine, and what they are doing (their processes) like this.

$ w

wall Command

wall command is used to send/display a message to all users on the system as follows.

$ wall "This is TecMint – Linux How Tos"

watch Command

watch command runs a program repeatedly while displaying its output on fullscreen. It can also be used to watch changes to a file/directory. The example below shows how to watch the contents of a directory change.

$ watch -d ls -l

wc Command

wc command is used to display newline, word, and byte counts for each file specified, and a total for many files.

$ wc filename

wget Command

wget command is a simple utility used to download files from the Web in a non-interactive (can work in the background) way.

$ wget -c http://ftp.gnu.org/gnu/wget/wget-1.5.3.tar.gz

whatis Command

whatis command searches and shows a short or one-line manual page descriptions of the provided command name(s) as follows.

$ whatis wget

which Command

which command displays the absolute path (pathnames) of the files (or possibly links) which would be executed in the current environment.

$ which who

who Command

who command shows information about users who are currently logged in like this.

$ who

whereis Command

whereis command helps us locate the binary, source and manual files for commands.

$ whereis cat

xargs Command

xargs command is a useful utility for reading items from the standard input, delimited by blanks (protected with double or single quotes or a backslash) or newlines, and executes the entered command.

The example below show xargs being used to copy a file to multiple directories in Linux.

$ echo /home/aaronkilik/test/ /home/aaronkilik/tmp | xargs -n 1 cp -v /home/aaronkilik/bin/sys_info.sh

yes Command

yes command is used to display a string repeatedly until when terminated or killed using [Ctrl + C] as follows.

$ yes "This is TecMint - Linux HowTos"

youtube-dl Command

youtube-dl is a lightweight command-line program to download videos and also extract MP3 tracks from YouTube.com and a few more sites.

The command below will list available formats for the video in the provided link.

$ youtube-dl   --list-formats
https://www.youtube.com/watch?v=iR

zcmp/zdiff Command

zcmp and zdiff minimal utilities used to compare compressed files as shown in the examples below.

$ zcmp domain-list.txt.zip basic_passwords.txt.zip

$ zdiff domain-list.txt.zip basic_passwords.txt.zip

zip Command

zip is a simple and easy-to-use utility used to package and compress (archive) files.

$ tar cf - . | zip | dd of=/dev/nrst0 obs=16k

$ zip inarchive.zip foo.c bar.c --out outarchive.zip

$ tar cf - .| zip backup -

zz Command

zz command is an alias of the fasd commandline tool that offers □uick access to files and directories in Linux. It is used to quickly and interactively cd into a previously accessed directory by selecting the directory number from the first field as follows.

$ zz

SECURE AND ANONYMOUS IN KALI LINUX BY USING TOR, PROXY SERVERS, VPN AND ENCRYPTED EMAILS

Now these days, almost everything we do on internet is tracked. Whoever is doing the tracking - it might be Google tracking our online searches, site sees, and e-mail or it may be the National Security Agency (NSA) cataloging all our every online action is being tape-recorded, indexed, and then mined for their advantage. The typical users and security professionals everybody requires to comprehend how to restrict this tracking and stay reasonably confidential on the internet and limitation this ubiquitous security.

we look how we can navigate the World Wide Web anonymously (or as close as we can get) and safely utilizing four techniques:

- The Onion Router
- Proxy servers
- Virtual Private Networks
- Personal encrypted email

Nobody method makes certain to keep our activities safe from prying eyes and offered adequate time and resources, anything can be tracked. Nevertheless we can utilize all techniques together, this will make the tracker's job almost difficult.

Let's start, finally we go over at a high level some of the methods our activity on the internet are tracked. We will not enter into all tracking techniques, or into too much details about only one method, as that would be beyond the scope of this post. Certainly such a discussion could use up a whole book on it's own.

Our IP address identifies us as we pass through the internet. Let's start by taking a look at how IP address offer us away on the internet.

When we send out an information package across the internet, it includes the IP address of the source and location for the data. In this way, the packet knows where it is going and where to return the response. Each packet hops through numerous internet routers up until it finds its location and then hops back to the sender. For general internet surfing each hop is a router the packages travels through to get to its location, but usually any packet will find its method to the location in fewer then 15 hops.

As the packet passes through the internet, anybody intercepting the packet can see who sent it, Where it has been, and it's going. This is one method sites can tell who we are when get here and log us in immediately, and it's also how someone can track where we have actually been on the internet.

To see what hops a package might make between we and our location, we can see the traceroute command in our Kali Linux treminal as following:

traceroute google.com

The screenshot is following:

```
root@kali:~# traceroute google.com
traceroute to google.com (172.217.26.174), 30 hops max, 60 byte packets
 1  3g.intex (192.168.10.1)  2.065 ms  2.318 ms  2.586 ms
 2  * * *
 3  10.172.19.26 (10.172.19.26)  679.329 ms  679.465 ms  679.521 ms
 4  192.168.17.5 (192.168.17.5)  678.794 ms * *
 5  100.64.0.111 (100.64.0.111)  679.493 ms  682.288 ms  682.404 ms
 6  182.19.108.191 (182.19.108.191)  726.677 ms  727.366 ms  726.896 ms
 7  72.14.210.238 (72.14.210.238)  736.654 ms  87.694 ms  89.540 ms
 8  108.170.253.97 (108.170.253.97)  83.021 ms  81.104 ms 108.170.253.113 (108.1
70.253.113)  106.914 ms
 9  74.125.253.65 (74.125.253.65)  88.340 ms  93.903 ms  84.442 ms
10  maa03s22-in-f14.1e100.net (172.217.26.174)  74.805 ms  89.661 ms  69.983 ms
root@kali:~#
```

As we can see in the screenshot Google.com is 10 hops across the web from us. Due to the fact that our demand would be coming from a various area and due to the fact that Google have numerous servers across the world, our outcomes will likely be different. Packages do not constantly take the same route across the internet, so we might send another packet from our address to the very same site and get different path. Let's see how we can camouflage all this with the Tor network.

Tor - The Onion Router

In the year 1990, the United States workplace of Naval Research (ONR) set out to establish a method for anonymously browsing the internet for espionage function. The strategy was to establish a network of routers that was separated from the web routers, that could encrypt the traffic, which just saved unencrypted IP address of our previous router.

That implies all other routers attend to along the way were encrypted. The idea was that anyone viewing the traffic could not identify the origin or destination of the information. This research study ended up being known as "The Onion Router (Tor) Project" In 2002, it is offered for everybody to utilize anonymous and safe navigation on the internet.

How Tor Works

Packages send over Tor are not sent over the routine routers so closely kept an eye on by a lot of rather are sent over a network of over 7000+ routers worldwide, unique thanks to volunteers who permit their computer systems to be utilized by Tor. On top of using a totally different router network, Tor encrypts the information, location, and sender IP address of each package. At each hop, the information is encrypted and then decrypted by the next hop when it is received. In this way, each package contains info about just the previous hop along the path and not the IP address of the traffic. If someone intercepts the traffic, they can see just the IP address of previous hop, and the website owner can see just the IP address of the last router that send the traffic. In this way Tor make sure relative privacy across the web.

To allow the use of Tor we need to install Tor web browser from https://www.torproject.org/download/

We can download Tor according to our OS, in our case that is Kali Linux. So after download the file we right click and select the "Extract Here" alternative.

We can run Tor internet browser from here but in Kali Linux it's bit hard to run Tor as root user. We do some configuration to run Tor in Kali Linux.

we will open this file in full-screen editor. We will search for root by utilizing Ctrl+F secret.

We added '#' in four lines here, see following screenshot:

```
            return
        fi
}

#if [ " id -u " -eq 0 ]; then
#       complain "The Tor Browser Bundle should not be run as root.  Exiting."
#       exit 1
#fi

if ! grep -q '^flags\s*:.* sse2' /proc/cpuinfo; then
       complain "Tor Browser requires a CPU with SSE2 support.  Exiting."
       exit 1
fi
```

Then we save this file now we can run Tor internet browser as root user. return to the main folder.

Now we open terminal here, and type following command

./ start-tor-browser. desktop.

Now we can click on link and after some seconds Tor will open:

It appears like any old web browser. By utilizing this internet browser, we will be navigating the internet through a different set of routers and will have the ability to go to without being tracked by anyone. Regrettably, the trade off is that by means of the Tor web browser can be bit slower, since there are not nearly as numerous routers, the bandwidth is limited in Tor network.

In addition, to being capable of accessing almost any website on the conventional web, the Tor web browser is capable of accessing the dark web. The websites that make up the dark web requires anonymity, for this factor they permit access only through the Tor internet browser, and dark sites have address ending with.onion for their leading level domain (TLD).

Security Concerns

The intelligence and spy services of the United States and other countries consider the Tor network as a threat to nationwide security, thinking such an anonymous network enables foreign governments and terrorists to interact without being watched. As a result, some robust, enthusiastic research tasks are working to break the privacy of Tor.

Tor's anonymity has been broken in the past prior to by these authorities and will likely broke again. The NSA, as one instance, runs it's own Tor routers, means that our traffic may be traversing the NSA's routers when we use Tor. If our traffic is leaving the NSA's routers, that is even worse, due to the fact that the exit router always knows our destination, however this will be really difficult to trace us. The NSA likewise has an approach called traffic correlation, which involves looking for patterns in outbound and inbound traffic, that has been able to break Tor's anonymity. Though these attempts to break Tor will not affect Tor's efficiency at obscuring our identity for industrial services, such as Google, they may limit the web browser's efficiency in keeping us anonymous from spy firms.

Proxy Servers

Another technique for attaining privacy on the web is to utilize proxies, which are intermediate systems that user connects to a proxy, and the traffic is given the IP address of the proxy before it's passed on. We can see the   following   image.

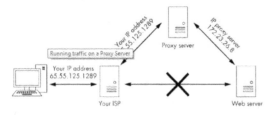

When the traffic returns from the locations the proxy sends the traffic back to the source. In this way, traffic appears to come from the proxy and not our IP address.

Certainly, the proxy servers most likely log our traffic, but a private investigator would have to get a subpoena or search warrant to get our logs. To make our traffic even harder to trace, we can utilize more then one proxy, this strategy known as proxy chain.

Security Concerns

A note on proxy security, make sure to pick your proxies sensibly. Proxychains is just as good as the proxies we use. We must not use totally free proxies if we are intention on staying anonymous. Experts use paid proxies that can be relied on. The totally free proxies are likely offering our IP address and browsing history. Bruce Schneier a popular security expert stated "If something is complimentary, you're no the consumer; you are the product." Simply put any free item likely event our information and offering it. Why else would they use a proxy for free?

The IP address of our traffic leaving the proxy will be confidential, there are other methods for security firms to recognize us. The owner or law enforcement firms with jurisdiction, might use up our identity to secure their organisation. It's crucial to be knowledgeable about the limitations of proxies as a source of anonymity.

Virtual Private Networks (VPN).

Using a virtual private network (VPN) can be effective method to keep our web traffic fairly confidential and safe and secure. A VPN is utilized to connect to an intermediary internet device such as a router that sends our traffic to it's supreme destination tagged with the IP address of the router.

Utilizing a VPN can definitely enhance our security and privacy, however it is not ensure of privacy. The internet device we connect to must tape-record our IP address can discover info about us.

We can open an account with a VPN service provider and then seamlessly link to the VPN each time we log on to our computer system. We can utilize our web browser as normal to navigate the web, but it will appear to anybody enjoying that our traffic is coming from the IP address and area of the web VPN device, not our own. In addition, all traffic in between us and the VPN devices is secured, so even our web company can't see our traffic.

- IPVanish.
- Nord VPN.
- ExpressVPN.
- Cyberghost.
- Goldenfrog VPN.
- Hide My Ass.

- Personal Internet Access.
- PureVPN.
- TorGuard.
- Buffered VPN.

The majority of these VPN services charge $50 - $100 each year, and numerous offers a free 30 day path. To find out more about how to set up a VPN, select one from the list and check out the website. We should find download, setup and utilizes instructions that are quite easy to follow.

The strength of a VPN is that all our traffic is secured when it leaves our PC/mobile, hence safeguarding us versus sleuthing, and our IP address is masked by the VPN IP address when we go to a website. Similar to a proxy server, the admin of the VPN has our stemming IP address (otherwise they could not send our traffic back to us). They might offer up our identity if they are pressed by espionage agencies or law enforcement. One method to prevent that is to utilize just VPN's that promised not to store or log any of this info (and we hope they are being sincere). In this way, if someone demand that the VPN service provider to check their data of users, there is no data.

Encrypted E-mail.

Free industrial email services like Gmail, Yahoo! In addition, the servers of the email supplier have access to the unencrypted content of our emails, even if we're utilizing HTTPS.

One way to prevent eavesdropping on our e-mail is to utilize encrypted email.

ProtonMail, encrypts our e-mail from end to end or browser to web browser. This implies that our e-mail is secured on ProtonMail servers. Even the ProtonMail owners can't read our e-mails.

The Swiss have a huge and storied history of protecting secrets (keep in mind the Swiss bank accounts), and ProtonMail's servers are based in the European Union, which has much more stringent laws concerning the sharing of personal information then does the US. It is crucial for some or all of the e-mail not to be secured.

We are constantly being surveilled by industrial firms and nationwide intelligence agencies. To keep our data and web takes a trip secure, we require to implement a minimum of one of the security determines discussed in this area.

By applying them in combination we can decrease our footprint online and keep our data much more safe. That's all. Be safe and assist pals to be protected.

HACKING TERMS YOU MUST KNOW

Phishing: basically, phishing is a method to hack online accounts (like Facebook, Gmail) by making phony login page similar to the original login page. When you open a phishing page it appears like an original page, for example, see this screenshot

Do yo believe it is initial however it is fake see the URL [Normally all online account login sites have SSL certificate indicate https [s indicate protected]

The advance version of phishing:

- Desktop Phishing

- Tabnapping.

Desktop Phishing: This is the advanced kind of phishing. It is like above method, but in this approach, URL is not replaced your computer system is impacted by this procedure and when you open facebook.com hacker phony page will open, however URL will not alter. Here I try to describe it.

All modern-day web browser discover desktop phishing and you need physical access to produce desktop phishing page.

Tabnapping: If you open many tabs on browsing the web then your account can be easily hacked by this technique. In this attack when the victim clicks the link from another website, for example, You and me are good friends on Facebook, and I send you to connect on Facebook by the message.

Then your facebook tab page Url will be changed by another page when you open the link and 2-3 another tab. You will think your account is logged out immediately. You will again Login your account and I will get your password you will be rerouted to facebook.com

Keylogger: this is software application of hardware which tapes every word typed by the victim from the keyboard. The primary purpose of keyloggers are for hacking online accounts like FB due to the fact that it tapes keyword, so it will likewise tape-record password and username. Here are two types of Keylogger

Software application keylogger: These are software application which records every keystroke. If you can excellent knowledge of programming, you can download complimentary keylogger from the internet or make own.

Hardware Keylogger: Hardware keylogger are is hardware device which requires to link to computer then it tape-records our keystrokes. These days Hardware keyloggers are connected to the keyboard for hacking charge card and so on. Here are some hardware keyloggers

Strength attack: Another fantastic way to hack passwords, Hacker simply think password length and characters utilized for the password. After that software mix all these elements and develop so many words and try to apply as every word as a password. It is a time-consuming approach.

Another software application uses every word as a password. Aircrack can attempt 969 words/second as the password.

File encryption: Generally it is utilized for encrypting the password in the database. In the database, it is saved in encrypted format. E.x.

Original message: This is a line

Encrypted   format: gfEDdWzoKboa9gTFLeb2D476vTg

It secures your password if a hacker hack website database. Then you know about paytm, if you are from India and.

Paytm use 128-bit file encryption suggest if it will increase your password length which has 2 128 combinations for applying brute force attack.

Ransomeware: It is a code program by Hacker which encrypts (imply make them so nobody can open that information) your entire Hard disk data then ask for some Money if you want to remover your information. you can format your complete hard drive or pay money to Hacker.

IP address: Ip represents internet protocol. It is the address of our Device. To discover your IP address type in google what is my IP.

There are two types of Ip address. I) Public IP II) private IP. We connected through the internet by Public IP address. It can be altered by Vpn or using the proxy.

Vpn: VPN means virtual private network. VPN basically change your IP address. If you are using a Vpn and doing anything, nobody can know up until VPN business does not expose you [If you doing something severe Ilegal] free VPN can. Here is the working of Vpn

Web Server: 90% of you understand what is web server however I you don't understand! Above image, text etc are stored on the computer system it is known as the web server.

Dos attack: it means Denial of service. Mainly utilized to make website down or not available. Phony traffic is sent out to the web server. Server crushes when information surpasses the limitation of bandwidth. Here is server down site screenshot when the server is down.

Service Unavailable - DNS failure

The server is temporarily unable to service your request. Please try again later.

Reference #11.e67e7a5c.1285274834.17bc0f|

The easiest way to protect Dos attack is a firewall which blocks activity from a particular computer.

DDOS attack: it means Distributed Denial of service. In dos attack, there is only one machine but it DDOS there is several phony gadgets as shown in the screenshot. There is only one method to secure DDOS attack. Again firewall software but here is working of the firewall program is various Firewall can endure this attack like me I am using CloudFlare CDN for safeguarding DDOS attack.

SQL injection: DDOS attack crush the server however SQL injection assists you to hack websites. Hacker injects inquiries in the website database.

Social engineering: It is not the hacking technique. It is Hacking by the typical person. Guessing password strategy is referred to as social engineering. I am not professional in this, and it takes a great deal of time. Various for the different person so really lengthy.

TEXT MANIPULATION

With numerous text files, manipulating text becomes essential in handling Linux and Linux applications. In this chapter, you'll use a number of commands and strategies for controling text in Linux.

For illustrative functions, I'll use files from the world's finest network intrusion detection system (NIDS), Snort, which was first developed by Marty Roesch and is now owned by Cisco. NIDSs are frequently used to discover intrusions by hackers, so if you want to be an effective hacker, you should recognize with the methods NIDSs can hinder attacks and the ways you can abuse them to avoid detection.

KEEP IN MIND

You can download the files from the Kali repository by getting in apt-get install snort if the variation of Kali Linux you're using doesn't come preinstalled with Snort.

SEEING FILES

As shown in Chapter 1, the most basic text screen command is most likely cat, but it has its limitations.

Use cat to display the Snort config file (snort.conf) found in/etc/snort (see Listing 2-1).

kali > feline/ etc/snort/snort. conf.

Listing 2-1: Displaying snort.conf in the terminal window.

Your screen should now display the entire snort.conf file, which will stream up until it comes to the end of the file, as revealed here. This isn't the most useful or hassle-free method to see and work with this file.

.

include $SO_RULE_PATH/exploit.rules

include $SO_RULE_PATH/exploit.rules

include $SO_RULE_PATH/exploit.rules

include $SO_RULE_PATH/exploit.rules

include $SO_RULE_PATH/exploit.rules

--snip--

event thresholding or suppressions commands...

kali >

In the following two areas, I will show you the head and tail commands, which are two methods for showing just part of a file's content in order to more easily view the crucial content.

Taking the Head

If you simply want to see the beginning of a file, you can use the head command. By default, this command shows the very first 10 lines of a file. The following command, for example, reveals you the very first 10 lines of snort.conf:

kali >head /etc/snort/snort.conf

#--

VRT Rules Packages Snort.conf

#

\#   For more information visit us at:

--snip--

\#Snort bugs:bugs@snort.org

If you want to see more or fewer than the default 10 lines, enter the quantity you want with the dash (-) switch after the call to head and before the filename. For example, if you want to see the first 20 lines of the file, you would enter the command shown at the top of Listing 2-2.

kali >head -20 /etc/snort/snort.conf

\#--
\#VRT Rule Packages Snort.conf
\#
\#For more information visit us at:
\#.

#.

#.

#Options : --enable-gre --enable-mpls --enable-targetbased

--enable-ppm --enable-perfprofiling enable-zlib -- enable-act

live-response --enable-normalizer --enable-reload -- enable-react

Listing 2-2: Displaying the first 20 lines of snort.conf in the terminal window

You should see only the first 20 lines of snort.conf displayed in your terminal window.

Grabbing That Tail

The tail command is similar to the head command, but it's used to view the last lines of a file. Let's use it on snort.conf:

kali >tail /etc/snort/snort.conf

#include $SO_RULE_PATH/smtp.rules

#include $SO_RULE_PATH/specific-threats.rules

#include $SO_RULE_PATH/web-activex.rules

#include $SO_RULE_PATH/web-client.rules

#include $SO_RULE_PATH/web-iis.rules

#include $SO_RULE_PATH/web-miscp.rules

#Event thresholding and suppression commands. See threshold.conf

Notice that this command displays a few of the last include lines of the rules files, however not all of them, because comparable to head, the default for tail is to show 10 lines. You can show more lines by getting the last 20 lines of snort.conf. Just like the head command, you can tell tail how many lines to show by getting in a dash (-) and then the variety of lines in between the command and the filename, as shown in Listing 2-3.

kali >tail -20 /etc/snort/snort.conf

#include $SO_RULE_PATH/chat.rules

#include $SO_RULE_PATH/chat.rules

#include $SO_RULE_PATH/chat.rules

--snip--

#Event thresholding or suppression commands. See theshold.conf

Listing 2-3: Displaying the last 20 lines of snort.conf in the terminal window

Now we can see nearly all the include lines of the rules files on one screen.

Numbering the Lines

Often-- especially with long files-- we may desire the file to display line numbers. Because snort.conf has more than 600 lines, line numbers would work here. This makes it simpler to reference changes and return to the exact same place within the file.

To display a file with line numbers, we use the nl (number lines) command. Simply enter the command shown in Listing 2-4.

kali >nl /etc/snort/snort.conf

612
###
######################

613 #dynamic library rules

614 #include $SO_RULE_PATH/bad-traffic.rules

615 #include $SO_RULE_PATH/chat.rules

--snip--

630 #include $SO_RULE_PATH/web-iis.rules

631 #include $SO_RULE_PATH/web-misc.rules

Listing 2-4: Displaying line numbers in terminal output

Each line now has a number, making referencing much easier.

FILTERING TEXT WITH GREP

The order grep is likely the most generally utilized content control direction. It lets you channel the substance of a record for show. In the event that, for example, you need to see all lines that incorporate the word yield in your snort.conf document, you could utilize feline and request that it show just those lines.

kali >cat /etc/snort/snort.conf | grep output

6) Configure output plugins

Step #6: Configure output plugins

output unified2: filename merged.log, limit 128, nostamp, mpls_event_types,

vlan_event_types

output unified2: filename merged.log, limit 128, nostamp, mpls_event_types,

vlan_event_types

output alert_unified2: filename merged.log, limit 128, nostamp

output log_unified2: filename merged.log, limit 128, nostamp

output alert_syslog: LOG_AUTH LOG_ALERT

output log_tcpdump: tcpdump.log

Listing 2-5: Displaying lines with instances of the keyword or phrase specified by grep

This command will initially view snort.conf and after that use a pipe (|) to send it to grep, which will take the file as input, try to find lines with incidents of the word output, and show just those lines. The grep command is a extremely powerful and necessary command for working in Linux, due to the fact that it can save you hours of looking for every incident of a word or command in a file.

VIEWING FILES WITH MORE AND LESS

Cat is a great energy for displaying files and creating little files, it definitely has its constraints when displaying big files. When you utilize cat with snort.conf, the file scrolls through every page until it comes to the end, which is not really useful if you wish to glean any information from it.

For dealing with larger files, we have 2 other seeing energies: more and less.

Managing the Display with more

The more command shows a page of a file at a time and lets you page down through it utilizing the ENTER secret. It's the energy that the man pages use, so let's take a look at it initially. Open snort.conf with the more command

kali >more /etc/snort/snort.conf

--snip--

Snort build options:

Options: --enable-gre   --enable-mpls   --enable-targetbased

--enable-ppm   --enable-perfprofiling   enable-zlib   --enable-active

-response   --enable-normalizer   --enable-reload   --enable-react

--enable-flexresp3

#

--More--(2%)

Utilizing more to show terminal output one page at a time

Notification that more display screens just the very first page and then stops, and it informs us in the lower-left corner how much of the file is revealed (2 percent in this case). To see additional lines or pages, press ENTER. To leave more, enter q (for quit).

Displaying and Filtering with less

The less command is extremely similar to more, but with extra performance-- hence, the common Linux aficionado quip, "Less is more." With less, you can not just scroll through a file at your leisure, however you can likewise filter it for terms. As in Listing 2-8, open snort.conf with less.

kali >less /etc/snort/snort.conf

--snip--

Snort build options:

Options: --enable-gre --enable-mpls --enable-targetbased

--enable-ppm --enable-perfprofiling enable-zlib --enable-active

-response --enable-normalizer --enable-reload --enable-react

/etc/snort/snort.conf

Listing 2-8: Using less to both display terminal output a page at a time and filter results

Notice in the base left of the screen that less has featured the way to the document. In the event that you press the forward slice (/) key, less will let you look for terms in the record. For example, when you originally set up Snort, you have to decide how and where you need to send your interruption ready yield. To find that segment of the design document, you could essentially look for yield, as so:

Snort build options:

Options: --enable-gre --enable-mpls --enable-targetbased

--enable-ppm --enable-perfprofiling enable-zlib -- enable-active

-response --enable-normalizer --enable-reload -- enable-react

/output

This will immediately take you to the first occurrence of output and highlight it. You can then look for the next occurrence of output by typing n (for next).

Step #6: Configure output plugins

For more information, see Snort Manual, Configuring Snort - Output Modules

##
#########################

#unified2

Recommended for most installs

output unified2: filename merged.log, limit 128, nostamp, mpls_event_types,

vlan_event_types

output unified2: filename snort.log, limit 128, nostamp, mpls_event_types,

vlan_event_types

Additional configuration for specific types of installs

output alert_unified2: filename snort.alert, limit 128, nostamp

output log_unified2: filename snort.log, limit 128, nostamp

syslog

output alert_syslog: LOG_AUTH LOG_ALERT

:

As you can see, less took you to the next occurrence of the word output and highlighted all the search terms. In this case, it went directly to the output section of Snort. How convenient!

ANALYZING AND MANAGING NETWORKS

In many circumstances, you'll be hacking something over a network, and a good hacker needs to know how to connect to and engage with that network. You might need to link to a computer system with your Internet Protocol (IP) address concealed from view, or you may require to redirect a target's Domain Name System (DNS) questions to your system; these kinds of tasks are relatively basic however require a little Linux network know-how.

ANALYZING NETWORKS WITH IFCONFIG

The ifconfig command is among one of the most standard tools for communicating and examining with active network interfaces. You can use it to query your active network connections by simply entering ifconfig in the terminal. Try it yourself, and you need to see output similar to Listing 3-1.

kali >ifconfig

❶eth0Linkencap:EthernetHWaddr 00:0c:29:ba:82:0f

❷inet addr:192.168.181.131 ❸Bcast:192.168.181.255
❹Mask:255.255.255.0

--snip--

❺lo Linkencap:Local Loopback

inet addr:127.0.0.1 Mask:255.0.0.0

--snip--

❻wlan0   Link   encap:EthernetHWaddr
00:c0:ca:3f:ee:02

Utilizing ifconfig to get network info

As you can see, the command ifconfig shows some helpful info about the active network user interfaces on the system. At the top of the output is the name of the very first spotted interface, eth0 ❶, which is short for Ethernet0 (Linux starts counting at 0 rather than 1). This is the very first wired network connection. If there were more wired Ethernet user interfaces, they would show up in the output utilizing the exact same format (eth1, eth2, and so on).

The kind of network being used (Ethernet) is noted next, followed by HWaddr and an address; this is the globally special address stamped on every piece of network hardware-- in this case, the network user interface card (NIC), generally described as the media access control (MAC) address.

The second line contains details on the IP address currently designated to that network user interface (in this case, 192.168.181.131 ❷); the Bcast ❸, or broadcast address, which is the address used to send out info to all IPs on the subnet; and finally the network mask (Mask ❹), which is utilized to determine what part of the IP address is connected to the local network. You'll also find more technical details in this section of the output, however it's beyond the scope of this Linux networking fundamentals chapter.

The next area of the output shows another network connection called lo ❺, which is short for loopback address and is in some cases called localhost. This is a special software address that connects you to your own system. Software application and services not operating on your system can't use it. You would utilize lo to test something on your system, such as your own web server. The localhost is usually represented with the IP address 127.0.0.1.

The 3rd connection is the user interface wlan0 ❻. This appears just if you have a wireless interface or adapter, as I do here. Note that it likewise displays the MAC address of that device (HWaddr).

This information from ifconfig enables you to link to and manipulate your local area network (LAN) settings, an essential skill for hacking.

EXAMINING WIRELESS NETWORK DEVICES WITH IWCONFIG

If you have a wireless adapter, you can use the iwconfig command to collect crucial details for cordless hacking such as the adapter's IP address, its MAC address, what mode it's in, and more. When you're utilizing wireless hacking tools like aircrack-ng, the info you can glean from this command is particularly important.

Utilizing the terminal, let's take a look at some wireless devices with iwconfig

kali >iwconfig

wlan0 IEEE 802.11bg ESSID:off/any

Mode:Managed Access Point: Not Associated Tx-Power=20 dBm

--snip--

lo   no wireless extensions

eth0 no wireless extensions

Utilizing iwconfig to get info on wireless adapters

The output here informs us that the only network user interface with cordless extensions is wlan0, which is what we would anticipate. Neither lo nor eth0 has any wireless extensions.

For wlan0, we learn what 802.11 IEEE cordless requirements our device is capable of: b and g, two early cordless interaction requirements. The majority of wireless devices now include n also (n is the most recent requirement).

We likewise gain from iwconfig the mode of the wireless extension (in this case, Mode: Managed, in contrast to monitor or promiscuous mode). We'll require promiscuous mode for cracking wireless passwords.

Next, we can see that the cordless adapter is not linked (Not Associated) to a gain access to point (AP) which its power is 20 dBm, which represents the strength of signal. We'll spend more time with this information in Chapter 14.

ALTERING YOUR NETWORK INFORMATION

Being able to change your IP address and other network info is a helpful skill since it will assist you access other networks while appearing as a relied on device on those networks. In a denial-of-service (DoS) attack, you can spoof your IP so that the attack appears to come from another source, therefore helping you avert IP capture throughout forensic analysis. This is a relatively easy task in Linux, and it's finished with the ifconfig command.

Changing Your IP Address

To change your IP address, enter ifconfig followed by the user interface you wish to reassign and the new IP address you desire assigned to that user interface. To assign the IP address 192.168.181.115 to interface eth0, you would get in the following:

kali >ifconfig eth0 192.168.181.115

kali >

When you do this correctly, Linux will simply return the command prompt and say nothing. This is a good thing!

Then, when you again check your network connections with ifconfig, you should see that your IP address has changed to the new IP address you just assigned.

Changing Your Network Mask and Broadcast Address

You can also change your network mask (netmask) and broadcast address with the ifconfig command. For instance, if you want to assign that same eth0 interface with a netmask of 255.255.0.0 and a broadcast address of 192.168.1.255, you would enter the following:

kali >ifconfig eth0 192.168.181.115 netmask 255.255.0.0 broadcast 192.168.1.255

kali >

By and by, on the off chance that you've done everything effectively, Linux reacts with another order brief. Presently enter ifconfig again to check that every one of the parameters has been changed in like manner.

Satirizing Your MAC Address

You can likewise utilize ifconfig to change your MAC address (or HWaddr). The MAC address is all around remarkable and is regularly utilized as a safety effort to keep programmers out of systems—or to follow them. Changing your MAC address to parody an alternate MAC address is practically minor and kills those safety efforts. Therefore, it's an extremely helpful procedure for bypassing system get to controls.

To parody your MAC address, basically utilize the ifconfig order's down alternative to bring down the interface (eth0 for this situation). At that point enter the ifconfig order pursued by the interface name (hw for equipment, ether for Ethernet) and the new ridiculed MAC address. At last, carry the interface back up with the up alternative for the change to happen. Here's a model:

kali >ifconfig eth0 down

kali >ifconfig eth0 hw ether 00:11:22:33:44:55

kali >ifconfig eth0 up

Now, when you inspect your settings with ifconfig, you must see that HWaddr has actually altered to your brand-new spoofed IP address!

Assigning New IP Addresses from the DHCP Server

Linux has a Dynamic Host Configuration Protocol (DHCP) server that runs a daemon-- a process that runs in the background-- called dhcpd, or the dhcp daemon. The DHCP server designates IP addresses to all the systems on the subnet and keeps log files of which IP address is assigned to which maker at any one time.

Normally, to connect to the internet from a LAN, you must have a DHCP-assigned IP. After setting a fixed IP address, you must return and get a new DHCP-assigned IP address. To do this, you can constantly reboot your system, however I'll reveal you how to recover a brand-new DHCP without having to shut your system down and restart it.

To ask for an IP address from DHCP, simply call the DHCP server with the command dhclient followed by the user interface you desire the address assigned to. Various Linux distributions utilize different DHCP clients, however Kali is built on Debian, which utilizes dhclient. For that reason, you can appoint a new address like this:

kali > dhclient eth0

The dhclient command sends out a DHCPDISCOVER demand from the network user interface defined (here, eth0). It then gets a deal (DHCPOFFER) from the DHCP server (192.168.181.131 in this case) and verifies the IP task to the DHCP server with a dhcp demand.

kali >ifconfig

eth0Linkencap:EthernetHWaddr 00:0c:29:ba:82:0f

inet addr:192.168.181.131 Bcast:192.168.181.131 Mask:255.255.255.0

Depending upon the configuration of the DHCP server, the IP address appointed in each case might be different.

Now when you get in ifconfig, you need to see that the DHCP server has appointed a new IP address, a new broadcast address, and new netmask to your network interface eth0.

CONTROLING THE DOMAIN NAME SYSTEM

Hackers can discover a treasure trove of details on a target in its Domain Name System (DNS). DNS is an important component of the web, and although it's created to equate domain to IP addresses, a hacker can use it to amass details on the target.

Analyzing DNS with dig

DNS is the service that translates a domain like hackers-arise. com to the suitable IP address; that way, your system knows how to get to it. Without DNS, we would all have to keep in mind countless IP addresses for our favorite sites-- no small task even for a savant.

Among the most useful commands for the hopeful hacker is dig, which offers a way to collect DNS information about a target domain. The saved DNS info can be a crucial piece of early reconnaissance to get prior to attacking. This info might consist of the IP address of the target's nameserver (the server that equates the target's name to an IP address), the target's email server, and possibly any subdomains and IP addresses.

Enter dig hackers-arise. The nameserver for hackers-arise.

kali >dig hackers-arise.com ns

--snip--

;; QUESTION SECTION:

;hackers-arise.com.   IN   NS

;; ANSWER SECTION:

hackers-arise.com. 5 IN   NS   ns7.wixdns.net.

hackers-arise.com. 5 IN   NS   ns6.wixdns.net.

;; ADDITIONAL SECTION:

ns6.wixdns.net.   5 IN   A   216.239.32.100

--snip--

Listing 3-3: Using dig and its ns option to get information on a domain nameserver

Likewise note in the ADDITIONAL SECTION that this burrow inquiry uncovers the IP address (216.239.32.100) of the DNS server serving programmers arise.com.

You can likewise utilize the burrow order to get data on email servers associated with a space by including the mx choice (mx is short for mail trade server). This data is basic for assaults on email frameworks. For instance, data on the www.hackers-arise.com email servers is appeared in the AUTHORITY SECTION of Listing 3-4.

kali >dig hackers-arise.com mx

--snip--

;; QUESTION SECTION:

;hackers-arise.com.   IN   MX

;; AUTHORITY SECTION:

hackers-arise.com.   5   IN   SOA   ns6.wixdns.net. support.wix.com 2016052216 10800 3600 604 800 3600

--snip--

Listing 3-4: Using dig and its mx option to get information on a domain mail exchange server

The most typical Linux DNS server is the Berkeley Web Call Domain (BIND). In some cases, Linux users will refer to DNS as BIND, however do not be puzzled: DNS and BIND both map specific domain to IP addresses.

Changing Your DNS Server

In some cases, you might desire to utilize another DNS server. To do so, you'll edit a plaintext file called/ etc/resolv. On your command line, get in the precise name of your editor followed by the location of the filename and the file.

kali >leafpad /etc/resolv.conf

will open the resolv.conf file in the /etc directory in my specified graphical text editor, Leafpad. The file should look something like this:

```
                              resolv.conf                         □ x
File  Edit  Search  Options  Help
    1 domain localdomain
    2 search localdomain
    3 nameserver 192.168.181.2
    4
```

As you can see on line 3, my nameserver is set to a local DNS server at 192.168.181.2. That works fine, but if I want to add or replace that DNS server with, say, Google's public DNS server at 8.8.8.8, I'd add the following line in the /etc/resolv.conf file to specify the nameserver:

nameserver 8.8.8.8

Then I would just need to save the file. However, you can also achieve the same result exclusively from the command line by entering the following:

kali >echo "nameserver 8.8.8.8"> /etc/resolv.conf

This command echoes the string nameserver 8.8.8.8 and redirects it (>) to the file /etc/resolv.conf, replacing the current content. Your /etc/resolv.conf file should now look like

Your system will now go out to the Google public DNS server to solve domain names to IP addresses. To keep speed however keep the alternative of using a public server, you may desire to retain the local DNS server in the resolv.conf file and follow it with a public

DNS server. The operating system queries each DNS server listed in the order it appears in/ etc/resolv.

KEEP IN MIND

The DHCP server will change the contents of the file when it renews the DHCP address if you're utilizing a DHCP address and the DHCP server offers a DNS setting.

Mapping Your Own IP Addresses

In other words, you can identify which IP address your browser goes to when you go into www.microsoft.com (or any other domain) into the internet browser, rather than let the DNS server decide. As a hacker, this can be helpful for hijacking a TCP connection on your regional location network to direct traffic to a malicious web server with a tool such as dnsspoof.

From the command line, key in the following command (you can replace your favored text editor for leafpad):.

kali >leafpad /etc/hosts

You should now see your hosts file, which will look something like

By default, the hosts file contains only a mapping for your localhost, at 127.0.0.1, and your system's hostname (in this case, Kali, at 127.0.1.1). But you can add any IP address mapped to any domain you'd like. As an example of how this might be used, you could map www.bankofamerica.com to your local website, at 192.168.181.131.

127.0.0.1   localhost

127.0.1.1   kali

192.168.181.131 bankofamerica.com

The following lines are desirable for IPv6 capable hosts

139

::1   localhost ip6-localhost ip6-loopback

ff02::1 ip6-allnodes

ff02::2 ip6-allrouters

Make certain you press TAB between the IP address and the domain key—not the spacebar.

As you get more involved in your hacking endeavors and learn about tools like dnsspoof and Ettercap, you'll be able to use the hosts file to direct any traffic on your LAN that visits www.bankofamerica.com to your web server at 192.168.181.131.

easy, right?

CONTROLLING FILE AND DIRECTORY PERMISSIONS

Not every user of a single operating system should have the very same level of access to files and directory sites. Like any enterprise-level or expert operating system, Linux has approaches for protecting file and directory gain access to. This security system permits the system administrator-- the root user-- or the file owner to secure their files from unwanted access or tampering by granting choose users consents to read, compose, or carry out files. For each file and directory, we can define the authorization status for the file's owner, for specific groups of users, and for all other users. This is a requirement in a multiuser, enterprise-level os. The alternative would be quite disorderly.

In this chapter, I'll reveal you how to look for and change consents on files and directory sites for select users, how to set default file and directory site consents, and how to set special consents. You will see how a hacker's understanding of authorizations may help them exploit a system.

DIFFERENT TYPES OF USERS

As you know, in Linux, the root user is all-powerful. The root user can do generally anything on the system. Other users on the system have more restricted abilities and authorizations and almost never have the gain access to that the root user has.

These other users are normally collected into groups that normally share a similar function. In a business entity, these groups might be financing, engineering, sales, and so on. In an IT environment, these groups may include developers, network administrators, and database administrators. The idea is to put people with comparable needs into a group that is given relevant authorizations; then each member of the group acquires the group consents. This is primarily for the ease of administering authorizations and, therefore, security.

The root user is part of the root group by default. Each new user on the system need to be contributed to a group in order to acquire the permissions of that group.

GRANTING PERMISSIONS

Each and every file and directory need to be allocated a particular level of approval for the various identities using it. The three levels of authorization are as follows:

r Permission to read. This grants permission only to open and view a file.

w Permission to write. This allows users to view and edit a file.

x Permission to execute. This allows users to execute a file (but not necessarily view or edit it).

In this way, the root user can grant users a level of authorization depending upon what they need the declare. When a file is created, generally the user who produced it is the owner of the file, and the owning group is the user's present group. The owner of the file can grant numerous gain access to privileges to it. Let's look at how to alter approvals to pass ownership to specific users and to groups.

Granting Ownership to an Individual User

To move ownership of a file to a different user so that they have the ability to manage consents, we can use the chown (or change owner) command:

kali > chown ❶ bob ❷/ tmp/bobsfile.

Here, we give the command, the name of the user we are providing ownership to, and after that the location and name of the pertinent file. This command grants the user represent Bob ❶ ownership of bobsfile ❷.

Approving Ownership to a Group.

To transfer ownership of a file from one group to another, we can use the chgrp (or change group) command.

Hackers are frequently more likely to work alone than in groups, but it's not unusual for several hackers or pentesters work together on a task, and in that case, utilizing groups is needed. You may have a group of pentesters and a group of security team members working on the very same job. The pentesters in this example are the root group, indicating they have all consents and access. The root group needs access to the hacking tools, whereas the security folk only require access to protective tools such as an intrusion detection system (IDS). Let's state the root group downloads and sets up a program named newIDS; the root group will need to alter the ownership to the security group so the security group can use it at will. To do so, the root group would simply enter the following command.:

kali >chgrp ❶security ❷newIDS

This command passes the security group ❶ ownership of newIDS ❷.

Now you require to know how to check whether these allocations have actually worked. You'll do that by examining a file's authorizations.

INSPECTING PERMISSIONS

When you want to find out what permissions are granted to what users for a file or directory site, utilize the ls command with the-- l (long) switch to show the contents of a directory in long format-- this list will consist of the consents. In Listing 5-1, I utilize the ls--1 command on the file/ usr/share/hashcat (among my preferred password-cracking tools) in order to see what we can discover the files there.

kali >ls –l /usr/share/hashcat

total 32952

❶ ❷   ❸ ❹   ❺   ❻   ❼

drwxr-xr-x 5 root root   4096   Dec 5 10:47 charsets

-rw-r--r-- 1 root root   33685504 June 28 2018 hashcat.hcstat

-rw-r--r-- 1 root root   33685504 June 28 2018 hashcat.hctune

drwxr -xr-x 2 root root   4096   Dec 5 10:47 masks

drwxr -xr-x 2 root root   4096   Dec 5 10:47 OpenCL

drwxr -xr-x 3 root root   4096   Dec 5 10:47 rules

Listing 5-1: Checking a file's permissions with the long listing command

146

On each line, we get info about:

❶ The file type

❷ The authorizations on the declare owner, groups, and users, respectively

❸ The variety of links (This topic is beyond the scope of the book.).

❹ The owner of the file.

❺ The size of the file in bytes.

When the file was produced or last customized, ❻.

❼ The name of the file.

For now, let's concentrate on the seemingly incomprehensible strings of letters and dashes on the left edge of each line. They tell us whether a product is a file or directory and what permissions, if any, are on it.

The very first character tells you the file type, where d represents a dash and a directory (--) indicates a file. These are the two most typical file types.

The next section defines the approvals on the file. There are three sets of three characters, made from some mix of read (r), write (w), and perform (x), because order. The very first set represents the authorizations of the owner; the second, those of the group; and the last, those of all other users.

Regardless of which set of three letters you're looking at, if you see an r first, that user or group of users has consent to open and check out that file or directory. Keep in mind that users can have approval to carry out only either scripts or binaries.

Let's utilize the 3rd line of output in Listing 5-1 as an example:.

- rw-r-- r-- 1 root 33685504 June 28 2018 hashcat.hcstat.

The file is called, as we know from the right end of the line, hashcat.hcstat. After the initial-- (which shows it's a file), the authorizations rw- tell us that the owner has read and compose consents but not execute approval.

The next set of permissions (r--) represents those of the group and reveals that the group has actually read permission but not compose or execute authorizations. And, lastly, we see that the remainder of the users likewise have just check out permission (r--).

These consents aren't set in stone. As a root user or file owner, you can change them. Next, we'll do just that.

ALTERING PERMISSIONS.

We can utilize the Linux command chmod (or alter mode) to change the permissions. Only a root user or the file's owner can alter consents.

In this section, we utilize chmod to alter approvals on hashcat.hcstat using two various approaches. First we use a mathematical representation of permissions, and after that we utilize a symbolic representation.

Altering Permissions with Decimal Notation.

We can use a shortcut to refer to authorizations by utilizing a single number to represent one rwx set of permissions. Like whatever underlying the operating system, permissions are represented in binary, so ON and OFF switches are represented by 1 and 0, respectively. You can think of the rwx permissions as 3 ON/OFF switches, so when all permissions are granted, this corresponds to 111 in binary.

A binary set like this is then easily represented as one digit by transforming it into octal, an eight-digit number system that begins with 0 and ends with 7. An octal digit represents a set of three binary digits, indicating we can represent a whole rwx set with one digit. Table 5-1 consists of all possible consent mixes and their binary and octal agents.

Table 5-1: Octal and Binary Representations of Permissions

Binary	Octal	rwx
000	0	---
001	1	--x
010	2	-w-
011	3	-wx
100	4	r--
101	5	r-x
110	6	rw-
111	7	rwx

Using this information, let's go through some examples. First, if we want to set only the read permission, we could consult Table 5-1 and locate the value for read:

r w x

4 - -

Next, if we want to set the authorization to wx, we might utilize the exact same method and look for what sets the w and what sets the x:

r w x.

- 2 1.

Notice in Table 5-1 that the octal representation for -wx is 3, which not so coincidently takes place to be the exact same value we get when we include the two worths for setting w and x separately: $2 + 1 = 3$.

When all three permissions are on, it looks like this:.

r w x.

4 2 1.

And $4 + 2 + 1 = 7$. Here, we see that in Linux, when all the approval switches are on, they are represented by the octal equivalent of 7.

If we desired to represent all permissions for the owner, group, and all users, we could write it as follows:.

7 7 7.

Here's where the faster way is available in. By passing chmod three octal digits (one for each rwx set), followed by a filename, we can alter approvals on that declare each kind of user. Go into the following into your command line:.

kali > chmod 774 hashcat.hcstat.

Looking at Table 5-1, we can see that this statement provides the owner all consents, the group all approvals, and everyone else (other) only the read authorization.

Now we can see whether those permissions have altered by running ls -l on the directory site and taking a look at the hashcat.hcstat line. Browse to the directory and run that command now.:

kali >ls -l

total 32952

drwxr-xr-x 5   root root   4096 Dec 5 10:47 charsets

❶ -rwxrwxr-- 1   root root 33685504   June 28 2018 hashcat.hcstat

-rw-r--r-- 1   root root 33685504 June 28 2018 hashcat.hctune

drwxr -xr-x 2   root root   4096 Dec 5 10:47 masks

drwxr -xr-x 2   root root   4096 Dec 5 10:47 OpenCL

drwxr -xr-x 3   root root   4096 Dec 5 10:47 rules

You should see - rwxrwxr- - on the left half of the hashcat.hcstat line ❶. This affirms the chmod consider effectively changed consents on the record to give both the proprietor and the gathering the capacity to execute the document.

Changing Permissions with UGO

In spite of the fact that the numeric strategy is likely the most well-known technique for changing authorizations in Linux, a few people locate chmod's emblematic technique progressively instinctive—the two strategies work similarly well, so simply locate the one that suits you. The emblematic strategy is frequently alluded to as the UGO linguistic structure, which represents client (or proprietor), gathering, and others.

UGO language structure is extremely straightforward. Enter the chmod direction and afterward the clients you need to change authorizations for, giving u to client, g for gathering, or o for other people, trailed by one of three administrators:

- Removes a permission

+ Adds a permission

= Sets a permission

After the administrator, incorporate the authorization you need to include or evacuate (rwx) and, at long last, the name of the record to apply it to.

Along these lines, on the off chance that you need to expel the compose authorization from the client that the record hashcat.hcstat has a place with, you could enter the accompanying:

kali >chmod u-w hashcat.hcstat

This direction says to expel (-) the compose (w) consent from hashcat.hcstat for the client (u).

Presently when you check the authorizations with ls – l once more, you should see that the hashcat.hcstat document never again has compose consent for the client:

kali >ls -l

total 32952

drwxr-xr-x 5   root root   4096   Dec 5 10:47 charsets

-r-xr-xr-- 1   root root   33685504   June 28 2018 hashcat.hcstat

-rw-r--r-- 1   root root   33685504   June 28 2018 hashcat.hctune

drwxr -xr-x 2   root root   4096   Dec 5 10:47 masks

drwxr -xr-x 2   root root   4096   Dec 5 10:47 OpenCL

drwxr -xr-x 3   root root   4096   Dec 5 10:47 rules

You can also alter numerous approvals with simply one command. If you want to offer both the user and other users (not consisting of the group) perform approval, you could enter the following:

chmod u+ x, o+ x hashcat.hcstat

This command tells Linux to add the execute consent for the user in addition to the execute consent for others for the hashcat.hcstat file.

Giving Root Execute Permission on a New Tool

As a hacker, you'll typically require to download new hacking tools, but Linux automatically appoints all files and directory sites default approvals of 666 and 777, respectively. This indicates that, by default, you will not have the ability to carry out a file right away after downloading it. If you try, you'll normally get a message that states something like "Permission rejected." For these cases, you'll need to offer yourself root and carry out authorizations using chmod in order to perform the file.

For instance, say we download a brand-new hacker tool called newhackertool and place it into the root user's directory (/).

kali >ls -l

total 80

drwxr-xr-x 7 root root 4096 Dec 5 11.17 Desktop

drwxr-xr-x 7 root root 4096 Dec 5 11.17 Documents

drwxr-xr-x 7 root root 4096 Dec 5 11.17 Downloads

drwxr-xr-x 7 root root 4096 Dec 5 11.17 Music

-rw-r--r-- 1 root root 1072 Dec 5 11.17 newhackertool❶

drwxr-xr-x 7 root root 4096 Dec 5 11.17 Pictures

drwxr-xr-x 7 root root 4096 Dec 5 11.17 Public

drwxr-xr-x 7 root root 4096 Dec 5 11.17 Templates

drwxr-xr-x 7 root root 4096 Dec 5 11.17 Videos

We can see newhackertool at ❶, alongside the remainder of the substance of the root registry. We can see that our newhackertool doesn't have execute authorization for anybody. This makes it difficult to utilize. It may appear to be weird that of course, Linux won't let you execute a record you downloaded, yet in general this setting makes your framework progressively secure.

We can give ourselves authorization to execute newhackertool by entering the accompanying:

kali >chmod 766 newhackertool

Presently, when we play out a long posting on the index, we can see that our newhackertool has execute authorization for the proprietor:

kali >chmod 766 newhackertool

kali >ls -l

total 80

--snip--

drwxr-xr-x 7 root root 4096 Dec 5 11.17 Music

-rwxrw-rw- 1   root   root   1072   Dec   5   11.17 newhackertool

drwxr-xr-x 7 root root 4096 Dec 5 11.17 Pictures

--snip--

As you now comprehend, this grants us (as the owner) all authorizations, including perform, and grants the group and everyone else just read and compose consents (4 + 2 = 6).

SETTING MORE SECURE DEFAULT PERMISSIONS WITH MASKS

As you have actually seen, Linux instantly appoints base permissions-- typically 666 for files and 777 for directories. You can alter the default consents allocated to directories and files produced by each user with the umask (or unmask) technique. The umask approach represents the permissions you want to eliminate from the base approvals on a file or directory to make them more safe.

The umask is a three-digit decimal number corresponding to the three approvals digits, however the umask number is subtracted from the approvals number to provide the brand-new approvals status. This means that when a brand-new file or directory is developed, its permissions are set to the default worth minus the worth in umask, as shown in Figure 5-1.

New files	New directories	
6 6 6	7 7 7	Linux base permissions
− 0 2 2	− 0 2 2	umask
6 4 4	7 5 5	Resulting permissions

How a umask value of 022 affects the permissions on new files and directories

For instance, if the umask is set to 022, a brand-new file with the initial default consents of 666 will now have the permissions 644, indicating the owner has both read and write consents, and the group and all other users have only check out authorization.

In Kali, just like the majority of Debian systems, the umask is preconfigured to 022, suggesting the Kali default is 644 for files and 755 for directory sites.

The umask worth is not universal to all users on the system. Each user can set an individual default umask worth for the files and directories in their personal.profile file. To see the existing worth when gone to as the user, just get in the command umask and note what is returned. To alter the umask worth for a user, modify the file/ home/username/. profile and, for example, include umask 007 to set it so just the user and members of the user's group have permissions.

UNIQUE PERMISSIONS

In addition to the three general-purpose authorizations, rwx, Linux has three special permissions that are somewhat more complex. These unique authorizations are set user ID (or SUID), set group ID (or SGID), and sticky bit. I'll talk about each in turn in the next 3 areas.

Approving Temporary Root Permissions with SUID

As you need to know by now, a user can execute a file just if they have consent to carry out that particular file. They can not execute if the user just has actually read and/or write consents. This might seem straightforward, however there are exceptions to this guideline.

You might have encountered a case in which a file needs the consents of the root user throughout execution for all users, even those who are not root. For instance, a file that permits users to alter their password would require access to the/ etc/shadow file-- the file that holds the users' passwords in Linux--which requires root user privileges in order to carry out. In such a case, you can momentarily grant the owner's opportunities to execute the file by setting the SUID bit on the program.

Basically, the SUID bit says that any user can execute the file with the approvals of the owner but those consents do not extend beyond using that file.

To set the SUID bit, go into a 4 before the regular approvals, so a file with a new resulting permission of 644 is represented as 4644 when the SUID bit is set.

Setting the SUID on a file is not something a common user would do, but if you wish to do so, you'll utilize the chmod command, as in chmod 4644 filename.

Granting the Root User's Group Permissions SGID

SGID also gives short-lived elevated permissions, however it grants the permissions of the file owner's group, rather than of the file's owner. This suggests that, with an SGID bit set, somebody without carry out consent can perform a file if the owner comes from the group that has consent to carry out that file.

The SGID bit works a little differently when applied to a directory: when the bit is set on a directory, ownership of new files developed in that directory goes to the directory creator's group, instead of the file developer's group. This is extremely useful when a directory site is shared by numerous users. All users because group can carry out the file(s), not simply a single user.

The SGID bit is represented as 2 prior to the routine authorizations, so a new file with the resulting consents 644 would be represented as 2644 when the SGID bit is set. Once again, you would use the chmod command for this-- for example, chmod 2644 filename.

The Outmoded Sticky Bit

The sticky bit is an authorization bit that you can set on a directory to allow a user to erase or relabel files within that directory site. Nevertheless, the sticky bit is a tradition of older Unix systems, and contemporary systems (like Linux) ignore it. I will not discuss it even more here, however you must be familiar with the term because you may hear it in the Linux world.

Unique Permissions, Privilege Escalation, and the Hacker

As a hacker, these unique authorizations can be used to exploit Linux systems through benefit escalation, where a regular user gains root or sysadmin advantages and the associated consents. With root privileges, you can do anything on the system.

A system administrator or software developer might set the SUID bit on a program to enable that program access to files with root advantages. You, the hacker, can utilize that permission to acquire momentary root benefits and do something harmful, such as get access to the passwords at/ etc/shadow.

Let's look for files with the SUID bit set on our Kali system to attempt this out. Back in Chapter 1, I presented you to the find command. We'll utilize its power to find files with the SUID bit set.

As you'll remember, the find command is powerful, however the syntax is bit more complex than a few of the other location commands, such as find and which. Take a moment to evaluate the discover syntax in Chapter 1, if you require to.

In this case, we want to discover files anywhere on the filesystem, for the root user or other sysadmin, with the permissions 4000. To do this, we can utilize the following discover command:

kali > discover/ -user root -perm -4000

With this command, we ask Kali to begin looking at the top of the filesystem with the/ syntax. It then looks everywhere below/ for files that are owned by root, defined with user root, and that have the SUID consent bit set (- perm -4000).

We get the output shown in Listing 5-2 when we run this command.

/usr/bin/chsh

/usr/bin/gpasswd

/usr/bin/pkexec

/usr/bin/sudo

/usr/bin/passwd

/usr/bin/kismet_capture

--snip--

Listing 5-2: Finding files with the SUID bit set

The yield uncovers various records that have the SUID bit set. How about we explore to the/usr/container index, where a significant number of these records dwell, and afterward run a long posting on that registry and look down to the sudo document, as appeared in Listing 5-3.

kali >cd /usr/bin

kali >ls -l

--snip--

-rwxr-xr-x 1   root   root   176272   Jul 18 2018
stunnel4

-rwxr-xr-x 1   root   root   26696   Mar 17 2018
sucrack

❶ -rwsr-xr-x 1 root root 140944   Jul 5 2018   sudo

--snip--

Listing 5-3: Identifying files with the SUID bit set

Note that at 1, the main arrangement of authorizations—for the proprietor—has a s instead of the x. This is the way Linux speaks to that the SUID bit is set. This implies any individual who runs the sudo document has the benefits of the root client, which can be a security worry for the sysadmin and a potential assault vector for the programmer. For example, a few applications need to get to the/and so forth/shadow document to effectively finish their undertakings. In the event that the aggressor can deal with that application, they can utilize that application's entrance to the passwords on a Linux framework.

Linux has a well-created arrangement of security that shields records and indexes from unapproved get to. The hopeful programmer needs to have a fundamental comprehension of this framework not exclusively to secure their records yet additionally to execute new instruments and documents. Sometimes, programmers can abuse the SUID and SGID consents to heighten benefits from a standard client to a root client.

MANAGING USER ENVIRONMENT VARIABLES

To get the most from your Linux hacking system, you need to comprehend environment variables and be adept at managing them for optimal efficiency, benefit, and even stealth. Amongst the areas that Linux beginners find bothersome, however, handling the user environment variables might be the most challenging to master. Technically, there are two types of variables: shell and environment. Environment variables are system-wide variables constructed into your system and interface that control the method your system looks, acts, and "feels" to the user, and they are inherited by any kid shells or processes. Shell variables, on the other hand, are generally noted in lowercase and are just legitimate in the shell they are set in. To avoid over-explanation, I just cover a few of the most basic and beneficial skills for environment and shell variables in this chapter and don't go too deeply into the differences between them.

Variables are simply strings in key-value pairs. Normally, each set will look like KEY= value. In cases where there are several values, they will look like KEY= value1: value2. Just like the majority of things in Linux, if there are spaces in the worth, it requires to be consisted of in quote marks. In Kali Linux, your environment is your bash shell. Each user, including root, has a default set of environment variables that identify how the system looks, acts, and feels. You can alter the values for these variables to make your system work more efficiently, customize your work environment to best satisfy your specific needs, and possibly cover your tracks if you require to.

VIEWING AND MODIFYING ENVIRONMENT VARIABLES

You can view all your default environment variables by getting in env into your terminal from any directory, like so:

kali >env

XDG_VTNR=7

SSHAGENT_PID=922

XDG_SESSION_ID=2

XDG_GREETER_DATA_DIR=/var/lib/lightdm/data/r
oot

GLADE_PIXMAP_PATH=:echo

TERM=xterm

SHELL=/bin/bash

--snip--

USER=root

--snip--

PATH=/usr/local/sbin :usr/local/bin:/usr/sbin:/sbin/bin

--snip--

HOME=/root

--snip--

Environment variables are constantly uppercase, as in HOME, PATH, SHELL, and so on. These are only the default environment variables that begin your system. A user can also produce their own variables, and as you will see, we require a different command to include those in the output.

Viewing All Environment Variables

To view all environment variables, consisting of shell variables, regional variables, and shell functions such as any user-defined variables and command aliases, utilize the set command. This command will note all environment variables distinct to your system, which for the most part will offer you an output so long you will not have the ability to view it all on a single screen. You can ask for to see each variable, line by line, in a more available fashion utilizing set and piping it to the more command, as follows:

kali >set | more

BASH=/bin/bash

BASHOPTS=checkwinsize:cmdlist:complete_fullquot e:expand_aliases:extglob.....

BASH_ALIASES=()

BASH_ARGC=()

BASH_ARGV=()

--snip--

Now the list of variables will fill up one screen, line by line, and then stop. When you press ENTER, the terminal advances to the next line, taking you to the next variable, so you can scroll through by pressing or holding ENTER. As you might recall from Chapter 2, whenever you use the more command for output, you can enter q to quit (or exit) and return to the command prompt.

Filtering for Particular Variables

Although using set with more gives more manageable results than looking through the huge chunk of variable names you get with set alone, it can still be rather tedious if you're looking for a particular variable. Instead, you can use the filtering command grep to find your variable of interest.

Let's use the variable HISTSIZE as an example. This variable contains the maximum number of commands your command history file will store. These commands are any ones you've previously typed into your command prompt in this session and can be recalled with your up- and down-arrow keys. Note that HISTSIZE doesn't store the commands themselves, just the number of them that can be stored.

Pipe your set output with grep to find the HISTSIZE variable, like so:

kali >set | grep HISTSIZE

HISTSIZE=1000

As you can see, this command finds the variable HISTSIZE and displays its value. The default value of this variable is probably set to 1000 on your system. This indicates that the terminal will store your last 1,000 commands by default.

Changing Variable Values for a Session

Now let's see how to change a variable's value. As noted, the HISTSIZE variable contains the value of the number of commands to store in the history file. Sometimes, you won't want your system to save past commands—perhaps because you don't want to leave any evidence of your activity on your own system or a target system. In that case, you can set the HISTSIZE variable to 0 so the system won't store any of your past commands. Because this variable has a single value, to change it, you assign it a new value in the familiar way shown in Listing 7-1.

kali >HISTSIZE=0

Listing 7-1: Changing the value of HISTSIZE

Now, when you try to use the up- and down-arrow keys to recall your commands, nothing happens because the system no longer stores them. This is stealthy, although it can be inconvenient.

Making Variable Value Changes Permanent

When you change an environment variable, that change only occurs in that particular environment; in this case, that environment is the bash shell session. This means that when you close the terminal, any changes you made are lost, with values set back to their defaults. If you want to make the changes permanent, you need to use the export command. This command will export the new value from your current environment (the bash shell) to the rest of the system, making it available in every environment until you change and export it again.

Variables are strings, so if you run on the cautious side, it isn't a bad idea to save the contents of a variable to a text file before you modify it. For example, since we're about to change the PS1 variable, which controls the information you display in the prompt, first run the following command to save the existing values to a text file in the current user's home directory:

kali >echo $HISTSIZE> ~/valueofHISTSIZE.txt

This way, you can always undo your changes. If you want to be even more cautious and create a text file with all the current settings, you can save the output of the set command to a text file with a command like this one:

kali >set> ~/valueofALLon01012017.txt

After you've changed a variable, as we did in Listing 7-1, you can make the change permanent by entering export and then the name of the variable you changed, as shown here:

kali >export HISTSIZE

Now the HISTSIZE variable will still be set to 0 when you leave this environment and enter another environment. If you want to reset the HISTSIZE variable to 1,000, simply enter this:

kali >HISTSIZE=1000

kali >export HISTSIZE

This code snippet will set your HISTSIZE variable's value to 1,000 and export it to all your environments.

CHANGING YOUR SHELL PROMPT

Your shell prompt, another environment variable, provides you with useful information such as the user you're operating as and the directory in which you're currently working. The default shell prompt in Kali takes the following format:

username@hostname:current_directory

If you're working as the root user, this translates to the following default prompt:

root@kali:current_directory

You can change the name in the default shell prompt by setting the value for the PS1 variable. The PS1 variable has a set of placeholders for information you want to display in the prompt, including the following:

\u The name of the current user

\h The hostname

\W The base name of the current working directory

This is very useful if you happen to have shells on multiple systems or are logged on as multiple accounts. By setting different \u and \h values for different shells or accounts, you can tell at a glance who you are and what your current system is.

Let's have a little fun and change the prompt in your terminal. For example, you could enter the following:

kali >PS1="World's Best Hacker: #"

World's Best Hacker: #

Now, every time you use this terminal, you'll be reminded that you are the "World's Best Hacker." But any subse□uent terminal you open will still have the default command prompt, because the PS1 variable only holds values for your terminal session. Remember, until you export a variable, it is only good for that session. If you really like this new command prompt and want to see it in every terminal, you need to export it, like so:

kali >export PS1

This will make the change permanent across all sessions.

How about a little more fun? Say you really want your terminal to look like a Windows cmd prompt. In this case, you could change the prompt name to C: and keep the \w to have the prompt show your current directory, as shown in Listing 7-2.

kali >export PS1='C:\w> '

C:/tmp>

Listing 7-2: Changing the prompt and showing the current directory

Having your prompt show your current directory can be generally useful, particularly to a beginner, so it's something to consider when you change your PS1 variable.

CHANGING YOUR PATH

One of the most important variables in your environment is your PATH variable, which controls where on your system your shell will look for commands you enter, such as cd, ls, and echo. Most commands are located in the sbin or bin subdirectory, like /usr/local/sbin or usr/local/bin. If the bash shell doesn't find the command in one of the directories in your PATH variable, it will return the error command not found, even if that command does exist in a directory not in your PATH.

You can find out which directories are stored in your PATH variable by using echo on its contents, like so:

kali >echo $PATH

/usr/local/sbin:usr/local/bin:/usr/sbin:/sbin/bin

These are the directories where your terminal will search for any command. When you enter ls, for example, the system knows to look in each of these directories for the ls command, and when it finds ls, the system executes it.

Each directory is separated by a colon (:), and don't forget to add the $ content symbol to PATH.

Adding to the PATH Variable

You can probably see why it's important to know what is in your PATH variable: if you downloaded and installed a new tool—let's say newhackingtool—into the /root/newhackingtool directory, you could only use commands from that tool when you're in that directory because that directory is not in the PATH variable. Every time you wanted to use that tool, you would first have to navigate to /root/newhackingtool, which is a bit inconvenient if you want to use the tool often.

To be able to use this new tool from any directory, you need to add the directory holding this tool to your PATH variable.

To add newhackingtool to your PATH variable, enter the following:

kali >PATH=$PATH:/root/newhackingtool

This assigns the original PATH variable plus the /root/newhackingtool directory to the new PATH variable, so the variable contains everything it did before, plus the new tool directory.

If you examine the contents of the PATH variable again, you should see that this directory has been appended to the end of PATH, as shown here:

kali >echo $PATH

/usr/local/sbin:usr/local/bin:/usr/sbin:/sbin/bin:/root/ne whackingtool

Now you can execute newhackingtool applications from anywhere on your system, rather than having to navigate to its directory. The bash shell will look in all directories listed for your new tool!

NOTE

Adding to PATH can be a useful technique for directories you use often, but be careful not to add too many directories to your PATH variable. Because the system will have to search through each and every directory in PATH to find commands, adding a lot of directories could slow down your terminal and your hacking.

How Not to Add to the PATH Variable

One mistake commonly made by new Linux users is assigning a new directory, such as /root/newhackingtool, directly to the PATH variable in this way:

kali >PATH=/root/newhackingtool

kali >echo $PATH

/root/newhackingtool

If you use this command, your PATH variable will only contain the /root/newhackingtool directory and no longer contain the system binaries directories such as /bin, /sbin, and others that hold critical commands. When you then go to use any of the system commands, you'll receive the error command not found, as shown next, unless you first navigate to the system binaries directory when you execute the command:

kali >cd

bash: cd: command not found

Remember that you want to append to the PATH variable, not replace it. If you're in doubt, save the contents of the variable somewhere before you modify it.

CREATING A USER-DEFINED VARIABLE

You can create your own custom, user-defined variables in Linux by simply assigning a value to a new variable that you name. This may be useful when you are doing some more advanced shell scripting or find you're often using a long command that you get tired of typing over and over.

The syntax is straightforward: enter the name of your variable, followed by the assignment symbol (=), and then the value to put in the variable, as shown here:

kali >MYNEWVARIABLE="Hacking is the most valuable skill set in the 21st century"

This assigns a string to the variable MYNEWVARIABLE. To see the value in that variable, use the echo command and the $ content symbol with the variable name, as we did earlier:

kali >echo $MYNEWVARIABLE

Hacking is the most valuable skill set in the 21st century

Just like our system environment variables, user-defined variables must be exported to persist to new sessions.

If you want to delete this new variable, or any variable, use the unset command. Always think before deleting a system variable, though, because your system will probably operate much differently afterward.

kali >unset MYNEWVARIABLE

kali >echo $MYNEWVARIABLE

kali >

As you can see, when you enter unset
MYNEWVARIABLE, you delete the variable along
with its value. If you use echo on that same variable,
Linux will now return a blank line.

BASH SCRIPTING

any self-respecting Linux administrator must be able to script. Hackers often need to automate commands, sometimes from multiple tools, and this is most efficiently done through short programs they write themselves.

In this chapter, we build a few simple bash shell scripts to start you off with scripting. We'll add capabilities and features as we progress, eventually building a script capable of finding potential attack targets over a range of IP addresses.

To become an elite hacker, you also need the ability to script in one of the widely used scripting languages, such as Ruby (Metasploit exploits are written in Ruby), Python (many hacking tools are Python scripts), or Perl (Perl is the best text-manipulation scripting language).

A CRASH COURSE IN BASH

A shell is an interface between the user and the operating system that enables you to manipulate files and run commands, utilities, programs, and much more. The advantage of a shell is that you perform these tasks immediately from the computer and not through an abstraction, like a GUI, which allows you to customize your task to your needs. A number of different shells are available for Linux, including the Korn shell, the Z shell, the C shell, and the Bourne-again shell, more widely known as bash.

Because the bash shell is available on nearly all Linux and UNIX distributions (including macOS and Kali), we'll be using the bash shell, exclusively.

The bash shell can run any system commands, utilities, or applications your usual command line can run, but it also includes some of its own built-in commands. Table 8-1 later in the chapter gives you a reference to some useful commands that reside within the bash shell.

In earlier chapters, you used the cd, pwd, set, and umask commands. In this section, you will be using two more commands: the echo command, first used in prevously, which displays messages to the screen, and the read command, which reads in data and stores it somewhere else. Just learning these two commands alone will enable you to build a simple but powerful tool.

You'll need a text editor to create shell scripts. You can use whichever Linux text editor you like best, including vi, vim, emacs, gedit, kate, and so on. I'll be using Leafpad in these tutorials, as I have in previous chapters. Using a different editor should not make any difference in your script or its functionality.

YOUR FIRST SCRIPT: "HELLO, HACKERS-ARISE!"

For your first script, we will start with a simple program that returns a message to the screen that says "Hello, Hackers-Arise!" Open your text editor, and let's go.

To start, you need to tell your operating system which interpreter you want to use for the script. To do this, enter a shebang, which is a combination of a hash mark and an exclamation mark, like so:

#!

You then follow the shebang (#!) with /bin/bash to indicate that you want the operating system to use the bash shell interpreter. As you'll see in later chapters, you could also use the shebang to use other interpreters, such as Perl or Python. Here, you want to use the bash interpreter, so enter the following:

#! /bin/bash

Next, enter the echo command, which tells the system to simply repeat (or echo) back to your monitor whatever follows the command.

In this case, we want the system to echo back to us "Hello, Hackers-Arise!", as done in Listing 8-1. Note that the text or message we want to echo back must be in double quotation marks.

#! /bin/bash

This is my first bash script. Wish me luck.

echo "Hello, Hackers-Arise!"

Listing 8-1: Your "Hello, Hackers-Arise!" script

Here, you also see a line that's preceded by a hash mark (#). This is a comment, which is a note you leave to yourself or anyone else reading the code to explain what you're doing in the script. Programmers use comments in every coding language. These comments are not read or executed by the interpreter, so you don't need to worry about messing up your code. They are visible only to humans. The bash shell knows a line is a comment if it starts with the # character.

Now, save this file as HelloHackersArise with no extension and exit your text editor.

Setting Execute Permissions

By default, a newly created bash script is not executable even by you, the owner. Let's look at the permissions on our new file in the command line by using cd to move into the directory and then entering ls -l. It should look something like this:

kali >ls -l

--snip--

-rw-r--r-- 1 root root 42 Oct 22 14:32 HelloHackersArise

--snip--

As you can see, our new file has rw-r--r-- (644) permissions. As you learned in Chapter 5, this means the owner of this file only has read (r) and write (w) permissions, but no execute (x) permissions. The group and all other users have only read permissions. We need to give ourselves execute permissions in order to run this script. We change the permissions with the chmod command, as you saw in Chapter 5. To give the owner, the group, and all others execute permissions, enter the following:

kali >chmod 755 HelloHackersArise

Now when we do a long listing on the file, like so, we can see that we have execute permissions:

kali >ls -l

--snip--

-rwx r-x r-x 1 root root 42 Oct 22 14:32
HelloHackersArise

--snip--

The script is now ready to execute!

Running HelloHackersArise

To run our simple script, enter the following:

kali >./HelloHackersArise

The ./ before the filename tells the system that we want
to execute this script in the file HelloHackersArise
from the current directory. It also tells the system that
if there is another file in another directory named
HelloHackersArise, please ignore it and only run
HelloHackersArise in the current directory. It may
seem unlikely that there's another file with this name

195

on your system, but it's good practice to use the ./ when executing files, as this localizes the file execution to the current directory and many directories will have duplicate filenames, such as start and setup.

When we press ENTER, our very simple script returns our message to the monitor:

Hello, Hackers-Arise!

Success! You just completed your first shell script!

Adding Functionality with Variables and User Input

So, now we have a simple script. All it does is echo back a message to standard output. If we want to create more advanced scripts, we will likely need to add some variables.

A variable is an area of storage that can hold something in memory. That "something" might be some letters or words (strings) or numbers. It's known as a variable because the values held within it are changeable; this is an extremely useful feature for adding functionality to a script.

In our next script, we will add functionality to prompt the user for their name, place whatever they input into a variable, then prompt the user for the chapter they're at in this book, and place that keyboard input into a variable. After that, we'll echo a welcome message that includes their name and the chapter back to the user.

Open a new file in your text editor and enter the script shown in Listing 8-2.

❶ #! /bin/bash

❷ # This is your second bash script. In this one, you prompt /

   # the user for input, place the input in a variable, and /

   # display the variable contents in a string.

❸ echo "What is your name?"

read name

❹ echo "What chapter are you on in Linux Basics for Hackers?"

read chapter

❺ echo "Welcome" $name "to Chapter" $chapter "of Linux Basics for Hackers!"

Listing 8-2: A simple script making use of variables

We open with #! /bin/bash to tell the system we want to use the bash interpreter for this script ❶. We then add a comment that describes the script and its functionality ❷. After that, we prompt the user for their name and ask the interpreter to read the input and place it into a variable we call name ❸. Then we prompt the user to enter the chapter they are currently

198

working through in this book, and we again read the keyboard input into a variable, this time called chapter ❹.

In the final line, we construct a line of output that welcomes the reader by their name to the chapter they are on ❺. We use the echo command and provide the text we want to display on the screen in double ☐uotes. Then, to fill in the name and chapter number the user entered, we add the variables where they should appear in the message. As noted in Chapter 7, to use the values contained in the variables, you must precede the variable name with the $ symbol.

Save this file as WelcomeScript.sh. The .sh extension is the convention for script files. You might have noticed we didn't include the extension earlier; it's not strictly re☐uired, and if you leave the extension off, the file will save as a shell script file by default.

Now, let's run this script. Don't forget to give yourself execute permission with chmod first; otherwise, the operating system will scold you with a Permission denied message.

```
kali >./WelcomeScript.sh
```

What is your name?

OccupytheWeb

What chapter are you on in Linux Basics for Hackers?

Welcome OccupytheWeb to Chapter 8 of Linux Basics for Hackers!

As you can see, your script took input from the user, placed it into variables, and then used those inputs to make a greeting for the user.

This is a simple script, but it taught you how to use variables and take input from the keyboard. These are both crucial concepts in scripting that you will need to use in more complex scripts in future.

YOUR VERY FIRST HACKER SCRIPT: SCAN FOR OPEN PORTS

Now that you have some basic scripting skills, let's move to some slightly more advanced scripting that has real-world application to hacking. We'll use an example from the world of black hat hacking. Black hat hackers are those with malicious intentions, such as stealing credit card numbers or defacing websites. White hat hackers are those with good intentions, such as helping software developers or system administrators make their systems more secure. Gray hat hackers are those who tend to move between these two extremes.

Before you continue, you need to become familiar with a simple yet essential tool named nmap that comes installed on Kali by default. You've likely heard the name; nmap is used to probe a system to see whether it is connected to the network and finds out what ports are open. From the open ports discovered, you can surmise what services are running on the target system. This is a crucial skill for any hacker or system administrator.

In its simplest form, the syntax for running an nmap scan looks like this:

nmap <type of scan><target IP><optionally, target port>

Not too difficult. The simplest and most reliable nmap scan is the TCP connect scan, designated with the -sT switch in nmap. So, if you wanted to scan IP address 192.168.181.1 with a TCP scan, you would enter the following:

nmap -sT 192.168.181.1

To take things a step further, if you wanted to perform a TCP scan of address 192.168.181.1, looking to see whether port 3306 (the default port for MySQL) was open, you could enter this:

nmap -sT 192.168.181.1 -p 3306

Here, -p designates the port you want to scan for. Go ahead and try it out now on your Kali system.

Our Task

At the time of this writing, there is a hacker serving time in US federal prison by the name of Max Butler, also known as Max Vision throughout the hacker world. Max was a kind of gray hat hacker. By day, he was an IT security professional in Silicon Valley, and by night, he was stealing and selling credit card numbers on the black market. At one time, he ran the world's largest credit card black market, CardersMarket. Now, Max is serving a 13-year prison term while at the same time assisting the Computer Emergency Response Team (CERT) in Pittsburgh with defending against hackers.

A few years before Max was caught, he realized that the Aloha Point of Sale (POS) system used by many small restaurants had a technical support backdoor built into it. In this case, the backdoor enabled tech support to assist their clients. Aloha tech support could access the end user's system through port 5505 to provide assistance when the user called for help. Max realized that if he found a system connected to the internet with the Aloha POS system, he could access the system with sysadmin privileges through port 5505. Max was able to enter many of these systems and steal tens of thousands of credit card numbers.

Eventually, Max wanted to find every system that had port 5505 open so that he could go from stealing thousands of credit card numbers to stealing millions.

Max decided to write a script that would scan millions of IP addresses looking for systems with port 5505 open. Of course, most systems do not have port 5505 open so, if they did, it was likely they were running the doomed Aloha POS. He could run this script while at work during the day, then by night hack into those systems identified as having port 5505 open.

Our task is to write a script that will be nearly identical to Max's script, but rather than scan for port 5505 as Max did, our script will scan for systems connected to the ubi☐uitous online database MySQL. MySQL is an open source database used behind millions of websites; we'll be working with MySQL in Chapter 12. By default, MySQL uses port 3306. Databases are the "Golden Fleece" that nearly every black hat hacker is seeking, as they often contain credit card numbers and personally identifiable information (PII) that is very valuable on the black market.

A Simple Scanner

Before we write the script to scan public IPs across the internet, let's take on much a smaller task. Instead of scanning the globe, let's first write a script to scan for port 3306 on a local area network to see whether our script actually works. If it does, we can easily edit it to do the much larger task.

In your text editor, enter the script shown in Listing 8-3.

❶ #! /bin/bash

❷ # This script is designed to find hosts with MySQL installed

   nmap   ❸-sT   192.168.181.0/24   ❹-p   3306 ❺>/dev/null ❻-oG MySQLscan

❼ cat MySQLscan | grep open > MySQLscan2 ❽

   cat MySQLscan2

Listing 8-3: The simplified scanner script

We start with the shebang and the interpreter to use ❶. Let's follow this with a comment to explain what the script does ❷.

Now let's use the nmap command to re☐uest a TCP scan ❸ on our LAN, looking for port 3306 ❹. (Note that your IP addresses may differ; in your terminal, use the ifconfig command on Linux or the ipconfig command on Windows to determine your IP address.) To stay stealthy, we also send the standard nmap output that would usually appear on the screen to a special place in Linux, where it disappears ❺. We're doing this on a local machine, so it doesn't matter so much, but if you were to use the script remotely, you'd want to hide the nmap output. We then send the output of the scan to a file named MySQLscan in a grep-able format ❻, meaning a format that grep can work on.

The next line displays the MySQLscan file we stored the output in and then pipes that output to grep to filter for lines that include the keyword open ❼. Then we put those lines into a file named MySQLscan2 ❽.

Finally, you display the contents of the file MySQLscan2. This final file should only include lines of output from nmap with hosts that have port 3306 open. Save this file as MySQLscanner.sh and give yourself execute permissions with chmod 755.

Execute the script, like so:

kali >./MySQLscanner.sh

host: 192.168.181.69 () Ports: 3306/open/tcp//mys□l///

As we can see, this script was able to identify the only IP address on my LAN with MySQL running. Your results may differ, depending on whether any ports are running MySQL installations on your local network, of course.

Improving the MySQL Scanner

Now we want to adapt this script to make it applicable to more than just your own local network. This script would be much easier to use if it could prompt the user for the range of IP addresses they wanted to scan and the port to look for, and then use that input. Remember, you learned how to prompt the user and put their keyboard input into a variable in "Adding Functionality with Variables and User Input" on page 84.

Let's take a look at how you could use variables to make this script more flexible and efficient.

Adding Prompts and Variables to Our Hacker Script

In your text editor, enter the script shown in Listing 8-4.

```
#! /bin/bash
```

❶ echo "Enter the starting IP address : "

❷ read FirstIP

❸ echo "Enter the last octet of the last IP address : "

read LastOctetIP

❹ echo "Enter the port number you want to scan for :
"

  read port

❺ nmap -sT $FirstIP-$LastOctetIP -p $port >/dev/null -oG MySQLscan

❻ cat MySQLscan | grep open > MySQLscan2

❼ cat MySQLscan2

Your advanced MySQL port scanner

The first thing we need to do is replace the specified subnet with an IP address range. We'll create a variable called FirstIP and a second variable named LastOctetIP to create the range as well as a variable named port for the port number (the last octet is the last group of digits after the third period in the IP address. In the IP address 192.168.1.101, the last octet is 101).

NOTE

The name of the variable is irrelevant, but best practice is to use a variable name that helps you remember what the variable holds.

We also need to prompt the user for these values. We can do this by using the echo command that we used in Listing 8-1.

To get a value for the FirstIP variable, echo "Enter the starting IP address : " to the screen, asking the user for the first IP address they want to scan ❶. Upon seeing this prompt on the screen, the user will enter the first IP address, so we need to capture that input from the user.

We can do this with the read command followed by the name of the variable we want to store the input in ❷. This command will put the IP address entered by the user into the variable FirstIP. Then we can use that value in FirstIP throughout our script.

210

We'll do the same for the LastOctetIP ❸ and port ❹ variables by prompting the user to enter the information and then using a read command to capture it.

Next, we need to edit the nmap command in our script to use the variables we just created and filled. To use the value stored in the variable, we simply preface the variable name with $, as in $port, for example. So at ❺, we scan a range of IP addresses, starting with the first user-input IP through the second user-input IP, and look for the particular port input by the user. We've used the variables in place of the subnet to scan and the port to determine what to scan for. The redirect symbol > tells the standard nmap output, which usually goes to the screen, to instead go to /dev/null (/dev/null is simply a place to send output so that it disappears). Then, we send the output in a grep-able format to a file we named MySQLscan.

The next line remains the same as in our simple scanner: it outputs the contents of the MySQLscan file, pipes it to grep, where it is filtered for lines that include the keyword open, and then sends that output to a new file named MySQLscan2 ❻. Finally, we display the contents of the MySQLscan2 file ❼.

If everything works as expected, this script will scan IP addresses from the first input address to the last input address, searching for the input port and then reporting back with just the IP addresses that have the designated port open. Save your script file as MySQLscannerAdvanced, remembering to give yourself execute permission.

A Sample Run

Now we can run our simple scanner script with the variables that determine what IP address range and port to scan without having to edit the script every time we want to run a scan:

kali >./MySQLscannerAdvanced.sh

Enter the starting IP address :

192.168.181.0

Enter the last IP address :

192.168.181.255

Enter the port number you want to scan for :

3306

Host: 192.168.181.254 ()Ports:3306/open/tcp//mys□l//

The script prompts the user for the first IP address, the last IP address, and then the port to scan for. After collecting this info, the script performs the nmap scan and produces a report of all the IP addresses in the range that have the specified port open. As you can see, even the simplest of scripting can create a powerful tool. You'll learn even more about scripting

COMMON BUILT-IN BASH COMMANDS

As promised, Table 8-1 gives you a list of some useful commands built into bash.

Table 8-1: Built-in Bash Commands

Command Function

: Returns 0 or true

. Executes a shell script

bg Puts a job in the background

break Exits the current loop

cd Changes directory

continue Resumes the current loop

echo Displays the command arguments

eval Evaluates the following expression

exec Executes the following command without creating a new process

exit Quits the shell

export Makes a variable or function available to other programs

fg Brings a job to the foreground

getopts Parses arguments to the shell script

jobs Lists background (bg) jobs

pwd Displays the current directory

read Reads a line from standard input

readonly Declares as variable as read-only

set Lists all variables

shift Moves the parameters to the left

test Evaluates arguments

[Performs a conditional test

times Prints the user and system times

trap Traps a signal

type Displays how each argument would be interpreted as a command

umask Changes the default permissions for a new file

unset Deletes values from a variable or function

wait Waits for a background process to complete

UNDERSTANDING AND INSPECTING WIRELESS NETWORKS

The ability to scan for and connect to other network devices from your system is crucial to becoming a successful hacker, and with wireless technologies like Wi-Fi (IEEE 802.1) and Bluetooth becoming the standard, finding and controlling Wi-Fi and Bluetooth connections is key. If someone can hack a wireless connection, they can gain entry to a device and access to confidential information. The first step, of course, is to learn how to find these devices.

Earlier we looked at some basic networking commands in Linux, including some of the fundamentals of wireless networking, with a promise of more wireless networking to come. As promised, here we examine two of the most common wireless technologies in Linux: Wi-Fi and Bluetooth.

WI-FI NETWORKS

We'll start with Wi-Fi. In this section, I'll show you how to find, examine, and connect to Wi-Fi access points. Before doing so, let's spend a bit of time going over some basic Wi-Fi terms and technologies to help you better understand the output from a lot of the queries we'll make in this chapter:

AP (access point) This is the device wireless users connect to for internet access.

ESSID (extended service set identifier) This is the same as the SSID, which we discussed in Chapter 3, but it can be used for multiple APs in a wireless LAN.

BSSID (basic service set identifier) This is the uni☐ue identifier of each AP, and it is the same as the MAC address of the device.

SSID (service set identifier) This is the name of the network.

Channels Wi-Fi can operate on any one of 14 channels (1–14). In the United States, Wi-Fi is limited to channels 1–11.

Power The closer you are to the Wi-Fi AP, the greater the power, and the easier the connection is to crack.

Security This is the security protocol used on the Wi-Fi AP that is being read from. There are three primary security protocols for Wi-Fi. The original, Wired Equivalent Privacy (WEP), was badly flawed and easily cracked. Its replacement, Wi-Fi Protected Access (WPA), was a bit more secure. Finally, WPA2-PSK, which is much more secure and uses a preshared key (PSK) that all users share, is now used by nearly all Wi-Fi APs (except enterprise Wi-Fi).

Modes Wi-Fi can operate in one of three modes: managed, master, or monitor. You'll learn what these modes mean in the following section.

Wireless range In the United States, a Wi-Fi AP must legally broadcast its signal at an upper limit of 0.5 watts. At this power, it has a normal range of about 300 feet (100 meters). High-gain antennas can extend this range to as much as 20 miles.

Fre□uency Wi-Fi is designed to operate on 2.4GHz and 5GHz. Modern Wi-Fi APs and wireless network cards often use both.

Basic Wireless Commands

In Chapter 3, you were introduced to the basic Linux networking command ifconfig, which lists each activated network interface on your system along with some basic statistics, including (most importantly) the IP address of each interface. Let's take another look at your results from running ifconfig and focus on the wireless connections this time.

kali >ifconfig

eth0Linkencap:EthernetHWaddr 00:0c:29:ba:82:0f

 inet addr:192:168.181.131 Bcast:192.168.181.255 Mask:255.255.255.0

--snip--

lo Linkencap:Local Loopback

inet addr:127.0.0.1 Mask:255.0.0.0

--snip--

❶   wlan0   Link   encap:EthernetHWaddr 00:c0:ca:3f:ee:02

The Wi-Fi interface here is shown as wlan0 ❶. In Kali Linux, Wi-Fi interfaces are usually designated as wlanX, with X representing the number of that interface. In other words, the first Wi-Fi adapter on your system would be labeled wlan0, the second wlan1, and so on.

If you just want to see your Wi-Fi interfaces and their statistics, Linux has a specific command that's similar to ifconfig but dedicated to wireless. That command is iwconfig. When you enter it, only your wireless interfaces and their key data are displayed:

kali >iwconfig

lo   no wireless extensions

wlan0 IEEE 802.11bg ESSID:off/any

    Mode:Managed   Access   Point:Not-Associated Tx-Power=20 dBm

    Retry short limit:7 RTS thr:off Fragment thr:off

    Encryption key:off

    Power Management:off

eth0 no wireless extensions

Here, we see just the wireless interfaces, also known as network cards, and key data about them, including the wireless standard utilized, whether the ESSID is off, and the mode. The mode has three settings: managed, which means it is ready to join or has joined an AP; master, which means it is ready to act as or already is an AP; and monitor, which we'll discuss a little later in the chapter. We can also see whether any client has associated with it and what its transmit power is, among other things. You can tell from this example that wlan0 is in the mode re□uired to connect to a Wi-Fi network but is not connected to any yet. We will revisit this command again once the wireless interface is connected to a Wi-Fi network.

If you are not certain which Wi-Fi AP you want to connect to, you can see all the wireless access points your network card can reach using the iwlist command. The syntax for iwlist is as follows:

iwlist interface action

You can perform multiple actions with iwlist. For our purposes, we'll use the scan action to see all the Wi-Fi APs in your area. (Note that with a standard antenna, your range will be 300–500 feet, but this can be extended with an inexpensive high-gain antenna.)

kali >iwlist wlan0 scan

wlan0   Scan completed:

      Cell 01 - Address:88:AD:43:75:B3:82

          Channel:1

          Frequency:2.412GHz (Channel 1)

          Quality=70/70   Signal level =-38 dBm

          Encryption key:off

          ESSID:"Hackers-Arise"

--snip--

The output from this command should include all Wi-Fi APs within range of your wireless interface, along with key data about each AP, such as the MAC address of the AP, the channel and fre☐uency it is operating on, its ☐uality, its signal level, whether its encryption key is enabled, and its ESSID.

You will need the MAC address of the target AP (BSSID), the MAC address of a client (another wireless network card), and the channel the AP is operating on in order to perform any kind of hacking, so this is valuable information.

Another command that is very useful in managing your Wi-Fi connections is nmcli (or the network manager command line interface). The Linux daemon that provides a high-level interface for the network interfaces (including the wireless ones) is known as the network manager. Generally, Linux users are familiar with this daemon from its graphical user interface (GUI), but it can also be used from the command line.

The nmcli command can be used to view the Wi-Fi APs near you and their key data, as we did with iwlist, but this command gives us a little more information. We use it in the format nmcli dev networktype, where dev is short for devices and the type (in this case) is wifi, like so:

kali >nmcli dev wifi

*	SSID	MODE	CHAN	RATE	SIGNAL	BARS	SECURITY
	Hackers-Arise	Infra	1	54 Mbits/s	100		WPA1 WPA2
	Xfinitywifi	Infra	1	54 Mbits/s	75		WPA2
	TPTV1	Infra	11	54 Mbits/s	44		WPA1 WPA2

--snip--

In addition to displaying the Wi-Fi APs within range and key data about them, including the SSID, the mode, the channel, the rate of transfer, the signal strength, and the security protocols enabled on the device, nmcli can be used connect to APs. The syntax to connect to an AP is as follows:

nmcli dev wifi connect AP-SSID password APpassword

So, based on the results from our first command, we know there is an AP with an SSID of Hackers-Arise. We also know it has WPA1 WPA2 security (this means that the AP is capable of using both the older WPA1 and the newer WPA2), which means we will have to provide the password to connect to the network. Fortunately, as it's our AP, we know the password is 12345678, so we can enter the following:

kali >nmcli dev wifi connect Hackers-Arise password 12345678

Device 'wlan0' successfully activated with '394a5bf4-8af4-36f8-49beda6cb530'.

Try this on a network you know, and then when you have successfully connected to that wireless AP, run iwconfig again to see what has changed. Here's my output from connecting to Hackers-Arise:

kali >iwconfig

lo   no wireless extensions

wlan0 IEEE 802.11bg   ESSID:"Hackers-Arise"

Mode:Managed   Fre□uency:2.452GHz Access Point:00:25:9C:97:4F:48

Bit Rate=12 Mbs Tx-Power=20 dBm

Retry short limit:7   RTS thr:off   Fragment thr:off

Encryption key:off

Power Management:off

Link Quality=64/70 Signal level=-46 dBm

Rx invalid nwid:0 Rx invalid crypt:0 Rx invalid frag:0

Tx excessive reties:0   Invalid misc:13   Missed beacon:0

eth0 no wireless extensions

Note that now iwconfig has indicated that the ESSID is "Hackers-Arise" and that the AP is operating at a fre□uency of 2.452GHz. In a Wi-Fi network, it is possible for multiple APs to all be part of the same network, so there may be many APs that make up the Hackers-Arise network. The MAC address 00:25:9C:97:4F:48 is, as you might expect, the MAC of the AP I am connected to. What type of security a

Wi-Fi network uses, whether it is running at 2.4GHz or 5GHz, what its ESSID is, and what the AP's MAC address is are all critical pieces of information that are necessary for Wi-Fi hacking. Now that you know the basic commands, let's get into some hacking.

Wi-Fi Recon with aircrack-ng

One of the most popular exploits for new hackers to try is cracking Wi-Fi access points. As mentioned, before you can even consider attacking a Wi-Fi AP, you need the MAC address of the target AP (BSSID), the MAC address of a client, and the channel the AP is operating on.

We can get all that information and more using the tools of the aircrack-ng suite. I've mentioned this suite of Wi-Fi hacking tools a few times before, and now it's time to actually use it. This suite of tools is included in every version of Kali, so you don't need to download or install anything.

To use these tools effectively, you first need to put your wireless network card into monitor mode so that the card can see all the traffic passing its way. Normally, a network card captures only traffic destined specifically for that card. Monitor mode is similar to promiscuous mode on wired network cards.

To put your wireless network card in monitor mode, use the airmon-ng command from the aircrack-ng suite. The syntax for this command is simple:

airmon-ng start|stop|restart interface

So, if you want to put your wireless network card (designated wlan0) into monitor mode, you would enter the following:

kali >airmon-ng start wlan0

Found three processes that could cause trouble

If airodump-ng, aireplay-ng, or airtun-ng stops working after

a short period of time, you may want to run 'airmon-ng check kill'

--snip--

PHY	INTERFACE	DRIVER	Chipset
phy0	wlan0	rtl8187	Realtek Semiconductor Corop RTL8187

(mac8311 monitor mode vif enabled for [phy0]wlan0 on [phy0]wlan0mon)

--snip--

The stop and restart commands, respectively, stop monitor mode and restart monitor mode if you run into trouble.

With your wireless card in monitor mode, you can access all the wireless traffic passing by you within the range of your wireless network adapter and antenna (standard is about 300–500 feet). Note that airmon-ng will rename your wireless interface: mine has been renamed "wlan0mon," though yours may be different. Make certain to note the new designated name of your wireless because you'll need that information in the next step.

Now we'll use another tool from the aircrack-ng suite to find key data from the wireless traffic. The airodump-ng command captures and displays the key data from broadcasting APs and any clients connected to those APs or within the vicinity. The syntax here is straightforward: simply plug in airdump-ng, followed by the interface name you got from running airmon-ng just now. When you issue this command, your wireless card will pick up crucial information (listed next) from all the wireless traffic of the APs nearby:

BSSID The MAC address of the AP or client

PWR The strength of the signal

ENC The encryption used to secure the transmission

#Data The data throughput rate

CH The channel the AP is operating on

ESSID The name of the AP

kali >airodump-ng wlan0mon

CH 9][Elapsed: 28 s][2018-02-08 10:27

BSSID   PWR Beacons #Data #/s CH MB ENC CIPHER AUTH ESSID

01:01:AA:BB:CC:22 -1   4   26 0 10 54e WPA2 CCMP PSK Hackers-Arise

--snip--

BSSID   Station   PWR   Rate   Lost Frames Probe

(not associated)   01:01:AA:BB:CC:22

01:02:CC:DD:03:CF   A0:A3:E2:44:7C:E5

Note that airodump-ng splits the output screen into an upper and lower portion. The upper portion has information on the broadcasting APs, including the

BSSID, the power of the AP, how many beacon frames have been detected, the data throughput rate, how many packets have traversed the wireless card, the channel (1–14), the theoretical throughput limit, the encryption protocol, the cipher used for encryption, the authentication type, and the ESSID (commonly referred to as SSID). In the client portion, the output tells us that one client is not associated, meaning it has been detected but is not connected to any AP, and that another is associated with a station, meaning it's connected to the AP at that address.

Now you have all the information you need to crack the AP! Although it's beyond the scope of this book, to crack the wireless AP, you need the client MAC address, the AP MAC address, the channel the target is operating on, and a password list.

So to crack the Wi-Fi password, you would open three terminals. In the first terminal, you would enter commands similar to the following, filling in the client and AP MAC addresses and the channel:

airodump-ng -c 10 --bssid 01:01:AA:BB:CC:22 -w Hackers-ArisePSK wlan0mon

This command captures all the packets traversing the AP on channel 10 using the -c option.

In another terminal, you can use the aireplay-ng command to knock off (deauthenticate) anyone connected to the AP and force them to reauthenticate to the AP, as shown next. When they reauthenticate, you can capture the hash of their password that is exchanged in the WPA2-PSK four-way handshake. The password hash will appear in the upper-right corner of the airodump-ng terminal.

aireplay-ng --deauth 100 -a 01:01:AA:BB:CC:22 -c A0:A3:E2:44:7C:E5 wlan0mon

Finally, in the final terminal, you can use a password list (wordlist.dic) to find the password in the captured hash (Hackers-ArisePSK.cap), as shown here:

aircrack-ng -w wordlist.dic -b 01:01:AA:BB:CC:22 Hacker-ArisePSK.cap

DETECTING AND CONNECTING TO BLUETOOTH

These days, nearly every gadget, mobile device, and system has Bluetooth built in, including our computers, smartphones, iPods, tablets, speakers, game controllers, keyboards, and many other devices. Being able to hack Bluetooth can lead to the compromise of any information on the device, control of the device, and the ability to send unwanted info to and from the device, among other things.

To exploit the technology, we need to understand how it works. An in-depth understanding of Bluetooth is beyond the scope of this book, but I will give you some basic knowledge that will help you scan for and connect to Bluetooth devices in preparation for hacking them.

How Bluetooth Works

Bluetooth is a universal protocol for low-power, near-field communication operating at 2.4–2.485GHz using spread spectrum, fre□uency hopping at 1,600 hops per second (this fre□uency hopping is a security measure). It was developed in 1994 by Ericsson Corp. of Sweden and named after the 10th-century Danish king Harald

Bluetooth (note that Sweden and Denmark were a single country in the 10th century).

The Bluetooth specification has a minimum range of 10 meters, but there is no limit to the upper range manufacturers may implement in their devices. Many devices have ranges as large as 100 meters. With special antennas, that range can be extended even farther.

Connecting two Bluetooth devices is referred to as pairing. Pretty much any two Bluetooth devices can connect to each other, but they can pair only if they are in discoverable mode. A Bluetooth device in discoverable mode transmits the following information:

Name

Class

List of services

Technical information

When the two devices pair, they exchange a secret or link key. Each stores this link key so it can identify the other in future pairings.

Every device has a unique 48-bit identifier (a MAC-like address) and usually a manufacturer-assigned name. These will be useful pieces of data when we want to identify and access a device.

Bluetooth Scanning and Reconnaissance

Linux has an implementation of the Bluetooth protocol stack called BlueZ that we'll use to scan for Bluetooth signals. Most Linux distributions, including Kali Linux, have it installed by default. If yours doesn't, you can usually find it in your repository using the following command:

kali >apt-get install bluez

BlueZ has a number of simple tools we can use to manage and scan Bluetooth devices, including the following:

hciconfig This tool operates very similarly to ifconfig in Linux, but for Bluetooth devices. As you can see in Listing 14-1, I have used it to bring up the Bluetooth interface and □uery the device for its specs.

hcitool This in□uiry tool can provide us with device name, device ID, device class, and device clock information, which enables the devices to work synchronously.

hcidump This tool enables us to sniff the Bluetooth communication, meaning we can capture data sent over the Bluetooth signal.

The first scanning and reconnaissance step with Bluetooth is to check whether the Bluetooth adapter on the system we're using is recognized and enabled so we can use it to scan for other devices. We can do this with the built-in BlueZ tool hciconfig, as shown in Listing 14-1.

kali >hciconfig

hci0: Type: BR/EDR Bus: USB

BD Address: 10:AE:60:58:F1:37 ACL MTU: 310:10 SCO MTU: 64:8

UP RUNNING PSCAN INQUIRY

RX bytes:131433 acl:45 sco:0 events:10519 errors:0

TX bytes:42881 acl:45 sco:0 commands:5081 errors:0

Listing 14-1: Scanning for a Bluetooth device

As you can see, my Bluetooth adapter is recognized with a MAC address of 10:AE:60:58:F1:37. This adapter has been named hci0. The next step is to check that the connection is enabled, which we can also do with hciconfig by providing the name and the up command:

kali >hciconfig hci0 up

If the command runs successfully, we should see no output, just a new prompt.

Good, hci0 is up and ready! Let's put it to work.

Scanning for Bluetooth Devices with hcitool

Now that we know our adapter is up, we can use another tool in the BlueZ suite called hcitool, which is used to scan for other Bluetooth devices within range.

Let's first use the scanning function of this tool to look for Bluetooth devices that are sending out their discover beacons, meaning they're in discovery mode, with the simple scan command shown in Listing 14-2.

kali >hcitool scan

Scanning...

    72:6E:46:65:72:66   ANDROID BT

    22:C5:96:08:5D:32   SCH-I535

Listing 14-2: Scanning for Bluetooth devices in discovery mode

As you can see, on my system, hcitool found two devices, ANDROID BT and SCH-I535. Yours will likely provide you with different output depending on what devices you have around. For testing purposes, try putting your phone or other Bluetooth device in discovery mode and see if it gets picked up in the scan.

Now let's gather more information about the detected devices with the inquiry function in □:

kali >hcitool inq

Inquiring...

    24:C6:96:08:5D:33   clock   offset:0x4e8b
class:0x5a020c

    76:6F:46:65:72:67   clock   offset:0x21c0
class:0x5a020c

This gives us the MAC addresses of the devices, the clock offset, and the class of the devices. The class indicates what type of Bluetooth device you found, and you can look up the code and see what type of device it is by going to the Bluetooth SIG site at https://www.bluetooth.org/en-us/specification/assigned-numbers/service-discovery/.

The tool hcitool is a powerful command line interface to the Bluetooth stack that can do many, many things. Listing 14-3 shows the help page with some of the commands you can use. Take a look at the help page yourself to see the full list.

kali >hcitool --help

hcitool - HCI Tool ver 4.99

Usage:

   hcitool   [options]   <command>   [command parameters]

Options:

   --help   Display help

   -i dev HCI device

Commands

```
dev   Display local devices

in☐   Inquire remote devices

scan  Scan for remote devices

name  Get name from remote devices
```

--snip--

Listing 14-3: Some hcitool commands

Many Bluetooth-hacking tools you'll see around simply use these commands in a script, and you can easily create your own tool by using these commands in your own bash or Python script—we'll look at scripting next.

Scanning for Services with sdptool

Service Discovery Protocol (SDP) is a Bluetooth protocol for searching for Bluetooth services (Bluetooth is suite of services), and, helpfully, BlueZ provides the sdptool tool for browsing a device for the services it provides. It is also important to note that the device does not have to be in discovery mode to be scanned. The syntax is as follows:

sdptool browse MACaddress

Listing 14-4 shows me using sdptool to search for services on one of the devices detected earlier in Listing 14-2.

kali >sdptool browse 76:6E:46:63:72:66

Browsing 76:6E:46:63:72:66...

Service RecHandle: 0x10002

Service Class ID List:

  ""(0x1800)

Protocol Descriptor List:

  "L2CAP" (0x0100)

    PSM: 31

  "ATT" (0x0007)

    uint16: 0x1

    uint16: 0x5

--snip--

Listing 14-4: Scanning with sdptool

Here, we can see that the sdptool tool was able to pull information on all the services this device is capable of using. In particular, we see that this device supports the ATT Protocol, which is the Low Energy Attribute Protocol. This can provide us more clues as to what the device is and possibly potential avenues to interact with it further.

Seeing Whether the Devices Are Reachable with l2ping

Once we've gathered the MAC addresses of all nearby devices, we can send out pings to these devices, whether they're in discovery mode or not, to see whether they are in reach. This lets us know whether they are active and within range. To send out a ping, we use the l2ping command with the following syntax:

l2ping MACaddress

Listing 14-5 shows me pinging the Android device discovered in Listing 14-2.

kali >l2ping 76:6E:46:63:72:66 -c 4

Ping: 76:6E:46:63:72:66 from 10:AE:60:58:F1:37 (data size 44)...

44 bytes 76:6E:46:63:72:66 id 0 time 37.57ms

44 bytes 76:6E:46:63:72:66 id 1 time 27.23ms

44 bytes 76:6E:46:63:72:66 id 2 time 27.59ms

--snip--

Listing 14-5: Pinging a Bluetooth device

This output indicates that the device with the MAC address 76:6E:46:63:72:66 is within range and reachable. This is useful knowledge, because we must know whether a device is reachable before we even contemplate hacking it.

MANAGING THE LINUX KERNEL AND LOADABLE KERNEL MODULES

All operating systems are made up of at least two major components. The first and most important of these is the kernel. The kernel is at the center of the operating system and controls everything the operating system does, including managing memory, controlling the CPU, and even controlling what the user sees on the screen. The second element of the operating system is often referred to as user land and includes nearly everything else.

The kernel is designed to be a protected or privileged area that can only be accessed by root or other privileged accounts. This is for good reason, as access to the kernel can provide nearly unfettered access to the operating system. As a result, most operating systems provide users and services access only to user land, where the user can access nearly anything they need without taking control of the operating system.

Access to the kernel allows the user to change how the operating systems works, looks, and feels. It also allows them to crash the operating system, making it unworkable. Despite this risk, in some cases, the system admin must very carefully access the kernel for operational and security reasons.

In this chapter, we'll examine how to alter the way the kernel works and add new modules to the kernel. It probably goes without saying that if a hacker can alter the target's kernel, they can control the system. Furthermore, an attacker may need to alter how the kernel functions for some attacks, such as a man-in-the middle (MITM) attack, where the hacker places themselves between a client and server and can eavesdrop on or alter the communication. First, we'll take a closer look at the kernel structure and its modules.

WHAT IS A KERNEL MODULE?

The kernel is the central nervous system of your operating system, controlling everything it does, including managing interactions between hardware components and starting the necessary services. The kernel operates between the user applications you see and the hardware that runs everything, like the CPU, memory, and hard drive.

Linux is a monolithic kernel that enables the addition of kernel modules. As such, modules can be added and removed from the kernel. The kernel will occasionally need updating, which might entail installing new device drivers (such as video cards, Bluetooth devices, or USB devices), filesystem drivers, and even system extensions. These drivers must be embedded in the kernel to be fully functional. In some systems, to add a driver, you have to rebuild, compile, and reboot the entire kernel, but Linux has the capability of adding some modules to the kernel without going through that entire process. These modules are referred to as loadable kernel modules, or LKMs.

LKMs have access to the lowest levels of the kernel by necessity, making them an incredibly vulnerable target for hackers. A particular type of malware known as a rootkit embeds itself into the kernel of the operating systems, often through these LKMs. If malware embeds itself in the kernel, the hacker can take complete control of the operating system.

If a hacker can get the Linux admin to load a new module to the kernel, the hacker not only can gain control over the target system but, because they're operating at the kernel level of the operating system, can control what the target system is reporting in terms of processes, ports, services, hard drive space, and almost anything else you can think of.

So, if a hacker can successfully tempt a Linux admin into installing a video or other device driver that has a rootkit embedded in it, the hacker can take total control of the system and kernel. This is the way some of the most insidious rootkits take advantage of Linux and other operating systems.

Understanding LKMs is absolutely key to being an effective Linux admin and being a very effective and stealthy hacker.

Let's take a look at how the kernel can be managed for good and ill.

CHECKING THE KERNEL VERSION

The first step to understanding the kernel is to check what kernel your system is running. There are at least two ways to do this. First, we can enter the following:

kali >uname -a

Linux Kali 4.6.0-kalil-amd64 #1 SMP Debian 4.6.4-lkalil (2016-07-21) x86_64

The kernel responds by telling us the distribution our OS is running is Linux Kali, the kernel build is 4.6.4, and the architecture it's built for is the x86_64 architecture. It also tells us it has symmetric multiprocessing (SMP) capabilities (meaning it can run on machines with multiple cores or processers) and was built on Debian 4.6.4 on July 21, 2016. Your output may be different, depending on which kernel was used in your build and the CPU in your system. This information can be required when you install or load a kernel driver, so it's useful to understand how to get it.

One other way to get this information, as well as some other useful information, is to use the cat command on the /proc/version file, like so:

kali >cat /proc/version

Linux version 4.6.0-kalil-amd64 (devel@kali.org) (gcc version 5.4.0 20160909

(Debian 5.4.0-6)   ) #1 SMP Debian 4.6.4-lkalil (2016-07-21)

Here you can see that the /proc/version file returned the same information.

KERNEL TUNING WITH SYSCTL

With the right commands, you can tune your kernel, meaning you can change memory allocations, enable networking features, and even harden the kernel against outside attacks.

Modern Linux kernels use the sysctl command to tune kernel options. All changes you make with sysctl remain in effect only until you reboot the system. To make any changes permanent, you have to edit the configuration file for sysctl directly at /etc/sysctl.conf.

A word of warning: you need to be careful when using sysctl because without the proper knowledge and experience, you can easily make your system unbootable and unusable. Make sure you've considered what you're doing carefully before making any permanent changes.

Let's take a look at the contents of sysctl now. By now, you should recognize the options we give with the command shown here:

```
kali >sysctl -a | less
dev.cdrom.autoclose = 1
dev.cdrom.autoeject = 0
dev.cdrom.check_media = 0
dev.cdrom.debug = 0
--snip--
```

In the output, you should see hundreds of lines of parameters that a Linux administrator can edit to optimize the kernel. There are a few lines here that are useful to you as a hacker. As an example of how you might use sysctl, we'll look at enabling packet forwarding.

In the man-in-the middle (MITM) attack, the hacker places themselves between communicating hosts to intercept information. The traffic passes through the hacker's system, so they can view and possibly alter the communication. One way to achieve this routing is to enable packet forwarding.

If you scroll down a few pages in the output or filter for "ipv4" (sysctl -a | less | grep ipv4), you should see the following:

net.ipv4.ip_dynaddr = 0

net.ipv4.ip_early_demux = 0

net.ipv4.ip_forward = 0

net.ipv4.ip_forward_use_pmtu = 0

--snip--

The line net.ipv4.ip_forward = 0 is the kernel parameter that enables the kernel to forward on the packets it receives. In other words, the packets it receives, it sends back out. The default setting is 0, which means that packet forwarding is disabled.

To enable IP forwarding, change the 0 to a 1 by entering the following:

kali >sysctl -w net.ipv4.ip_forward=1

Remember that that sysctl changes take place at runtime but are lost when the system is rebooted. To make permanent changes to sysctl, you need to edit configuration file /etc/sysctl.conf. Let's change the way the kernel handles IP forwarding for MITM attacks and make this change permanent.

To enable IP forwarding, open the /etc/sysctl.conf file in any text editor and uncomment the line for ip_forward. Open /etc/sycstl.conf with any text editor and take a look:

#/etc/sysctl.conf - Configuration file for setting system variables

See /etc/sysctl.d/ for additional system variables.

See sysctl.conf (5) for information.

#

#kernel.domainname = example.com

Uncomment the following to stop low-level messages on console.

#kernel.printk = 3 4 1 3

##

##################3

Functions previously found in netbase

#

Uncomment the next two lines to enable Spoof protection (reverse-path

Turn on Source Address Verification in all interfaces to

prevent some spoofing attacks.

#net.ipv4.conf.default.rp_filter=1

#net.ipv4.conf.all.rp_filter=1

Uncomment the next line to enable TCP/IP SYN cookies

#

Note: This may impact IPv6 TCP sessions too

#net.ipv4.tcp_syncookies=1

See http://lwn.net/Articles/277146/

Uncomment the next line to enable packet forwarding for IPv4

❶ #net.ipv4.ip_forward=1

The relevant line is at ❶; just remove the comment (#) here to enable IP forwarding.

From an operating system–hardening perspective, you could use this file to disable ICMP echo re☐uests by adding the line net.ipv4.icmp_echo_ignore_all=1 to make it more difficult—but not impossible—for hackers to find your system. After adding the line, you will need to run the command sysctl -p.

MANAGING KERNEL MODULES

Linux has at least two ways to manage kernel modules. The older way is to use a group of commands built around the insmod suite—insmod stands for insert module and is intended to deal with modules. The second way, using the modprobe command, we will employ a little later in this chapter. Here, we use the lsmod command from the insmod suite to list the installed modules in the kernel:

kali >lsmod

Module	Size	Used by
nfnetlink_queue	20480	0
nfnetlink_log	201480	0
nfnetlink	16384	2 nfnetlink_log, nfnetlink_queue
bluetooth	516096	0
rfkill	0	2 bluetooth

--snip--

As you can see, the lsmod command lists all the kernel modules as well as information on their size and what other modules may use them. So, for instance, the nfnetlink module—a message-based protocol for communicating between the kernel and user space—is 16,384 bytes and used by both the nfnetlink_log module and the nf_netlink_☐ueue module.

From the insmod suite, we can load or insert a module with insmod and remove a module with rmmod, which stands for remove module. These commands are not perfect and may not take into account module dependencies, so using them can leave your kernel unstable or unusable. As a result, modern distributions of Linux have now added the modprobe command, which automatically loads dependencies and makes loading and removing kernel modules less risky. We'll cover modprobe in a moment. First, let's see how to get more information about our modules.

Finding More Information with modinfo

To learn more about any of the kernel modules, we can use the modinfo command. The syntax for this command is straightforward: modinfo followed by the name of the module you want to learn about. For example, if you wanted to retrieve basic information on the bluetooth kernel module you saw when you ran the lsmod command earlier, you could enter the following:

kali >modinfo bluetooth

filename: /lib/modules/4.6.0-kali-amd64/kernel/net/bluetooth/bluetooth.ko

alias: net-pf-31

license: GPL

version: 2.21

description:Bluetooth Core ver 2.21

author: Marcel Holtman <marcel@holtmann.org>

srcversion: FCFDE98577FEA911A3DAFA9

depends: rfkill, crc16

intree: Y

vermagic: 4.6.0-kali1-amd64   SMP   mod_unload modversions parm: disable_esco: Disable eSCO connection creation (bool)

parm: disable_ertm: Disable enhanced retransmission mode (bool)

As you can see, the modinfo command reveals significant information about this kernel module which is necessary to use Bluetooth on your system. Note that among many other things, it lists the module dependencies: rfkill and crc16. Dependencies are modules that must be installed for the bluetooth module to function properly.

Typically, this is useful information when troubleshooting why a particular hardware device is not working. Besides noting things like the dependencies, you can get information about the version of the module and the version of the kernel the module was developed for and then make sure they match the version you are running.

Adding and Removing Modules with modprobe

Most newer distributions of Linux, including Kali Linux, include the modprobe command for LKM management. To add a module to your kernel, you would use the modprobe command with the -a (add) switch, like so:

kali >modprobe -a <module name>

To remove a module, use the -r (remove) switch with modprobe followed by the name of the module:

kali >modprobe -r <module to be removed>

A major advantage of using modprobe instead of insmod is that modprobe understands dependencies, options, and installation and removal procedures and it takes all of these into account before making changes. Thus, it is easier and safer to add and remove kernel modules with modprobe.

Inserting and Removing a Kernel Module

Let's try inserting and removing a test module to help you familiarize yourself with this process. Let's imagine that you just installed a new video card and you need to install the drivers for it. Remember, drivers for devices are usually installed directly into the kernel to give them the necessary access to function properly. This also makes drivers fertile ground for malicious hackers to install a rootkit or other listening device.

Let's assume for demonstration purposes (don't actually run these commands) that we want to add a new video driver named HackersAriseNewVideo. You can add it to your kernel by entering the following:

```
kali >modprobe -a HackersAriseNewVideo
```

To test whether the new module loaded properly, you can run the dmesg command, which prints out the message buffer from the kernel, and then filter for "video" and look for any alerts that would indicate a problem:

```
kali >dmesg | grep video
```

If there are any kernel messages with the word "video" in them, they will be displayed here. If nothing appears, there are no messages containing that keyword.

Then, to remove this same module, you can enter the same command but with the -r (remove) switch:

kali >modprobe -r HackersAriseNewVideo

Remember, the loadable kernel modules are a convenience to a Linux user/admin, but they are also a major security weakness and one that professional hackers should be familiar with. As I said before, the LKMs can be the perfect vehicle to get your rootkit into the kernel and wreak havoc!

PYTHON SCRIPTING BASICS FOR HACKERS

Without having developed some basic scripting skills, a beginner hacker who simply uses tools created by someone else will be condemned to the realm of script kiddies. This means that you will be limited to using tools developed by someone else, which decreases your probability of success and increases your probability of detection by antivirus (AV) software, intrusion detection systems (IDSs), and law enforcement. With some scripting skills, you can elevate yourself to the upper echelon of the master hackers!

Earlier we covered bash scripting basics and built some simple scripts, including MySQLScanner.sh, which finds systems running the ubi☐uitous MySQL database system. In this chapter, we begin looking at the scripting language most widely used by hackers: Python. Many of the most popular hacker tools are written in Python, including s☐lmap, scapy, the Social-Engineer Toolkit (SET), w3af, and many more.

Python has some important features that make it particularly well-suited for hacking, but probably most importantly, it has a huge variety of libraries—prebuilt modules of code that can be imported externally and reused—that provide some powerful functionality. Python ships with over 1,000 modules built in, and many more are available in various other repositories.

Building hacking tools is possible in other languages too, such as bash, Perl, and Ruby, but Python's modules make building these tools much easier.

ADDING PYTHON MODULES

When you install Python, you also install its set of standard libraries and modules that provide an extensive range of capabilities, including built-in data types, exception handling, numeric and math modules, file handling, cryptographic services, internet data handling, and interaction with internet protocols (IPs).

Despite all the power offered by these standard libraries and modules, you may need or want additional third-party modules. The third-party modules available for Python are extensive and are probably the reason most hackers prefer Python for scripting. You can find a comprehensive list of third-party modules at PyPI at http://www.pypi.org/.

Using pip

Python has a package manager specifically for installing and managing Python packages known as pip (Pip Installs Packages). Since we are working with Python 3 here, you will need pip for Python 3 to download and install packages. You can download and install pip from the Kali repository by entering the following:

kali >apt-get install python3-pip

Now, to download modules from PyPI, you can simply enter this:

kali >pip3 install <package name>

When you download these packages, they are automatically placed in the /usr/local//lib/<python-version>/dist-packages directory. So, for instance, if you had used pip to install the Python implementation of the SNMP protocol for Python 3.6, you would find it at /usr/local/lib/python3.6/pysnmp. If you aren't sure where a package has been placed on your system (sometimes different distributions of Linux use different directories), you can enter pip3 followed by show and the package name, as shown here:

kali >pip3 show pysnmp

Name: pysnmp

Version: 4.4.4

Summary: SNMP library for Python

Home-page: https://github.com/etingof/pysnmp

Author: Ilya Etingof <etingof@gmail.com>

Author-email: etingof@gmail.com

License: BSD

Location: usr/local/lib/python3.6/dist-packages

Requires: ptsmi, pyansl, pycryptodomex

You can see this gives you a lot of information about the package, including the directory that holds it.

As an alternative to using pip, you can download a package directly from the site (make certain that is downloaded to the proper directory), unpack it (see Chapter 9 on how to unpack software), and then run the following:

kali >python setup.py install

This will install any unpacked packages that haven't yet been installed.

Installing Third-Party Modules

To install a third-party module created by another member of the Python community (as opposed to an officially released Python package), you can simply use wget to download it from wherever it is being stored online, uncompress the module, and then run the python setup.py install command.

As an example, let's download and install the Python module for the port-scanning tool we used in Chapter 8, nmap, from its online repository at https://xael.org.

First, we need to download the module from xael.org:

```
kali    >wget    http://xael.org/norman/python/python-
nmap/python-nmap-0.3.4.tar.gz

--2014-12-28                          17:48:32--
http://xael.org/norman/python/python-nmap/python-
nmap-0.3.4.tar.gz

Resolving xael.org (xael.org)...194.36.166.10

Connecting             to             xael.org
(xael.org)|194.36.166.10|:80...connected.



--snip--



2018-21-28 17.48:34 (113 KB/s)  - 'python-nmap-
0.3.4.tar.gz' saved

[40307/40307]
```

Here, you can see we use the wget command and the full URL for the package. After the package has downloaded, you need to uncompress it with tar, as you learned in Chapter 9:

kali >tar -xzf python-nmap-0.3.4.tar.gz

Then change directories to the newly created directory:

kali >cd python-nmap-.03.4/

Finally, in that directory, install the new module by entering the following:

kali >~/python-nmap-0.3.4 >python setup.py install

running install

running build

running build_py

creating build

--snip--

running install_egg_info

writing   /usr/local/lib/python2.7/dist-
packages/python_nmap-0.3.4.egg.info

Innumerable other modules can be obtained this way
as well. Once you've installed this nmap module, you
can use it in your Python scripts by importing the
module. More on this later. Now let's get started on
some scripting.

GETTING STARTED SCRIPTING WITH PYTHON

Now that you know how to install modules in Python,
I want to cover some of the basic concepts and
terminology of Python, then the basic syntax. After
that, you'll write some scripts that will be useful to
hackers everywhere and that I hope will demonstrate
the power of Python.

Just as with bash or any other scripting language, we
can create Python scripts using any text editor. For this
chapter, to keep things simple, I advise you to use a
simple text editor such as Leafpad, but it's useful to
know that a number of integrated development
environments, or IDEs, are available for use with
Python. An IDE is like a text editor with other

271

capabilities built in, such as color-coding, debugging, and compiling capabilities. Kali has the IDE PyCrust built in, but there are many more IDEs available to download, of which the best is arguably JetBrain's PyCharm. This is an excellent IDE with a lot of enhancements that make learning Python easier and ⬚uicker. There is a professional version for purchase and a community edition that is free. You can find them at https://www.jetbrains.com/pycharm/.

Once you've completed this chapter, if you want to keep learning Python, PyCharm is an excellent tool that will help you in your development. For now, we will use a basic text editor like Leafpad to keep things simple.

Note that learning any programming language takes time and a lot of hard work. Be patient with yourself—attempt to master each of the small scripts I provide before moving on.

FORMATTING IN PYTHON

One difference between Python and some other scripting languages is that formatting is critically important in Python. The Python interpreter uses the formatting to determine how code is grouped. The particulars of the formatting are less important than simply being consistent, particularly with your indentation levels.

If you have a group of code lines that you start with double indentation, for example, you must be consistent with the double indentation throughout the entire block in order for Python to recognize that these code lines belong together. This is different from scripting in other programming languages, where formatting is optional and a best practice, but not re□uired. You'll notice this as you go through and practice; it's something to always keep in mind!

Variables

Now, on to some more practical concepts in Python. A variable is one of the most basic data types in programming, and you encountered it earlier in Chapter 8 with bash scripting. In simple terms, a variable is a name associated with a particular value such that whenever you use that name in your program, it will invoke the associated value.

The way it works is that the variable name points to data stored in a memory location, which may contain any kind of value, such as an integer, real number, string, floating-point number, Boolean (true or false statement), list, or dictionary. We'll briefly cover all of these in this chapter.

To become familiar with the basics, let's create a simple script, shown in Listing 17-1, in Leafpad and save it as hackers-arise_greetings.py.

```
#! /usr/bin/python3


name="OccupyTheWeb"


print ("Greetings to " + name + " from Hackers-Arise. The Best Place to Learn Hacking!")
```

Listing 17-1: Your first Python program

The first line simply tells your system that you want it to use the Python interpreter to run this program, rather than any other language. The second line defines a variable called name and assigns a value to it (in this case, "OccupyTheWeb"). You should change this value to your own name. The value of this variable is in the string character data format, meaning the content is enclosed in quotation marks and is treated like text. You can put numbers in strings, too, and they will be treated like text, in that you won't be able to use them in numerical calculations.

The third line creates a print() statement concatenating Greetings to with the value in the name variable, followed by the text from Hackers-Arise. The Best Place to Learn Hacking! A print() statement will display whatever you pass to it within the parentheses on your screen.

Now, before you can run this script, you need to give yourself permission to execute it. We need the chmod command to do that. (For more information on Linux permissions, see Chapter 5).

kali >chmod 755 hackers-arise_greetings.py

Just as you did in Chapter 8 with bash scripting, to execute your script, precede the script name with a period and forward slash. Your current directory is not in the $PATH variable for security reasons, so we need to precede the script name with ./ to tell the system to look in the current directory for the filename and execute it.

To run this particular script, enter the following:

kali >./hackers-arise_greetings.py

Greetings to OccupyTheWeb from Hackers-Arise. The Best Place to Learn Hacking!

In Python, each variable type is treated like a class. A class is a kind of template for creating objects. See "Object-Oriented Programming (OOP)" on page 192 for more information. In the following script, I have attempted to demonstrate a few of the types of variables. Variables can hold more than just strings.

Listing 17-2 shows some variables containing different data types.

```
#! /usr/bin/python3


HackersAriseStringVariable = "Hackers-Arise Is the Best Place to Learn

Hacking"


HackersAriseIntegerVariable = 12


HackersAriseFloatingPointVariable = 3.1415


HackersAriseList = [1,2,3,4,5,6]


HackersAriseDictionary = {'name' : 'OccupyTheWeb', 'value' : 27)


print (HackersAriseStringVariable)
```

```
print (HackersAriseIntegerVariable)
```

```
print (HackersAriseFloatingPointVariable)
```

Listing 17-2: A series of data structures associated with variables

This creates five variables that contain different data types: a string, treated as text; an integer, which is a number type without decimals that can be used in numerical operations; a float, which is a number type with decimals that can also be used in numerical operations; a list, which is a series of values stored together; and a dictionary, which is an unordered set of data where each value is paired with a key, meaning each value in the dictionary has a uni☐ue identifying key. This is useful for when you want to refer to or change a value by referring to a key name. For example, say you have a dictionary called fruit_color configured like the following:

fruit_color = {'apple' : 'red', 'grape' : 'green', orange : 'orange'}

If later in your script you want get the fruit_color of the grape, you simply call it by its key:

```
print (fruit_color['grape'])
```

You could also change values for particular keys; for example, here we change the color of the apple:

```
fruit_color['apple'] : 'green'
```

We will discuss lists and dictionaries in more detail later in the chapter.

Create this script in any text editor, save it as secondpythonscript.py, and then give yourself permission to execute it, like so:

kali >chmod 755 secondpythonscript.py

When we run this script, it prints the values of the string variable, the integer variable, and the floating-point number variable, like so:

kali >./secondpythonscript.py

Hackers-Arise Is the Best Place to Learn Hacking

12

3.1415

NOTE

In Python, there is no need to declare a variable before assigning a value to it, as in some other programming languages.

Comments

Like any other programming and scripting language, Python has the capability for adding comments.

Comments are simply parts of your code—words, sentences, and even paragraphs—that explain what the code is meant to do. Python will recognize comments in your code and ignore them. Although comments are not required, they're incredibly helpful for when you come back to your code two years later and can't remember what it should do. Programmers often use comments to explain what a certain block of code does or to explain the logic behind choosing a particular method of coding.

Comments are ignored by the interpreter. This means that any lines designated as comments are skipped by the interpreter, which simply continues until it encounters a legitimate line of code. Python uses the # symbol to designate the start of single-line comment. If you want to write multiline comments, you can use three double quotation marks (""") at the start and end of the comment section.

As you can see in the following script, I have added a short, multiline comment to our simple hackers-arise_greetings.py script.

#! /usr/bin/python3

"""

This is my first Python script with comments. Comments are used to help explain code to

ourselves and fellow programmers. In this case, this simple script creates a greeting for

the user.

"""

name = "OccupyTheWeb"

print ("Greetings to "+name+" from Hackers-Arise. The Best Place to Learn Hacking!")

When we execute the script again, nothing changes compared to the last time it was executed, as you can see here:

kali >./hackers-arise_greetings.py

Greetings to OccupyTheWeb from Hackers-Arise. The Best Place to Learn Hacking!

It runs exactly the same as it did in Listing 17-1, but now we have some info about our script when we return to the code at a later time.

Functions

Functions in Python are bits of code that perform a particular action. The print() statement you used earlier, for example, is a function that displays whatever values you pass to it. Python has a number of built-in functions you can immediately import and use. Most of them are available on your default installation of Python in Kali Linux, although many more are available from the downloadable libraries. Let's take a look at just a few of the thousands of functions available to you:

exit() exits from a program.

float() returns its argument as a floating-point number. For example, float(1) would return 1.0.

help() displays help on the object specified by its argument.

int() returns the integer portion of its argument (truncates).

len() returns the number of elements in a list or dictionary.

max() returns the maximum value from its argument (a list).

open() opens the file in the mode specified by its arguments.

range() returns a list of integers between two values specified by its arguments.

sorted() takes a list as an argument and returns it with its elements in order.

type() returns the type of its argument (for example, int, file, method, function).

You can also create your own functions to perform custom tasks. Since there are so many already built into the language, it's always worth checking whether a function already exists before going through the effort of building it yourself. There are many ways to do this check. One is to look at the official Python documentation available at https://docs.python.org. Choose the version you are working with and then select Library Reference.

LISTS

Many programming languages use arrays as a way to store multiple separate objects. An array is a list of values that can be retrieved, deleted, replaced, or worked with in various ways by referencing a particular value in the array by its position in the list, known as its index. It's important to note that Python, like many other programming environments, begins counting indexes at 0, so the first element in a list is index 0, the second is index 1, the third is index 3, and so on. So, for instance, if we wanted to access the third value in the array, we could do so with array[2]. In Python, there are a few implementations of arrays, but probably the most common implementation is known as lists.

Lists in Python are iterable, which means that the list can provide successive elements when you run all the way through it (see "Loops" on page 198). This is useful because ☐uite often when we use lists, we are looking through them to find a certain value, to print out values one by one, or to take values from one list and put them into another list.

So, let's imagine we need to display the fourth element in our list HackersAriseList from Listing 17-2. We can access that element and print it by calling the list's name, HackersAriseList, followed by the index of the element we want to access enclosed in s☐uare brackets.

To test this, add the following line to the bottom of your secondpythonscript.py script to print the element at index 3 in HackersAriseList:

--snip--

print (HackersAriseStringVariable)

print (HackersAriseIntegerVariable)

print (HackersAriseFloatingPointVariable)

print (HackersAriseList[3])

When we run this script again, we can see that the new print statement prints 4 alongside the other output:

kali >./secondpythonscript.py

Hackers-Arise Is the Best Place to Learn Hacking

12

3.1415

4

MODULES

A module is simply a section of code saved into a separate file so you can use it as many times as you need in your program without having to type it all out again. If you want to use a module or any code from a module, you need to import it. As discussed earlier, using standard and third-party modules is one of the key features that makes Python so powerful for the hacker. If we wanted to use the nmap module we installed earlier, we would add the following line to our script:

import nmap

Later in this chapter, we will use two very useful modules: socket and ftplib.

OBJECT-ORIENTED PROGRAMMING (OOP)

Before we delve deeper into Python, it's probably worth taking a few minutes to discuss the concept of object-oriented programming (OOP). Python, like most programming languages today (C++, Java, and Ruby, to name a few) adheres to the OOP model.

Figure 17-2 shows the basic concept behind OOP: the language's main tool is the object, which has properties in the form of attributes and states, as well as methods that are actions performed by or on the object.

The idea behind OOP-based programming languages is to create objects that act like things in the real world. For example, a car is an object that has properties, such as its wheels, color, size, and engine type; it also has methods, which are the actions the car takes, such as accelerating and locking the doors. From the perspective of natural human language, an object is a noun, a property is an adjective, and a method is generally a verb.

Objects are members of a class, which is basically a template for creating objects with shared initial variables, properties, and methods. For instance, say we had a class called cars; our car (a BMW) would be a member of the class of cars. This class would also include other objects/cars, such as Mercedes and Audi, as shown

Classes may also have subclasses. Our car class has a BMW subclass, and an object of that subclass might be the model 320i.

Each object would have properties (make, model, year, and color) and methods (start, drive, and park), as shown

In OOP languages, objects inherit the characteristics of their class, so the BMW 320i would inherit the start, drive, and park methods from class car.

These OOP concepts are crucial to understanding how Python and other OOP languages work, as you will see in the scripts in the following sections.

NETWORK COMMUNICATIONS IN PYTHON

Before we move on to more Python concepts, let's use what you've learned so far to write a couple of hacking scripts to do with network connections.

Building a TCP Client

We'll create a network connection in Python using the socket module. I've already mentioned that Python comes with a library of modules for a multitude of tasks. In this case, we will need the socket module to create a TCP connection. Let's see it in action.

Take a look at the script in Listing 17-3 named HackersAriseSSHBannerGrab.py (I know, it's a long name, but bear with me here). A banner is what an application presents when someone or something connects to it. It's kind of like an application sending a greeting announcing what it is. Hackers use a technique known as banner grabbing to find out crucial information about what application or service is running on a port.

```
#! /usr/bin/python3
```

❶ import socket

❷ s = socket.socket()

❸ s.connect(("192.168.1.101", 22))

❹ answer = s.recv(1024)

❺ print (answer)

```
s.close
```

A banner-grabbing Python script

First, we import the socket module ❶ so we can use its functions and tools. Here, we're going to use the networking tools from the socket module to take care of interfacing a connection over the network for us. A socket provides a way for two computer nodes to communicate with each other. Usually, one is a server and one is a client.

Then we create a new variable, s, and associate it with the socket class from the socket module ❷. This way, we don't have to reference the full socket.socket() syntax whenever we want to use the socket class—we can simply use the s variable name.

We then use the connect() method from the socket module ❸ to make a network connection to a particular IP and port. Remember that methods are functions that are available for a particular object. The syntax is object.method (for example, socket.connect). In this case, I'm connecting to IP address 192.168.1.101, which is the IP address of a machine on my network, and port 22, which is the default SSH port. You can test this on another instance of Linux or Kali. Most have port 22 open by default.

Once you make the connection, there are a number of things you can do. Here, we use the receive method recv to read 1024 bytes of data from the socket ❹ and store them in a variable named answer; these 1024 bytes will contain the banner information. Then we print the contents of that variable to the screen with the print() function ❺ to see what data has been passed over that socket, allowing us to spy on it! On the final line, we close the connection.

Save this script as HackersAriseSSHBannerGrab.py and then change its permissions using the chmod command so that you can execute it.

Let's run this script to connect to another Linux system (you might use an Ubuntu system or even another Kali system) on port 22. If SSH is running on that port, we should be able to read the banner into our answer variable and print it to the screen, as shown here:

kali >./HackersAriseSSHBannerGrab.py

SSH-2.0-OpenSSH_7.3p1 Debian-1

We have just created a simple banner-grabbing Python script! We can use this script to find out what application, version, and operating system are running at that IP address and port. This gives us key information a hacker needs before attacking a system. This is essentially what the website Shodan.io does for nearly every IP address on the planet, and it catalogs and indexes this information for us to search.

Creating a TCP Listener

We just created a TCP client that can make a connection to another TCP/IP address and port and then spy on the information being transmitted. That socket can also be used to create a TCP listener, to listen to connections from outsiders to your server. Let's try doing that next.

In the Python script shown in Listing 17-4, you'll create a socket on any port of your system that, when someone connects to that socket, collects key information about the connector's system. Enter the script and save it as tcp_server.py. Make sure to give yourself execute permissions with chmod.

```python
#! /usr/bin/python3

import socket
```

❶ TCP_IP = "192.168.181.190"

TCP_PORT = 6996

BUFFER_SIZE = 100

❷ s = socket.socket(socket.AF_INET, socket.SOCK_STREAM)

❸ s.bind((TCP_IP, TCP_PORT))

❹ s.listen (1)

❺ conn, addr = s.accept()

print ('Connection address: ', addr)

while 1:

```
data=conn.recv(BUFFER_SIZE)

if not data:break

print ("Received data: ", data)

  conn.send(data)  #echo


conn.close
```

Listing 17-4: A TCP-listening Python script

We declare that we want the script to run with the Python interpreter and then import the socket module as before, so we can use its capabilities. We then define variables to hold information for the TCP/IP address, the port to listen on, and the buffer size of the data we want to capture from the connecting system ❶.

We define the socket ❷ and bind the socket to the IP address and port ❸ using the variables we just created.

We tell the socket to listen using the listen() method from the socket library ❹.

We then capture the IP address and port of the connecting system using the socket library's accept method, and we print that information to the screen so the user can see it ❺. Notice the while 1: syntax here; we'll discuss this more later in the chapter, but for now just know that it is used to run the indented code that comes after it indefinitely, meaning Python keeps checking for data until the program is stopped.

Finally, we place the information from the connecting system into a buffer, print it, and then close the connection.

Now, go to another computer on your network and use a browser to connect to the 6996 port designated in our script. Run the tcp_server.py script, and you should be able to connect and collect key information about that system, including the IP address and port of the connecting system, as shown here:

kali >./tcp_server.py

Connection Address: ('192.168.181.190', 45368)

Received data: Get /HTTP/1.1

Host:192.168.181.190:6996

User -Agent:Mozilla/5.0 (X11; Linux x86_64; rv:45.0) Gec

--snip---

This is critical information for a hacker to gather before deciding on an exploit. Exploits (or hacks) are very specific to the operating system, application, and even language being used, so the hacker needs to know as much information as possible about the target before proceeding. This act of gathering information prior to a hack is often referred to as reconnaissance. You just developed a tool that will gather key reconnaissance information on a potential target, very similar to the popular hacker tool p0F!

DICTIONARIES, LOOPS, AND CONTROL STATEMENTS

Let's keep expanding your understanding of Python and then use everything you've learned so far to build a password cracker for an FTP server.

Dictionaries

Dictionaries hold information as unordered pairs, where each pair contains a key and an associated value. We can use a dictionary to store a list of items and give each item a label so we can use and refer to that item individually. We might use a dictionary to store, for example, user IDs and their associated names, or to store known vulnerabilities associated with a specific host. Dictionaries in Python act like associative arrays in other languages.

Like lists, dictionaries are iterable, meaning we use a control structure such as a for statement to go through the entire dictionary, assigning each element of the dictionary to a variable until we come to the end of the dictionary.

Among other things, you might use this structure in building a password cracker that iterates through each password stored in a dictionary until one works or until the cracker comes to the end of the dictionary.

The syntax for creating a dictionary is as follows:

dict = {key1:value1, key2:value2, key3:value3...}

Note that for dictionaries, you use curly brackets and separate items with a comma. You can include as many key-value pairs as you like.

Control Statements

Control statements allows your code to make decisions based on some condition. There are a number of ways in Python to control the flow of the script.

Let's look at some of these structures in Python.

The if Statement

The if structure in Python, as in many other programming languages including bash, is used to check whether a condition is true or not and run different sets of code for each scenario. The syntax looks like this:

if conditional expression

  run this code if the expression is true

The if statement contains a condition that might be something like if variable < 10, for example. If the condition is met, the expression evaluates to true, and then the code that follows, known as the control block, is executed. If the statement evaluates to false, then the statements in the control block are skipped over and not executed.

In Python, the control block must be indented. This indentation identifies the control block to the interpreter. The next statement that is not indented is outside the control block and therefore not part of the if statement, and this is how Python knows where to skip to if the condition is not met.

if...else

The if...else structure in Python looks like this:

if conditional expression

    *** # run this code when the condition is met

else

    *** # run this code when the condition is not met

As before, first the interpreter checks the condition in the if expression. If it evaluates to true, the interpreter executes the statements in the control block. If the conditional statement evaluates to false, the control block following the else statement is executed instead.

For example, here we have a code snippet that checks the value of a user ID; if it is 0 (the root user in Linux is always UID 0), then we print the message "You are the root user." Else, if it is any other value, we print the message "You are NOT the root user."

if userid == 0

302

```
    print ("You are the root user")

else

    print ("You are NOT the root user")
```

Loops

Loops are another very useful structure in Python. Loops enable the programmer to repeat a code block multiple times, depending on a value or a condition. The two most widely used are while and for.

The while Loop

The while loop evaluates a Boolean expression (an expression that can evaluate only to true or false) and continues execution while the expression evaluates to true. For example, we could create a code snippet that prints each number from 1 to 10 and then exits the loop, like so:

```
count = 1

while (count <= 10):

    print (count)
```

```
count += 1
```

The indented control block then runs for as long as the condition is true.

The for Loop

The for loop can assign values from a list, string, dictionary, or other iterable structure to an index variable each time through the loop, allowing us to use each item in the structure one after the other. For example, we can use a for loop to attempt passwords until we find a match, like so:

```
for password in passwords:

    attempt = connect (username, password)


    if attempt == "230"


        print ("Password found: " + password)
```

```
sys.exit (0)
```

In this code snippet, we create a for statement that continues through a list of passwords we have provided and attempts to connect with a username and password. If the connection attempt receives a 230 code, which is the code for a successful connection, the program prints "Password found:" and then the password. It then exits. If it does not get a 230, it will continue through each of the remaining passwords until it receives a 230 or until it exhausts the list of passwords.

IMPROVING OUR HACKING SCRIPTS

Now with a bit more background in Python looping structures and conditional statements, let's return to our banner-grabbing script and add some capabilities.

We'll add a list of ports that we want to grab the banner from, rather than just listening on one port, and then loop through the list using a for statement. In this way, we can search for and grab banners for multiple ports and display them to the screen.

First, let's create a list and put additional ports in it. Open HackersAriseSSHBannerGrab.py, and we'll work from there. Listing 17-5 shows the full code. Note that the grayed-out lines have stayed the same; the black lines are the ones you need to change or add. We'll try to grab banners for ports 21 (ftp), 22 (ssh), 25 (smtp), and 3306 (mys□l).

```
#! /usr/bin/python3


import socket


❶ Ports = [21,22,25,3306]


❷ for i in range (0,4):


    s = socket.socket()


❸   Ports = Port[i]
```

```
print ('This Is the Banner for the Port')


print (Ports)


❹  s.connect (("192.168.1.101", Port))


answer = s.recv (1024)


print (answer)


s.close ()
```

Listing 17-5: Improving the banner grabber

We create a list called Ports ❶ and add four elements, each representing a port. Then we create a for statement that iterates through that list four times, since it has four items ❷.

Remember that when you're using a for loop, the code associated with the loop must be indented beneath the for statement.

We need to alter the program to reflect the use of a variable from the list on each iteration through. To do so, we create a variable named Port and assign it to the value from the list at each iteration ❸. Then we use that variable in our connection ❹.

When the interpreter comes to that statement, it will attempt to connect to whichever port is assigned to the variable at the IP address.

Now, if you run this script on a system with all the ports listed open and enabled, you should see something like Listing 17-6.

kali >./HackersArisePortBannerGrab.py

This is the Banner for the Port

21

220 (vsFTPd 2.3.4)

This Is the Banner for the Port

22

SSH-2.0-OpenSSH_4.7p1 Debian-8ubuntu1

This Is the Banner for the Port

25

220   metasploitable.localdomain   ESMTP   Postfix
(Ubuntu)

This Is the Banner for the Port

3306

5.0.51a-3ubuntu5

Listing 17-6: Output for the port banner grabber

Note that the script has found port 21 open with
vsFTPd 2.3.4 running on it, port 22 open with
OpenSSH 4.7 running on it, port 25 with Postfix, and
port 3306 with MySQL 5.0.51a.

We have just successfully built a multiport banner-grabbing tool in Python to perform reconnaissance on a target system. The tool tells us which service is running on the port and the version of that service! This is key information a hacker needs before proceeding with an attack.

EXCEPTIONS AND PASSWORD CRACKERS

Any code you write will be at risk of errors or exceptions. In programming terms, an exception is anything that disrupts the normal flow of your code—usually an error caused by incorrect code or input. To deal with possible errors, we use exception handling, which is simply code that handles a particular problem, presents an error message, or even uses an exception for decision making. In Python, we have the try/except structure to handle these errors or exceptions.

A try block tries to execute some code, and if an error occurs, the except statement handles that error. In some cases, we can use the try/except structure for decision making, similar to if...else. For instance, we can use try/except in a password cracker to try a password and, if an error occurs due to the password not matching, move to the next password with the except statement. Let's try that now.

Enter the code in Listing 17-7 and save it as ftpcracker.py; we'll go through it in a moment. This script asks the user for the FTP server number and the username of whichever FTP account they want to crack. It then reads in an external text file containing a list of possible passwords and tries each one in an effort to crack into the FTP account. The script does this until it either succeeds or runs out of passwords.

```
#! /usr/bin/python3


import ftplib


❶ server = input(FTP Server: ")


❷ user = input("username: ")


❸ Passwordlist = input ("Path to Password List > ")
```

❹ try:

  with open(Passwordlist, 'r') as pw:

    for word in pw:

❺   word = word.strip ('\r').strip('\n')

❻   try:

      ftp = ftplib.FTP(server)

      ftp.login(user, word)

❼   print (Success! The password is ' + word)

❽   except:

```
        print('still trying...')

    except:

        print ('Wordlist error')
```

Listing 17-7: FTP password cracker Python script

We're going to use tools from the ftplib module for the FTP protocol, so first we import that. Next, we create a variable named server and another variable named user, which will store some commands for user input. Your script will prompt the user to enter the IP address of the FTP server ❶ and the username for the account ❷ the user is trying break into.

Then we ask the user for the path to the password list ❸. You can find numerous password lists in Kali Linux by entering locate wordlist in a terminal.

We then begin the try block of code that will use the password list provided by the user to attempt to crack the password for the username supplied by the user.

Note that we use a new Python function called strip() ❺. This function removes the first and last character of a string (in this case, the Passwordlist). This is necessary if the passwords in this list have a preceding whitespace or comma. The strip() function removes these and leaves just the string of characters of the potential password. If we don't strip the whitespace, we might get a false negative.

Then, we use a second try ❻ block. Here, we use the ftplib module to first connect to the server using the IP address the user supplied and then try the next password from the password list on that account.

If the combination of the username and password results in an error, the block exits and goes to the except clause ❽, where it prints still trying and then returns to the top of the for clause and grabs the next password from the password list to try.

If the combination succeeds, the successful password is printed to the screen ❼. The final line picks up any other situations that would otherwise result in errors. An example would be if the user input something the program couldn't process, such as bad path to the wordlist or a missing wordlist.

Now, let's run this script against the FTP server at 192.168.1.101 and see whether we can crack the password of the root user. I am using a password list named bigpasswordlist.txt in my working directory. You may need to provide the entire path to whichever password list you are using if it is not in your working directory (for example, /usr/share/bigpasswordlist.txt).

kali >./ftpcracker.py

FTP Server: 192.168.1.101

username: root

Path to PasswordList >bigpasswordlist.txt

still trying...

still trying...

still trying...

--snip--

Success! The password is toor

As you can see, ftpcracker.py successfully found the password for the user root and presented it onscreen.

CONCLUSION

This manual is going to provide us with all of the info that we require to understand about Hacking with Linux. Lots of people worry that hacking is a bad procedure which it is not the right option for them. Fortunately here is that hacking can work well for not just taking details and harming others but also for assisting you keep your own network and personal info as safe as possible.

Inside this manual, we are going to spend some time to explore the world of hacking, and why the Kali Linux system is among the best to assist you get this done. We check out the different types of hacking, and why it is beneficial to discover a few of the techniques that are needed to perform your own hacks and to see the outcomes that we want with our own networks.

In this manual, we will take a look at a lot of the various topics and strategies that we require to know when it concerns working with hacking on the Linux system. A few of the subjects that we are going to have a look at here include:

The different kinds of hackers that we might experience and how they are various and comparable.

How to set up the Kali Linux onto your os to begin.

The basics of cybersecurity, web security, and cyberattacks and how these can impact your computer system and how a hacker will attempt to use you.

The various types of malware that hackers can use versus you.

How a male in the middle, DoS, Trojans, infections, and phishing can all be tools of the hacker.

And so a lot more.

Hacking is typically a choice that most people will rule out due to the fact that they stress that it is going to be evil, or that it is just used to damage others. As we will go over in this guidebook, there is so much more to the process than this.

DISCLAIMER

This book is not intended as a substitute for the medical advice of physicians. The reader should regularly consult a physician in matters relating to his/her health and particularly with respect to any symptoms that may require diagnosis or medical attention.

(kali linux, cyber security)

ABOUT THE AUTHOR

MY NAME IS

I really love educating people on how to stay healthy and live the life of their dreams.

Do Not Go Yet; One Last Thing To Do

If you enjoyed this book or found it useful, I'd be very grateful if you'd post a short review on Amazon. Your support does make a difference, and I read all the reviews personally so I can get your feedback and make this book even better.

Thanks again for your support!